QUALITY EDUCATION FOR LATINOS AND LATINAS

Joe R. and Teresa Lozano Long Series
in Latin American and Latino Art and Culture

Rita and Marco Portales

QUALITY EDUCATION
FOR LATINOS AND LATINAS

Print and Oral Skills for All Students, K–College

 UNIVERSITY OF TEXAS PRESS
Austin

Copyright © 2005 by the University of Texas Press

All rights reserved
Printed in the United States of America

First edition, 2005

Requests for permission to reproduce material from this work should be sent to Permissions, University of Texas Press, Box 7819, Austin, TX 78713-7819.

♾ The paper used in this book meets the minimum requirements of ANSI/NISO z39.48-1992 (R1997) (Permanence of Paper).

LIBRARY OF CONGRESS
CATALOGING-IN-PUBLICATION DATA
Portales, Rita.
    Quality education for Latinos and Latinas : print and oral skills for all students, K–college / Rita and Marco Portales. — 1st ed.
        p.   cm. — (Joe R. and Teresa Lozano Long series in Latin American and Latino art and culture)
    Includes bibliographical references.
    ISBN 0-292-70633-2 (cloth : alk. paper) —
    ISBN 0-292-70664-2 (pbk. : alk. paper)
    1. Latin Americans—Education—United States.
2. Latin American students—United States—Social conditions.   3. Multicultural education—United States.
I. Portales, Marco, 1948-   II. Title.   III. Series.
    LC2670.3.P67 2005
    371.82968′073—dc22
                                                2004024718

We dedicate these pages to the selfless educators of this nation who often spend countless after-school hours preparing lessons and grading assignments that motivate and excite students to learn.

We also want to express appreciation for administrators who work diligently, in cooperation with their staffs, to achieve the type of everyday working school conditions that produce quality education for all students.

May all members of society learn to appreciate their true value!

Contents

PREFACE *ix*

ACKNOWLEDGMENTS *xiii*

INTRODUCTION *1*

PART I. *Education and Latino amd Latina Students Today* 7

Chapter 1. THINKING ABOUT OUR SPANISH-SPEAKING STUDENTS IN THE SCHOOLS *9*

Chapter 2. LATINO AND LATINA STUDENTS AND THE SCHOOLS WE COULD CREATE *19*

Chapter 3. BUT OUR EDUCATION SYSTEMS ARE DISTENDED *40*

Chapter 4. WHY STUDENTS DROP OUT *52*

Chapter 5. A MEXICAN AMERICAN MOTHER WHO WILL NOT VISIT SCHOOL *70*

Chapter 6. THE TRIBAL MENTALITY AND FAVORITISM *76*

Chapter 7. CRIME AND PROPERLY FUNDED SCHOOLS *89*

PART II. *How to Repair an Education System* 101

Chapter 8. TEACHERS, ADMINISTRATORS, BOARD MEMBERS, STATE EDUCATION AGENCIES, LEGISLATORS, AND TAXPAYERS: WHICH IS THE MOST IMPORTANT GROUP? *103*

Chapter 9. THE K–12 SCHOOL DISTRICT TEAM *112*

Chapter 10. TEACHERS AND STUDENTS IN THE CLASSROOM *116*

Chapter 11.   UNDERSTANDING AND EDUCATING ALL STUDENTS   *128*

Chapter 12.   THE FOUR K–16 CULTURES   *136*

PART III.   *A Print and Oral Approach*   *143*

Chapter 13.   EMPHASIZING ALL PRINT AND ORAL SKILLS   *145*

Chapter 14.   BLUEPRINT FOR REINSTATING SOCIAL VALUES AND CIVIC VIRTUES   *162*

Chapter 15.   A PRINT AND ORAL APPROACH THAT CHAMPIONS THE IMPORTANCE OF CLAUSES   *166*

Chapter 16.   A THIRD DIMENSION TO WORDS: CHOREOGRAPHING WRITING   *177*

CONCLUSION   *185*

Chapter 17.   QUALITY EDUCATION AND THE TEACHERS IN THE CLASSROOM   *187*

NOTES   *191*

BIBLIOGRAPHY   *211*

INDEX   *217*

$\mathcal{P}$REFACE

$\mathcal{A}$s a husband-and-wife team of educators, we have written this book to make Americans aware of the nature of the interactions that often make learning particularly difficult for Latino and Latina students. We have written *Quality Education* to show that the failure and dropout rates among such students and among students of all backgrounds and ethnicities can be considerably reduced through a unified effort that repairs our schools.

Only after experiencing problems in different schools and in different states, after finding confirmation in the research of other educators, and after knocking futilely on the doors of people empowered to effect change in the schools did we finally resort to writing this volume. We decided to pursue this option because we have been frustrated in our efforts and we want to demonstrate how and why education systems that succeed for some students are dismally failing others.

By doing so, we hope to enlist educators and American society in helping not only Latino and Latina students but all students not served well enough by current educational approaches. We focus attention on Latinos and Latinas because demographic statistics since the 2000 U.S. Census inform us that Spanish-speaking students now comprise the largest ethnic minority population in U.S. schools.

Throughout this volume, we refer to female and male Spanish-speaking students as Latinos, the masculine form, because when both genders are intended the male form is used in the Spanish language. When not grammatically cumbersome, though, we have included the word Latinas, the feminine form, specifically in the title and where appropriate in the text. Readers will notice that our stories concern not only Latinos and Latinas but African Americans and people of other races and backgrounds. In every instance, we intend inclusion, not exclusion.

We believe quality education can be made equally available to all students from kindergarten not only through the twelfth grade but including college. For proficiency in the skills that we promote is a lifelong issue for all of our citizens. In order to provide a quality education to every student, however, we have learned that it is necessary to make viable suggestions that can be implemented within the real-life constraints that educators face daily. Actual classroom teaching time has been substantially reduced by other school tasks that, while often well-intended, are not directly extending the knowledge of students or stimulating their learning capacities. Learning assignments for this and other reasons that we discuss in the following pages tend toward rote classroom tasks that do not sufficiently engage students' interest nor their imaginations and creativity.

Our extensive teaching experiences have taught us that most educators simply do not have enough time in their busy schedules to think about how they can also deliver quality education to a greater number of educationally underserved students. Based on our observations and on the experiences of students in our classrooms, we are convinced that one of the best contributions that educators of our generation can make to the general welfare of society is to offer a higher quality of education to more students, regardless of color or ethnicity. That objective, we believe, can be responsibly and sensibly achieved by examining and adjusting the ideas that we highlight in the following chapters to the different realities that each school and every school district face.

We hope that no readers will feel singled out by our analysis of the current education scene. For this reason, we want to state clearly at the outset that we have not written our book to criticize or fault the schools or anyone in or related to the education establishment. We hasten, in fact, to recognize the courageous efforts of many teachers, administrators, and citizens who, despite considerable stressful challenges, continue to devote their best energies to improving the increasingly difficult environment in which U.S. schools function.

Some of our ethnographic stories will be distressing to read. Indeed, when we have related a few of these factual school events to different audiences over the years, occasionally we have been told, "You're so negative," and once even, "You sound un-American." We have listened to such responses with dismay because we realize that the points of the stories we have carefully attempted to narrate have not been accepted. Such responses, in turn, delay the desired improvements. Our intention in describing the school incidents is to raise awareness about the messages that words, looks, and actions send to youngsters in our schools. The impact of what some adults may dismiss as seeming trivialities, especially when reinforced by life's cares and what some students see and interpret as indifference or ignorance, can cripple and sometimes even devastate children and teenagers who have little recourse and who do not quite understand how the classes they attend ought to and can benefit their future lives.

To move toward improving student learning, in the following pages we describe situations that we have personally experienced. We are aware that throughout the years Latino and Latina students in particular have shared their problems and frustrations with us more readily because we are Spanish-speaking educators ourselves. Given this reality, we have gradually and somewhat reluctantly arrived at the realization that our schools and education systems are not as effective as many people want to think.

The suggestions that we put forth in these pages have considerably improved the education of students with whom we have worked. Encouraging students has been constantly required, but by emphasizing a gradual increase in sophistication in the basic skills of reading, interpreting, thinking, writing, and speaking, we have successfully enabled many students. We are convinced that the skills and ideas we recommend, especially when communicated by teachers using approaches and methods with which they feel comfortable, can smoothly improve the quality of education delivered at every grade level.

Even though we grew up in different parts of the country, we are both first-generation Americans. Rita was born on the commonwealth of Puerto Rico. Although her parents were schooled in English during their time, Spanish has always been the language of the island, making *el español* Rita's mother tongue. When she came to the United States at the age of eight, Rita entered the third grade. Knowing little English, she suffered emotionally from culture shock, a response that was only ameliorated by an English-speaking third-grader who became a steadfast friend. That experience and other events in her young life progressively turned her into a lifelong defender of students of English as a second language. Since then, she has worked on developing nurturing, understanding, and properly implemented approaches to education that best address the needs of Spanish-speaking students.

In Marco's case, his father learned only what English he could before his schooling abruptly ended in the fifth grade. He stopped there because at that grade level schooling stopped for the great majority of Mexican children in Central and South Texas in the 1920s, as Guadalupe San Miguel points out in *Let All of Them Take Heed* (1987) and as Américo Paredes suggests in *George Washington Gómez* (which was finished in 1940 and not published until 1990). Marco's Costa Rican mother, who immigrated to the United States as an adult in 1946, knew no English; and since his parents lived along the border area next to Mexico in the Rio Grande Valley all their married life, bilingualism was a way of life.

We both know that if our separate and different schooling experiences had not sufficiently equipped us with the necessary print and oral skills that each of us was fortunate to develop due to the care and support of our parents and teachers as we moved from grade to grade, the schools would not have transformed our lives by what we learned and were taught. Like many of the Spanish-speaking students who attend school today, we also might have failed and ended up without the quality education that has allowed us to care for our needs and the future of our children. From personal experience, then, we feel compelled to say that when schools do not offer students ample opportunities to succeed, all members of society have to endure the consequences.

ACKNOWLEDGMENTS

The Race and Ethnic Studies Institute (RESI) at Texas A&M University supplied start-up funding for the early research needed to write this book. During the past two years, our Mexican American/U.S. Latino Faculty Association (MALFA) has also been working steadfastly to establish the Mexican American/U.S. Latino Research Center (MALRC) at Texas A&M. In May 2004, we are pleased to report, the Board of Regents approved MALRC, formally encouraging other new research efforts on Latinos and Latinas like the current one. Our hope is that *Quality Education for Latinos and Latinas* will substantially enhance the education and thus the life and career options available to students like the ones we describe in these pages. We believe the testimonial stories we have taken from our teaching experiences call for and even demand the kind of changes we advocate. From the enthusiastic responses we have received from Texas A&M junior and senior students, most of whom will be teachers, we believe we have written a book that readers will find eye-opening and compelling. We are convinced that to produce more educated citizens and better teachers and administrators, all Americans need to contribute in some way to the communal obligation of helping students who through no fault of their own struggle academically. Only by recognizing the lack of resources and by uniting to provide the kind of community support that such students require will all learn to capitalize on school opportunities that deliver quality education.

We particularly want to thank the students at Texas A&M, too many to name individually, who carefully read earlier versions of this study and who provided us with helpful responses. Graduate students Kerri Barton and Hilary Standish and educational administration professor Maynard Bratlien of Texas A&M offered helpful suggestions during the early stages of the manuscript. We want to express our appreciation to David A. Sustaita, Virgilio Martínez, and Richard Sanchez, too, for their computer assistance at different junctures of this book. The final work, however, expresses our own views. Although we have discussed some of these views with sympathetic friends who have kindly listened and asked questions that have helped us articulate our ideas over the years, no other person is responsible for our diagnoses of the schools or for the solutions that we recommend.

*I*NTRODUCTION

$\mathcal{E}$ ducational foundations like the Carlos H. Cantu Hispanic Education and Opportunity Endowment increasingly recognize both the seriousness and the depth of the problems that Latina and Latino students face. The Cantu endowment is a million-dollar gift to Texas A&M University's College Station campus donated in the fall of 1999 for the purpose of addressing the shockingly high dropout rates among U.S. Latino students. When he dedicated this sum to the university to reduce that unconscionable human loss, Mr. Carlos Cantu, an Aggie Former Student, Class of 1955, observed that more than "half a million Hispanic children drop out of school every year. That is disastrous."[1] Although educators have long known that many Latino and Latina students drop out of school without graduating year after year, the schools have not effectively addressed this appalling human wreckage.

Given today's wave of standardized testing and accountability, thousands of schools nationwide are in the process of being declared "failing" by state education agencies and other education watch organizations.[2] Such reports suggest the extent of the problem that we endeavor to curb and to rectify. Primarily because most minority students are not yet receiving quality education, academically competitive colleges and universities cannot find enough qualified Hispanic, black, and other minority students capable of pursuing higher education successfully. Two-thirds of all Latino and Latina students in higher education are enrolled at the community college level, largely because they lack the financial means, adequate transcripts from kindergarten through twelfth grade (K–12), and competitive college entrance test scores to attend four-year colleges and universities. With these demographics in mind, our objective is to demonstrate how long-standing social and economic disparities among Hispanic, black, and other disadvantaged students can be gradually surmounted year in and year out by good, consistent teaching.[3]

We believe that schools have an obligation to help students improve the quality of their lives. The best way to achieve this goal is to show students what knowledge can do for them. The idea of "quality education" is to engage the natural curiosity and interest of all students in learning and in improving their skills and talents so they can be academically prepared to achieve success as adults.

For years scholars and educators have studied the complex nature of the K–12 issues that our schools and higher education institutions have faced, and many have offered recommendations. In our experience and observations, we recognize that education recommendations, if they are to be taken seriously, should not necessarily depend on incurring new costs or on securing new funding that often is uncertain or wishful at best. We also have discovered that education cannot be improved unless the changes being contemplated and implemented actually facilitate the lives of the people charged with making the improvements, namely the educators and the administrators themselves. While being encouraged to teach up to their full potential, these professionals have become so regulated by policies and mandates that a good amount of their best energies are daily consumed by activities that are only tangentially connected to the teaching mission and their classroom assignments.

Schools, too, often become boring places for students, prompting many of them to seek more interesting activities on which to spend their considerable youthful energies. But in strongly urging educators to return to the business of teaching the fundamental skills that all students can progressively continue to develop until they achieve their full potential, we are keenly aware that the assistance of many different audiences has to be enlisted. Indeed, if a constructive national dialogue and practical academic changes that promote the public good in the schools are to ensue, we should not delay. We believe that the quality schools that minority as well as nonminority students urgently need can be communally created by diagnosing the different problems that exist in the individual schools. The task then becomes a matter of locally and nationally repairing the school systems on which so much of civilization depends.

When we look at the history of education and how schools function today, it is clear to us that the great majority of educators and citizens tend to see quality education and Latino students in separate and highly unrelated realms. Quality education is extremely desirable and sought after by members of society who know its value, for good schooling has traditionally secured economic advantages and social privileges for its beneficiaries. We have learned, however, that over the years Latina and

Latino students more often unfortunately have been seen as problem pupils whom educators have not been able to teach successfully enough. But these realities and distinctions are no longer acceptable. The narratives we share in this volume illustrate personal encounters that reflect some educators' lack of understanding or skill in relating to such pupils and their families. Throughout the twentieth century, a small number of students of color attained a quality education year after year, helping them shape their destinies productively, but the great majority of such students did not.

The twenty-first century, we are convinced, has to be different.

National discussions about how best to educate students, such as the debate over the No Child Left Behind Act, cannot overlook the demographic dimension of school populations. Given evolving realities in American society, solving the schools' problems cannot be postponed or ignored much longer. Our schools today require a renewed emphasis on actually teaching students how to understand and how to master the use of all print symbols as well as fully understanding the necessity to communicate very well orally. To accomplish these two goals, we must first repair our existing education systems. We believe that the structures and the organizations of our schools are basically sound. But often they do not work because the adults involved in the education of our students do not sufficiently appear to understand how their particular roles, responsibilities, and challenges are compromised by continual changes that pervade school policies, procedures, and practices. A constantly changing school environment directly impinges on the lives of students, and it is the education of the students that suffers. Ironically, often the students themselves end up as casualties of many good intentions. We believe that the relationships between parents and the educators and other employees within a school system need to be clarified sensibly so that everybody understands who is responsible for what. By doing so, all citizens involved in the business of delivering effective education to all students can help each other instead of working against each other, as often happens.

We believe it is time to initiate a transformation of the schools into the learning environments they can be. We possess such confidence in our colleagues that we know we can all provide quality education for all students once we learn how to repair our school systems. For quality education cannot be provided with the school systems functioning as uncertainly as they do. We believe society understands that an uneducated child of any socioeconomic background is a failure that will continue to affect all of us, a harder or more difficult life that will not easily go away. For every school failure is a life that ever after calls into question the great hopes and aspirations that the Constitution promises to all of our citizens and residents.

We have related existing problems in order to encourage educators and the schools to initiate the task of improving their own school systems, if that is needed. We tell the stories we have selected to underscore the urgency of the challenge. We did not exaggerate the difficulties described here; no one wishes more than we do that these school experiences did not exist. They are simply part of the daily reality for many students, and we encourage educators to be courageous enough to admit the problems we discuss and to work steadfastly in any way they can to remedy the nature of the education extended to all students. Until problems like the ones that we describe in this text are accurately diagnosed and addressed and students can feel free to relate them to any confidant in education, the American system of education will remain besieged by forces and factors that educators have not entirely understood.

To address the problems brought out in Part I and Part II of this book, we believe that our education systems need immediate repair. Part III is designed to show how all members of society can help educators overhaul the school systems for which we pay to produce better students. In *Quality Education for Latinos and Latinas* we place emphasis on the skills that every teacher in every discipline can teach within a classroom while staying within the normal parameters of a school district's grade course curriculum. We are hopeful that school district leaders will see that they are responsible for hiring teachers who know their disciplines well enough to provide quality education for their students while following school guidelines. The idea in these closing chapters is to show administrators, teachers, and all interested citizens the extent to which every person associated with a school district has to work with colleagues and other members of society to help the schools provide all students with quality education. The alternative is what we have today: to continue with cross-purpose school relationships that frequently impede the delivery of first-rate education to the students. Such relationships are often built more on school district power and position than on delivering the knowledge and information that students need to be successful. Given this objective, we approach the issue of improving an education system by reminding educators again that the schools exist to achieve the full potential of students, not to provide adults with opportunities to demonstrate that they are accountable, competent professionals. This goal of featuring learning by the students nonetheless still leaves considerable room for administrators and teachers to run the schools, including shaping the curriculum that each grade level requires.

Although Latino and Latina, black, and other minority and disadvantaged students are often seen as academically less competitive, we write to encourage educators and concerned citizens to raise the academic expectations and dispel incorrect perceptions particularly associated with students of color. By preparing and working to deliver high-quality instruction to them on a consistent daily basis, good educators can make every classroom a transforming environment that changes and can end up improving the lives of all students.

When educators are allowed and encouraged to work to their full potential, education becomes capable of actually changing the nature of the lives of students. Hispanic and non-Hispanic students who are now languishing in our schools can be energized by pedagogical challenges that allow such students to participate actively in their own education, reducing boredom, fatigue, and classroom disruptions. We hope that our book will be used by educators and readers seriously engaged in providing Latinos and Latinas as well as all other students with the quality education that should supply the ensuing generations with success in school and throughout their lives.

PART I | **ƐDUCATION AND LATINO AND LATINA STUDENTS TODAY**

<table>
<tr><td>

Chapter 1

</td><td>

THINKING ABOUT OUR
SPANISH-SPEAKING
STUDENTS IN THE SCHOOLS

</td></tr>
</table>

*W*hy do Latino and Latina youngsters tend to lag behind their peers in the same schools? Gaining proficiency in English, to be sure, is a major barrier for students who speak only Spanish, but even the great majority of Hispanic students who communicate mainly in English usually receive lower grades and less competitive college entrance test scores. No doubt many people in the schools continue to try different approaches as we write, but why are the more competitive universities still finding it so difficult to admit and enroll promising Latino and Latina applicants? Millions of Americans know that educators throughout the country suffer from unsatisfactory working conditions in the form of large classes, low salaries, increased accountability, school shootings, and all sorts of other problems and violent behaviors that have changed the nature of teaching. What used to be a fairly well-regulated working environment has become a frustrating, unpredictable workplace at some schools. Our children and our school communities often are caught up in a whirlwind of changing school requirements, activities, and policies that sometimes overwhelm and unnerve even the most experienced and best educators. Teachers and administrators complain that they do not have a life away from school any more, and we know that too many K–12 students cannot wait to finish their school days. If that experience was the case here and there, school critics might be more understanding. But these circumstances prevail in many of the schools in Texas, California, Florida, New Jersey, Pennsylvania, and many other states across the nation. The same kinds of reports concerning teaching dissatisfaction arrive daily from educators not only in the large school districts in New York, Los Angeles, Chicago, Houston, Philadelphia, Dallas, San Antonio, El Paso, and Phoenix, for example, but in much of rural and suburban America as well, despite all efforts to reform education.

Due to the difficult working environment of the schools, the everyday experiences of Latino and Latina students and other minority young-sters in particular have not been articulated in ways that have afforded teachers opportunities to develop an understanding of the educational problems such students face. Do teachers know, for example, that His-panic youngsters are usually instructed by parents and relatives to re-spect teachers as much as and sometimes even more than their very own parents? Many Latino and Latina parents, indeed, value education so highly that immigrants are often willing to undergo perilous journeys to enter the United States not only to work but to provide better education for their children, as any cursory inquiry will uncover. We have come to recognize over the years that the school experiences of many minority students are different from the experiences of their white, mainstream peers, even though both groups are often exposed to the same activities. We have reluctantly concluded that the professionals responsible for education in the schools are so involved with record-keeping and other required tasks that paying the kind of academic attention that will allow minority youngsters to turn their lives around often appears quite dif-ficult. Such realities have led us to ask: If the schools are not properly educating minority students, what experiences will adequately prepare such youngsters for higher education and for their future social success, given the demographic numbers?

By working with a great number of educators and people interested in education on a daily basis for many years, we have learned that most Americans do not want to hear that Hispanic students are receiving infe-rior educations. Many would rather hear that Latino and Latina young-sters are as likely to succeed as other students. Veteran educators like us, in fact, are generally expected to make encouraging statements about the progress that school district officials like to promote for public relations. Given that the education of minority youngsters has not been a high pri-ority, we want to say unequivocally that some schools have nonetheless made noticeable progress. Still, we know that most people will agree that the schools are not yet providing the kind of widespread quality educa-tion that minority students require in the twenty-first century. Indeed, we would not be exaggerating if we were to say that only by educating all students as if they were being prepared to attend Harvard will education make a real difference in their lives.

Since some minority students nowadays attend the same schools with the same teachers and programs as mainstream white students, one un-derstandably could assume that the education of such students is com-parable. But teaching in a good number of schools in different parts of the country has allowed us to see that even students sitting in the same room often receive surprisingly different lessons. Why? Because the relationships that frequently develop between teachers and students, depending on both the expectations and the nature of their interactions, often end up promoting very different school cultures.

We believe different educational outcomes are the result of quite different kinds of relationships that students establish with their teachers, parents, counselors, and other community people. Such relationships require careful analysis, diagnosis, and then attention. A student's home experience and school environment, as well as the ways adults assess and respond to the student's skills, talents, and personality, are factors that shape educational outcomes. We have learned that unless education professionals discern, better understand, and capitalize on the talents, skills, and cultural backgrounds that different youngsters bring to the classroom as they move through the grades, first-rate teaching that enhances a student's potential will remain elusive.[1]

Students with more parental resources undeniably tend to attend the better schools where quality education is the standard fare. But why are some schools known for performing very well academically while others with similar demographics fail students? We believe that school systems directly reflect the nature of the professional relationships that exist within school districts. Relationships between educators and students that are not continually encouraged and cultivated quickly fall into disrepair, impairing the progress of students, educators themselves, and the academic reputations of schools. Human relationships in the schools either mesh smoothly, helping to produce well-educated students, or they do not. Due to the ways teachers and education systems often respond to different cultural mores, norms, and home lives, experience has taught us that Latino and Latina students tend to experience quite uneven kinds of education—the nature of the education often depending on some of the multiple factors that we discuss in this text. Various studies have shown that the quality of the courses usually offered to Latino and Latina students is academically less competitive, particularly at the middle and high school levels. Building on what should be the firm foundations that the elementary grades provide, the secondary grades are the consequential school years when students either are adequately prepared for higher education or they are not. If we are thus to understand and improve the nature of the school experiences that Hispanic and most other minority students receive, current realities force us to say that educators need to study experiences like the ones we describe here as such students move from kindergarten to high school and into college.[2]

Given our combined K–12 and higher education experience, we have prepared a number of suggestions to help educators teach more effectively. We offer some practical ways to approach school problems that especially tend to beset minority students and American society as the twenty-first century opens. In sharing these ideas, we hope to persuade educators to examine how the whole educational establishment shapes student behavior and achievement. When examining such issues, we have found systems theory particularly useful. We are convinced that educators need to focus attention on how school systems need to work if we are to revitalize the actual classroom experience between teachers and students. We believe that quality education is not being sufficiently delivered to all students because our school systems are overburdened; schools labor in ponderous ways. That is, instead of making the delivery of a quality education the central priority, in practice school districts often discourage fine teaching and end up promoting acceptable teaching and moderate student learning. Some educators may disagree with this assessment, but we are nonetheless confident that our education systems can be effectively repaired by the very people who lead our schools, especially when school personnel are supported by political leaders who make it their business to provide proper financial support for education.

Systems theory holds that all the elements contained within a system must work well together in a certain environment in order for the system to accomplish the goals that it is designed or intended to achieve. Harmony and congruity are essential, and how well a system functions depends largely on how smoothly the people responsible for operating and sustaining it work together to accomplish its stated purpose. The purpose of an education system, we should be reminded, is to educate the student, a good that unfortunately is often lost when other concerns are given primacy. Thinking about systems has considerably shaped and influenced much of American society since World War II. Systems theory is most evident both in how we conceptualize this study and in how we discuss organizations and the groups of people who necessarily have to work together to educate students properly.[3]

In education, academic success is rooted in stimulating learning and then on using what has been learned so that the material assimilated becomes an integral part of a student's life. If students are prepared at any juncture that they enter a school system so that they will enjoy the learning process, they will learn to perform competently as superior students as they continue to move from grade to grade. But if they have not had the benefit of being told, for example, why algebra and calculus are worth studying and if they never learn how or why biology, chemistry, and physics will later build on the basic middle and high school science courses, students will not be interested in these disciplines, largely because they will be studying with a distinct disadvantage. Part of the reality, of course, is that there is a scarcity of teachers. Connie Mabin has reported on this scarcity in Texas schools: "About 17 percent of the state's math positions could not be filled last fall, and nearly a quarter of the 38,500 teachers hired last year were not trained in their subjects. That means a grammar teacher could have taught math, according to a Texas A&M University study released in March."[4]

So between the lack of qualified teachers and the fact that the importance of disciplines is not properly explained primarily to Latinos, Latinas, and blacks, such minority students are often left behind academically. Both the nature of the instruction and the academic resources that they receive in too many minority-dominant schools fall short of what students require to move toward superior academic learning and performance. Such students are simply not provided with the type of quality school experiences that will produce academically competitive students—meaning that they are, instead, being subjected to some of the same kinds of disempowering experiences that we describe in this book.[5]

In this text we carefully attempt to fashion a different way of working within current education system infrastructures so that educators can deliver quality education not only to the traditional beneficiaries of such instruction but to all students. Our recommendations result from many discussions that we have wrestled with in the communities where we have taught. To air and to encourage other readers to talk about school problems that we have personally experienced, we have included some of the difficulties that minority students undergo every semester year after year. The education problems that such students encounter almost every day of their lives are legion, and we hope that the stories we have chosen will lead readers who may be skeptical to be persuaded by our arguments.

Although current test scores show that most educators have not historically transformed minority children into first-rate students, we believe educators are perfectly capable of creating superior minority students. If school districts were to embrace this objective as a defined, articulated goal, we know all students would receive a quality education. The goal should not be merely to pass classroom and state-mandated tests and turn in satisfactory homework assignments, but indeed to strive for and to achieve academic excellence. We know this objective is particularly difficult for Latino and Latina students because, aside from the normal cares and concerns of growing up in the topsy-turvy adolescent world of American society, most Spanish-dominant youngsters also tend to go through difficult identity crises that educational experts and other American citizens are just beginning to investigate in our ethnic populations.

Our emphasis on understanding and employing excellent print and oral skills addresses the actual academic needs of Hispanic as well as non-Hispanic students. The approach we recommend is also effectively designed to help educators see how they can repair our education systems by working communally. We believe that educators can pedagogically employ this approach with all students in any grade of the academic spectrum from kindergarten to the last year of the college experience. Students who have not previously been taught to pay much attention to words, to print symbols and signs, nor to how language can be effectively used to communicate both on paper and orally tend to feel newly empowered when they learn that they can shape their own futures. In the work world, almost everything depends on how adults control and represent themselves and on our ability to impress others with our communication skills.

When students are taught to pay special attention to the art and the task of improving their writing and speaking skills, they begin to understand how the world functions and what success requires. We propose this highly practical bread-and-butter way of educating students because this approach does not encroach on the academic freedom of teachers, encouraging instructors to capitalize on their teaching strengths. This method of approaching and instructing students also complements existing pedagogical theories and philosophies, since it does not require teachers to teach only certain materials in ways that may constrain or limit their talents and/or skills. In today's classroom, an instructor has to begin teaching a student wherever the pupil is academically when the teacher meets the student. A print and oral skills approach, we believe, offers the kind of latitude and freedom that can create positive school experiences for all students and teachers, an emphasis that can be daily reinforced by other members of our schools and communities. This claim may initially sound overly optimistic, but these days not many programs can deliver quality education in the disturbing education world that most educators inhabit.

For too many years, education programs have nominally been designed to create leaders and to educate mainly the students who have learned to test well. Since class sizes grew throughout the twentieth century, one can see how, pressed for time and resources, teachers have been unable to address the needs of every single student. The brighter children who have also enjoyed the benefits of better socioeconomic wherewithal and/or nurturing parental support invariably have been the main beneficiaries. Such students have traditionally shown that they can learn because they have been encouraged from their earliest years; they have been taught how to respond appropriately to the materials that teachers devise. This process has assured American society of the kind of social stability that has elevated the United States to a world power. But the demographics of the U.S. population have changed, and so have the number of students from working-class and poor parents.

Before the Civil Rights Act of 1964, most minority children were relegated to an inferior education in segregated schools.[6] If minority children succeeded, that success could usually be attributed to one or more teachers, parents, or other adults who created opportunities that made a difference in their lives. As a nation we need to recognize that quality education programs have not been traditionally constructed for minority students. This history explains why transforming the schools to address the needs of minority youngsters today may appear a monumental challenge. Since educators resisted equally educating minority children well before *Brown v. Board of Education* declared race-segregated schools unconstitutional in 1954, securing properly prepared teachers and adequate funding has not been easy.

During the past half-century, the education of American students, primarily due to the inclusion of minority youngsters, has emerged as one of the most contested political issues.[7] Today most education programs attempting to provide the type of help that minority students need are usually add-on programs that receive federal, state, or local funds to support initiatives seldom seen as high-priority programs. Such supplemental funding assures less stable service and maintenance by most school districts throughout the United States. Since school districts also often pride themselves on being locally run entities, most school board members understandably believe that their first obligation is to meet the needs of their leading traditional citizens. Serving newer, developing populations for this reason has remained a matter of teaching such youngsters as time allows. The days when minority children were not educated properly, in other words, are still with us, and this reality complicates the school environment because it remains largely unaddressed. In many school districts, that exclusionary legacy has not been left behind; such practices continue to shape the expectations that communities and educators have when the academic needs of minority students are considered.

Because Latinos and Latinas are being left out of too many diversity and multicultural dialogues, quality education for U.S. Spanish speakers has not elicited the attention this need deserves. We believe that Hispanic Americans should be at the center of new education ideas and reforms because this is the largest population that will be attending the schools in the next several decades.[8] The best-paying jobs require at least some postsecondary education, and disparities between jobs and education will undoubtedly translate into very clear social and economic differences. The costs that Hispanic students will have to pay for their educational underachievement will be enormous unless we take strong measures to reverse the current circumstances. The following lead editorial in the August 30, 2002, *Houston Chronicle*, which we will quote at length, underscores this point:

> Earlier this summer, state Sen. Rodney Ellis complained that $17 million in college scholarship money was going begging because no student had applied for it. The senator said the money, appropriated for the Toward Excellence, Access and Success grant program, could help 6,500 students attend college.
>
> A more recent development reveals why lack of financial means is not the greatest obstacle to higher education in Texas. Figures released this week show Texas ranks fifth from the bottom on average SAT College entrance exam scores. Nationwide, the average math score was 516; the average verbal score was 504. In Texas, the average scores were 500 and 491, respectively.
>
> Particularly disturbing, the average scores of black and Mexican American Texans (other Hispanics were tracked separately) lagged the state average by 50 to 80 points.
>
> About half of Texas' children drop out of school before graduating. Of those who graduate, 45 percent do not take the SAT test required for admission to competitive universities and some open-enrollment campuses. The poor scores of many who take the test indicate woefully inadequate preparation for higher education.

The high dropout rate and poor preparation guarantee low college attendance and graduation rates. Many of those who do not receive higher education are doomed to unemployment or jobs with low wages and inadequate benefits—becoming as much a drag on society as a boon to business.

Texas students are making slow, painful progress on high school exit exams. Despite the exams' increasing difficulty, the tests represent only the minimum attainment necessary to earn a high school diploma.

The more urgent task for Texas is not to hand out all the scholarship money at its disposal, but to make sure that many more of its children are educated well enough to benefit from a college scholarship.[9]

The issue is not that scholarship money remains unclaimed but that most Latino, Latina, and black students do not receive adequate educations to qualify them to apply successfully for the scholarships. This same circumstance is encountered by many minority students not only in Texas but across the country. For reasons like these, it is essential to show people interested in educating tomorrow's citizens why minority students often feel more discouraged than nourished by the education they are receiving in today's schools.

Changing the unacceptable conditions that most minority students experience from kindergarten to college will be difficult. But having successfully tested the print and oral skills approach in our own classrooms, we believe that our suggestions, if implemented according to the needs of school districts, are capable of transforming the educational landscape for Latino and Latina students. In the following case, for instance, we offer the narrative of a student who made it out of her barrio into college despite an unsupportive high school environment:

How I made it this far still boggles my mind. My high school did not push students to go further than a high school diploma. My high school did not even have pre-calculus. When I first came to Texas A&M I was put in a remedial math class because my SAT math scores were so low. I had a 20 average in the class because I had no understanding of math whatever. So, I dropped the class and took math the next semester at a community college. It took a tutor and a lot of hard work to pass the class and I made a B. I had been third in my graduating class of 250 students. Beginner math should have been a breeze. I felt like Esperanza, the narrator of Sandra Cisneros's The House on Mango Street *when her teachers made her feel like nothing. This reminded me of a similar experience in school. I was going to make a speech at a teachers' meeting asking for their assistance with a student program. I was waiting for my turn to speak in the back of the room and I guess no one noticed me. The principal was speaking to the teachers about implementing a new program that would help the students, which at my high school were 90 percent Hispanic, graduate and continue to go to college. A teacher stood up and said, "Why should we help a bunch of Mexicans that don't want to be helped!" The principal responded that as educators they had to help.*

The school board of my district was not much help. I definitely want to go back to San Antonio and be on the school board that supposedly "works" for the students. When I was going to school, our school board was so corrupt. It was all about who you knew. Most of the men and women on the board were only there to help their future political careers. The position was simply something to put on a résumé. Every once in a while a member would come along that actually wanted to work for the students, but it was rare and he did not serve long. Members of the board were always being accused of embezzlement, fraud, affairs, etc. There were always scandals. One year cheerleader tryouts were said to have been discriminatory and the case was taken to the school board for review. Since the head cheerleader's father was on the school board, somehow the case was miraculously dismissed. Recently a bond worth $65,770,000 was passed that was supposed to be used to build new elementary schools. Some of the money did go to build new schools but a big portion of the amount went to new turf for the football field. The turf was millions of dollars and not even the NFL has it. The school district may not have the money to implement new courses and programs to ensure a quality education, but it surely has enough money for a nice football field. This upsets me so much.

I believe in education more than anything. From the time a child can walk and talk he/she is being influenced and taught by teachers, whether at day care or pre-school. Latinos need to be provided with the proper education in order to grow up and become something worth being proud of. Education is a key factor in succeeding, and Latinos deserve the same type of education that any wealthy Anglo would receive. I cannot say that I hope to improve this one day because I WILL improve this one day!

Chapter 2	# LATINO AND LATINA STUDENTS AND THE SCHOOLS WE COULD CREATE

College entrance examination scores and other college admissions criteria regularly document the fact that most minority students do not receive a K–12 education that allows them to compete evenly with non-Hispanic white college applicants. Every year we learn through the media, surveys, and research studies that minorities are academically less prepared than their white counterparts, often while attending the same schools. Why these differences in academic achievement continue is a question that baffles many observers.

Minority students are not any less intelligent than whites, and their genes are not inferior, as some researchers have posited.[1] Our contention is that quality education simply is not being made readily available to a great many minority students. Despite improvements in some pedagogical areas, quality education still remains largely the province of students who are not minorities. Students who receive steady support and attention from parents and teachers and who sensibly are taught to encourage each other's efforts invariably acquire a better education. Among Hispanic and other minority and even among some majority students, quality education is less common because such students seldom receive the advantages and the long-term nurturing provided by close parent-teacher relationships and good communal support. Such students, consequently, often pass their academic assignments or they fail, but most do not strive for nor are they seriously encouraged to pursue academic excellence. When minority students benefit and enjoy similar care and attention from parents and teachers, however, they also succeed, as William Bowen and Derek Bok demonstrate in *The Shape of the River*. But when students do not have parents who are culturally comfortable in working with the schools, that is, establishing and maintaining good relationships with teachers and school personnel, such students leave the schools ill-equipped for success as adults.

What do we mean by culturally comfortable parents?

Rafael's mother went to her son's high school three times to check on his progress. The first time, no one at the front office spoke Spanish. She found a school custodian and asked him to translate, to inform the secretaries that she needed to speak with Rafael's teachers. The secretaries told her that no one there spoke Spanish, even though the school has a Spanish department with at least five teachers teaching that discipline. Mrs. A., Rafael's mother, returned a second time, this time with a translator, a friend from her neighborhood who drove her to the school. They were told that Mrs. A. needed to make an appointment with his teachers because "all the teachers are teaching now." The third time, another friend called to make an appointment for her with Rafael's math teacher. When she arrived, Rafael's mother was told, again at the front office, that the teacher was at a faculty meeting and that she could not be called out! Since she had no car, each time she went to the high school, Mrs. A. had to find someone to bring her to the school and make the necessary arrangements where she worked. Despite all of these efforts, she remained unsuccessful in meeting with and in talking to any of Rafael's teachers. She ended by informing us that she is very unwilling to return to that school again.

If schools have Latino and Latina students with parents who do not speak English, we believe there is no excuse for not having both teachers and professional staff who can communicate with Spanish-speaking members of the school's community. Not to do so is irresponsible, sending the unwelcome message that Mrs. A. very clearly received. With experiences like these occurring and being talked about in the Hispanic community, should school officials wonder why Hispanic students and their parents tend to remain uninvolved in the schools?

*I*n the school environment, it is widely known that academic comfort and nourishment begin at the preschool level and strongly develop in the first, second, third, fourth, and fifth grades.[2] This necessary academic foundation, built by educators on care and attention, then has to be reinforced by educators and parents in the difficult middle school years of the sixth, seventh, and eighth grades. By the time students transfer to high school, college expectations have to be well in place; otherwise, higher education in not a real, viable option in a student's mind. Educators and counselors engaged in addressing the learning needs of students understandably place freshmen with better grades in the college-bound and advanced placement courses. The goal is to provide students with curricula that increase their knowledge base, challenging them to grow increasingly sophisticated during their ninth, tenth, junior, and senior years of high school. Students not selected for such challenges, on the other hand, are in effect discouraged from developing intellectually and often leave school from ennui. We know because we have seen and heard from a number of bright Latino and Latina students who were excited about education in the earlier grades. When we encountered a few of them years later, they informed us that school had turned them off. Usually they blamed the teachers, the difficulty of the courses, and the fact that they were essentially left alone to figure out class materials.

We identify every single grade from preschool to the senior year in high school in the above paragraph to remind readers of the thirteen years it takes to graduate a person from our American school system. Failure at any grade level, or even in any one subject, often affects a student's entire subsequent psychological development. This lengthy school process is a little-acknowledged reality that partly helps explain why too many minority students fail to arrive at the twelfth grade. Since the expectation is not only to pass but to excel in one's studies, failure anywhere in the progress of minority youngsters as they move year to year through school stigmatizes them and is not easily forgotten. How one or two such incidents in a young life are affected by the responses of teachers and peers, shaping actual learning and progress, influences a student's self-esteem, frequently determining a student's adult future.

School is psychologically so important that unresolved or unaddressed problems in the lives of students, from the time they are three or four years old until graduation from high school at eighteen or so, usually continue to shape their subsequent lives. Everything that a student experiences in life, in other words, influences his or her education either positively or negatively.[3]

The immediate effect of gaps in vocabulary and education present themselves when the child starts school. Two significant studies of student vocabularies in first through third grades showed children from high-income families with a 30 to 50 percent larger vocabulary than peers in low-income families, a factor that allows them to understand and decode words faster, read more, and thus widen the gap further. In order for the poverty child to make up ground before fifth grade, he would need to learn an extra 170 vocabulary words for each week of the school year, along with the 116 words he already is supposed to be learning—a daunting task, to say the least. We state what may be an obvious but fundamental point, that the nature of the experiences that students have while learning should amply tell us whether we are meeting our obligation to prepare today's young people to become responsible, taxpaying citizens tomorrow. The case of Ramón Ramos is instructive:

There is little as gratifying to an educator as hearing students speaking about higher education and how they hope to reach that goal. Imagine my surprise one day, when, as I stood outside my high school classroom door awaiting my students between changes of class to hear a voice saying in a heavily accented English to another student, "Do you know where I go to get a scholarship?" I jumped to find the voice among the many students passing in the hallway and found it belonged to Ramón. This young man, I learned, was on his way to his ESL (English as a second language) class. He was not one of my classroom students, but I was always looking for such students to let them know I spoke Spanish and to encourage them in any way possible.

We became friends as the year progressed. Ramón told me his mom and dad had immigrated to give his brothers and sisters and himself a better education and life. His dad was a cook at a local Mexican restaurant, and his mom was not yet working. Later on I met both parents, and their eyes sparkled as they spoke to me, "la maestra," of the dreams that immigrant parents have for their children. Ramón continued well in his studies, stopping occasionally by my room to chat but mainly to ask questions in subject areas he found difficult. He usually sought clarification of material he had heard in class or to assure himself he was understanding and working problems and assignments correctly. One morning I saw him coming down the hall with head down and a red face. He seemed to halt at my door a moment and then continued. I stepped out and called, "Qué pasa, Ramón?" I saw the face of a sixteen-year-old young man with tears running down his face. Alarmed, I asked again, but he did not want to tell me. After a few minutes alone with me in my room, me wishing that he would relax before proceeding to ESL, he told me that after turning to a Spanish-speaking friend in the previous class to ask for an explanation, the teacher had said, "In this room we speak English. Don't speak Spanish in my room!" One could see he was deeply hurt, and "fighting" with him all the way, we went to see that teacher. She was my friend. I knew her from the good comments made about her by the students she taught and our own col-

legial lunch breaks and after-school talks, when I heard an insightful and caring teacher.

With Ramón beside me, I told her what he had said. "Yes," she readily replied, "but I did not mean it that way. In my room I teach English, and so I wanted him to speak only in English." I explained that was not what "came across" to Ramón. She saw his tears and said she was sorry, BUT the damage was done. Ramón would never again feel comfortable in one of his most important classes. AND what was particularly sad was that her comment was made on the heels of another one by another school adult. While supervising the lunch hour, that second adult had told Ramón and a group of his friends to stop talking so loudly, and then referred to him and his friends, even at this late date, as "wetbacks." I had worked hard to take away the sting of that word from his friends and himself, yet having one's culture twice berated is difficult for any person who loves his country, let alone one so freshly arrived.

Ramón is a strong youth, cognizant of what he is facing, yet these instances cut to his heart and it took me time to bring him back. We all have frustrating days, and I know that sometimes, by third period, some teachers have had plenty of talks regarding "attitude" with our students. The force and power of insensitive remarks must nevertheless be communicated to all teachers. As I have told my students, "I would rather be cut with a knife than cut by words that a person never forgets."

How can we educate students like Ramón? Hispanics, blacks, Native Americans, and other minority students who have not historically been taught how to become successful learners are our primary target audience, mainly because such students greatly need educational attention today. The suggestions we propose, however, benefit all students in nearly all education systems. The actual curricular content, which changes as educators discover more relevant and effective ways to improve student learning, are best left, we believe, to the creativity and imaginations of classroom teachers and the school's principal or district area supervisor. For that reason, we focus little attention on what specific materials to teach, choosing instead to highlight the basic skills that students have to learn and the manner that such knowledge can be creatively delivered to them.

The education system and the actual skills imparted to all students are our proper subjects because once the schools focus attention on teaching and expanding skills and knowledge, students will continue to develop to their full potential. We believe that the main problem with K–12 education today is that there is too much interference with the central relationship in education, that is, the classroom relationship that teachers need to establish anew with each and every student. This traditional association, as we see it, needs to be reasserted, protected, championed, and then carefully nourished and sustained by the existing educational infrastructures. Our basic pedagogical position is that either learning communicated by a mentor to a pupil is facilitated by the leaders of a school district following school policies designed to encourage that primary purpose, or learning is not first and foremost. Either everything and everyone in a school system fosters and encourages healthy professional relationships that teachers establish with their students, or school districts labor under conditions that work against such ideals.

One of our three main objectives is to describe how education systems must function to support the teacher-student relationships that need building if schools are to succeed. Only when we recognize this need will administrators and concerned citizens improve the quality of education available to all of America's students.

During one of my beginning teaching years, I was assigned to teach a third-grade class in a school very near a ghetto area. This particular group of children was a mix of three ethnic groups, African American, Anglo, and Latino. They were third-graders from impoverished socioeconomic backgrounds and neighborhoods. They were lively, full of energy and excitement. Their energies were extended outward toward anything that was not what the teacher needed. Each morning, as I passed the other third-grade classrooms, I noticed that the more experienced third-grade teachers were always at their doors watching to see my class as we passed by. I had not been given any information regarding the placement of the students as far as the curriculum was concerned. It took me one day to realize that not one third-grader in that class could read, write, or perform basic arithmetic. I soon realized why the other teachers, who had lovely, well-behaved classes, looked at my students as we went by — my class was composed of all of the "discipline" students in the third-grade classes. I was the proverbial "new kid on the block." So many difficulties in my class took me to a behavioral modification teacher friend of mine, and together we worked on a specific plan designed for that group. Through some fun activities and exercises, I started to spend my mornings talking to them, making them believe in themselves again. They were apparently used to arguments and fights. They had to "defend" their property. And they made valiant efforts to shield and to obscure and hide their personal shame — their inability to read or write in the third grade, and their personal grief and sorrow, since some had jailed family members, and others had other woes from living in their impoverished neighborhoods.

Little by little I was able to begin teaching them arithmetic, the alphabet, and reading. I began to show them how to work as members of a class group, to help each other. The rapidity with which most of them learned and soaked in the information I was teaching them surprised all of us. As a group, we discussed how others in our class needed extra help, and I told them that no one but us was around to help. We discussed the manner in which people can help each other and the patience that we would need to help the slower students. The maturity of our discussions and their total focus and attention to these talks is forever etched in my mind. Although not much actual teaching from any district curriculum took place for a few weeks, the class and I came to an understanding of civility within the school walls and toward each other.

Since discipline had been unknown to the class, I later discovered that the nature of the class was perfectly known and understood by the administration. It had just never been verbalized to the new teacher. As the new teacher, it took every ounce of strength within me to face the administrators with my problems and to tell them of my need to direct the class in the fashion that I saw necessary if this group was to achieve. To my great relief, the principal and the assistant principal and counselors agreed, and, in effect, young as I was, I was given carte blanche and left to teach the students as I saw their needs. I also learned much later that they, too, had hoped someone would come along and find the strength to properly guide, encourage, and teach this group of particularly difficult kids. I just wished that someone had been kind enough at least to inform me of the task that I had when I was given the class, because, looking at it from my angle as the teacher, my job was to meet the challenges of my profession head on. That became my philosophy after that. Throughout my career, without a doubt the most successful teaching years that I have had with students have been ones when school administrators have allowed me to teach unhindered by a set diagnosis of a class.

Again, Hispanic and other minority students are our focus because too many students of color continue educationally disenfranchised, despite professed pedagogical advances. Although considerable research is published yearly, educators like the ones in the above narrative have not figured out how to address the needs of minority students.[4] In the classroom, learning progressively depends on teaching students how to understand and how to interpret everything that is communicated in the adult world through the printed word or other widely understood symbols. Once this goal is incrementally accomplished, the evolving task of educators is to show students how to think and how to express their views more and more effectively both orally and in writing. Once these basic skills are learned, students will continue to grow in sophistication, expanding their knowledge and expertise as they move from K–12 toward higher education and beyond. In adulthood, they will reach whatever level of mastery their talents and skills facilitate.

*W*hy focus attention on the school systems if the primary relationship is the one between the teacher and the student? Many years of teaching and observation have convinced us that the teacher-student relationship cannot work properly if the schools do not function as an education "system." In this complex set of professional and human relationships, every person who is part of a school district is expected to work in harmony with everyone else to achieve the single purpose of educating students better.

To educate all students better, we need to recognize that every single individual hired by a school district has designated duties and responsibilities that cumulatively ought to enhance the overall quality of the education delivered by a district's schools. Education systems for this reason need to be structured around the academic and social needs of students, and they have to be continually maintained so that they remain student-centered. This means that school districts and the teachers and administrators in the individual schools should constantly be required, and require themselves, to demonstrate how their students are progressively learning. The problem, of course, is that people who work in education systems are aware that not all components of our education systems work together efficiently enough, and that is why not all school systems are sufficiently student-centered.

In some places, for example, education systems have not kept learning as the uppermost good for students. Over the years, school boards and local leaders, in effect, have allowed school personnel to weaken, politicize, or otherwise decentralize academic goals, and the curriculum shows that marginalization. In such school districts, the educational needs of the students are not the primary factors that shape school district policy anymore. Other considerations, such as athletics, to name one, have clearly become at least as important as the materials that students should be learning. Once a school system has been destabilized by competing interests and concerns, district officials have the responsibility to intervene. If student learning is still not the first consideration, then public accountability requires that other measures and adjustments take place until student learning is established once more as the top and first priority.

Many different types of education systems exist in the United States, and each one has its own set of advantages and drawbacks. Although most Americans take pride in controlling their school districts, part of the reason the education of students often remains mainly a rhetorical goal is that other administrative and teaching problems and concerns crowd out student learning. Depending on the personnel selected to make decisions within school districts, some are quite successful, while other districts remain dysfunctional year after year. When relationships and operations run well, such efforts can usually be attributed to a good superintendent, great teachers, or a well-run board supported by strong parental presence. Unsuccessful schools, we believe, can be effectively repaired by studying where the problems are and by propping or adjusting an education system so it will equally deliver quality education to all students. Even the most successful of our education systems can be improved. Our view is that since schools exist within the education systems that sustain them, educators need to recognize what a good school education system is so that all American citizens fully understand what makes one work properly — so that we can all recognize those that require repairing.

As education systems stand, some tend to work better for some students than for others. That, of course, should not be the case, since in a public school system, as in a private one, every student ought to receive the same kind of quality education. The reason that education systems do not work as well as they might, particularly for Hispanics and other students of color, is that some educators and administrators have shown that they apparently do not sufficiently know how to teach minority youngsters who bring different cultural attitudes and philosophies to school. Such students, in other words, too often are identified and perceived as students who bring "difficult problems" to school. These students are not seen as bringing altogether different ways of looking at the world, given, of course, the nature of their socialization and the upbringing they have had. And when such students do not discernibly bring "problems," minority students are nonetheless treated differently enough so that eventually they become the "problem" youngsters that educators have learned to expect. The task, then, is how to construct education systems that embrace culturally different youngsters like Latinos, Latinas, and other minority students so that quality education is successfully provided to all students.

On another occasion, I taught ESL in a K–8 environment. A young fifth-grade Puerto Rican student, short and slight of built but very athletically oriented, attended my classes. He was very bright and inquisitive. On a certain report card day, he came in unusually quiet. His report card reflected good grades for an ESL learner, each six-week period higher than the one before—except in P.E.

This particular time, his P.E. grade was a 60 and neither of us was happy. He would not answer my questions about the grade, except to say that the P.E. teacher "did not like spics." I half-bolted at the word, asking him where he had heard it. Very matter-of-factly, he told me that was what the P.E. coach always called him, sometimes saying "You short, dark spic, come over here." I asked him if he knew what the teacher meant by that. He said he didn't when he first heard the word, but by the tone and the way the students laughed in class, it couldn't be anything nice. He didn't know enough English at the time to defend himself or to ask about it, but his other Puerto Rican friends told him after class. I asked him if he had misbehaved in that class. His enthusiastic answer in Spanish was "No, I love P.E. That is one of my most favorite classes." I figured that kids are kids and that he must have been in some manner fooling around, so I asked Michael, the teacher, if Francisco gave him any problems. No, he stated, other than not doing what he asked immediately and that irritated him. Michael did not know Spanish, so I asked if he knew that Francisco attended ESL. Sure, was his reply, "but that is an excuse they all use to get their way." As a matter of fact, Francisco's favorite words in his P.E. class were "I no understand." I asked Michael if he could perhaps ask another student to explain to Francisco when he said that. Michael said he would think about it. When Francisco attended my class the next time, he asked me not to talk to the P.E. teacher any more. He could handle it.

I heard nothing about P.E. from Francisco for many weeks, though his grades continued at 60. June and finals were approaching, and Francisco said he was sure he would fail the exam. I asked him to ask if I could be allowed to translate the test questions for him. Not without some resistance, Michael gave in to my request, but only after having a serious closed-door session with the principal. The first part of the test was a multiple choice section that went well, since the questions were related to health, body part functions, and well-being. Any teacher could tell that Francisco had studied. The second part consisted of five essays. I translated them for Francisco, and he wrote the answers in English, as Michael requested. There were grammar and spelling errors, but the basic explanations were perfect.

Two weeks after school let out, I ran into Francisco chasing some younger children on his bicycle and throwing rocks at them. "Why are you doing that?" I asked. With a look that I had not seen on his face before, he told me that he was "malo," bad. That's not so, I replied. To change the topic, I asked him about his P.E. final exam. He said he got a 30. Did you ask the coach to show you the errors, I asked. Yes, and he said he would not show anything to a cheater who had a teacher help him. I was totally taken back, yet I tried not to have a reaction. I told him that the first thing in September, he and I would go to the principal to ask for a different P.E. teacher. Looking with a faraway look, his hands on the handlebars of his bike, he said not to bother because he would not be returning to school next year. I explained that, by law, he had to. "No, Miss," he stated. He knew many who skipped daily, and no one from "el gobierno" (the government) came for them after two or three tries. Finally, he shouted as he took off in a flying whizz, "And if they make me come back, I will NOT learn because I am a 'malo spic.'"

To educate all students so that they are capable of reaching their full potential, we believe that American educators and our entire society need to place the class relationships that teacher and students establish at the center of the pedagogical enterprise. This is not a new idea, to be sure. Almost everyone associated with education in one way or another pays at least lip service to this important teaching and learning relationship. But few education systems are actually set up to empower teachers, and few endeavor to do everything possible to promote the one central relationship on which the education of the young either succeeds or fails. In this age of accountability, making sure that this inviolable relationship functions well has never been more important.

Often our school experiences do not work properly because in too many school districts other issues, expectations, and relationships besides the one between the teachers and the students are treated as more important. Actual classroom teaching in such cases is then consigned to being a lesser activity, as teaching is widely seen in too many education environments. When that happens, other interests and relationships elbow out the essential classroom relationships between teachers and students that ought to have first consideration. In those instances, we need to recognize that such an education system is not functioning smoothly any more, for stakeholders are engaged in promoting any number of other objectives. They are not working primarily for the education of the young as a team any more, regardless of claims. Such a school system then needs to be efficiently and effectively reorganized so that every single member is again reminded that teachers and students are central to the education enterprise.

Readers at this point may ask why we "side" with the classroom teachers? Why not sympathize and understand the difficult positions of the administrators and the other stakeholders in a school district, like the parents and the taxpayers? After all, teachers are employees hired by the administrators and the school board. The latter are the members who actually make the tough decisions for a school district, and they are responsible to the voters, since they are specifically charged with seeing that an education system works. So, if the schools do not work, won't the administrators and the board members be removed by the voters during the next election? Not necessarily. Voters tend to vote for people with whom they feel comfortable. Such people, of course, may not be competent educators.

But readers should not wonder why we side with the teachers instead of the administration, as those lines have traditionally existed, or as some degree of enmity has sometimes developed between the two groups. All of us, rather, should know that if the education of the young is going to occur successfully, that desired outcome mainly happens in the classroom, that is, where teachers directly interface with students. Everybody else who is positioned outside the classroom, from the principal to the governor of a state, for this basic reason can only facilitate, encourage, and promote the teacher-student relationship that, again, has to be placed at the center of all education systems. For learning can happen only when a student's mind is engaged by the manner in which a teacher communicates the material taught. If effective learning is to occur, good teaching has to start with the teacher, and it must flow out toward the student. Administrators, to be sure, show leadership and supervise and evaluate teachers, but these functions should be carried out with the clear understanding that it is the teacher's professional relationship with a student that is the central most important activity that occurs in any school district, in any school, in any classroom.

We are not, to be sure, interested in pointing to specific education systems that work and to others that do not, as some studies have been inclined. It seems to us that education stakeholders spend too much time defending practices that, if they worked well enough, we would not be writing this book. Also, we are not interested in continuing to encourage educators to think of themselves as members of separate or antagonistic teams. Teachers, for example, sometimes define themselves as not administrators, and the latter usually depict themselves as employees subordinated to the boards of education that hired them. State education agencies make up yet another academic entity, that is, as groups of people who help legislators set standards and policies and periodically evaluate school districts. Common ground, however, is achieved when educators and all education stakeholders recognize—not only in their rhetoric but also in their practice—that we are all part of a societal team whose primary objective is to teach all students successfully.

Having worked in a number of school districts, our sense is that some school systems function well because of the personnel or for a variety of reasons that outside evaluators can often pinpoint. Either the leadership of a school or an area knows what it is doing, or the teachers themselves make an education system look good; or, of course, there are as many reasons that explain why some school districts are successful and why others fail.

We, rather, are more interested in proposing ideas about how all school personnel can collectively go about repairing and making the education systems that exist today work. Once more, we are not interested in finding fault with the schools or the people who make their living through education. Like many taxpaying citizens, we simply want the number of schools that provide quality education to all students to increase substantially throughout the nation. We believe education systems can be successful when school district leaders consciously follow philosophies that allow and encourage all members to work as teams so every student will benefit, regardless of background, instead of mainly serving the interests of students traditionally prepared to graduate from college.

Most people who work in education agree that the schools can function more efficiently, and nearly all educators have ideas about what exactly is wrong with education and what ought to be done. When there are as many educational theories and methods as we have today in the

United States, nearly all pedagogical practices can be found operating somewhere. Teaching methods that have been advanced and that have proven successful usually continue in use in some parts of this great country. Nevertheless, it is also generally acknowledged that the education pipeline is not working properly enough. So, how can educators approach and successfully educate all students?

*W*e believe that a good education system should function like a good baseball or football team. Every member of a school system should know what his or her job is and what the expectations are, from the elected school board members to the top administrators to the secretarial and custodial staff. Every member of the education system team should also know that the entire school district can only be as good as the quality of the mentor and pupil relationships that a school district encourages and supports between teachers and students. Strange as it may seem, often many members do not know what the duties and the responsibilities of the other members in a school district are. Systems theory teaches us that everything both within and without a system either helps a system to function well or it does not. In a baseball or football team, for instance, everybody, fans included, works in unison to accomplish the single purpose of winning. If the baseball team is playing out on the field, the defensive objective is to cause the opposing team to make three outs so that the team on the field can bat and score some runs to win the game. Every player has to remain alert, ready to play his or her position to benefit the entire team. If everyone contributes to the effort and no one botches the work of other team members, the team is more likely to win. If some team members fail to carry out their assigned duties, the team is more likely to lose.

The same theory is applicable to an education system and to the individual schools in a school district. In today's education systems, too often teachers are trying to teach students, while administrators, board members, and education agencies are engaged in activities that do not always directly help the teachers with the school district's main objective. Every member may be working very hard, but some of their efforts may be at cross purposes. In such cases, there is little overall coordination. People are not reminded, or they may not have been told, that everyone ought to be contributing to the effort of educating the young students who daily sit in the school district's classrooms.

Teachers may feel that they have to find or to create extra time from somewhere in their busy schedules to actually teach students because other assigned tasks have very effectively kept them from giving their best energies to the learning that their students need to do. Administrators, in turn, have other activities and charges that have been levied on them by state agencies and school boards, aside from supervising and facilitating matters for their teachers. The education system players are not, unfortunately, all working to help the teacher dispense the knowledge that students need. Sometimes, in fact, many of these school activities and professional personnel are delaying and frustrating one another instead of helping teachers educate the students. Providing time during the week, for example, to take care of state-mandated paperwork would relieve stress and allow teachers more time to prepare their lessons — their most important job.

In baseball, the central activity is the nature of the agreement that takes place between the pitcher and the catcher. The game does not proceed until the pitcher hurls the ball for the batter to hit. At that point, every player on the field, including the coaches and the other team members in the dugout, strategize, communally working to win, even while some fans encourage the players and others don't. At such a point, the objective is not to show how much any one player knows or to require another person to take care of a certain task, but to help strike out or to put out the batter on the opposing team. That is team effort.

In a school, teachers are the main deliverers of knowledge. Their task is to educate the youngsters who have been placed in their charge. Every educator and education leader knows this, but many education systems do not function to advance and support the interactive relationship between the teacher and the student. Often teaching becomes, in real life, only one of the many duties that teachers are hired and required to accomplish. Nowadays, teachers are charged with a myriad number of other responsibilities, depending on the particular school district.

But students should be the main beneficiaries in an education system, while teachers and administrators who earn their livelihoods in the field of education should be rewarded for their efforts. Talk to almost any K–12 educator today, however, and we encounter increasingly frustrated and dissatisfied professionals who are kept, by one obstacle or another that most educators will spell out, if we inquire, from doing a better job. In such conversations, the "educational system" is often represented as a kind of ogre that no one person or individual fully controls, that no one is capable of successfully explaining, and, worse, that no one can understand well enough to improve it. When we inquire, we learn that something militates against good teaching — some intractable factor or person, who may be a principal, a teacher, a counselor, an administrator, a school board member, a benefactor, or even the governor or the president. One or several of these education stakeholders interposes with one more task or responsibility, keeping educators from carrying out their teaching duties to their students.

> *School spirit was high in the middle school, and the principal often helped out by providing weekly small tokens of appreciation, such as new pens with "Teachers are #1" tags or fresh fruit or even sundaes, treats which he asked the parent-teacher organizations to bring. For many days I had noticed my colleague Sonia looking weary, but since she was not one to talk, I did not want to intrude. I knew this teacher to be a very responsible, experienced, nurturing instructor who took her career seriously. She had been teaching more than twenty years. When I asked her how her classes were going, she said, "I love my classes, but I am so fatigued by the paperwork that the state and the district require for all of this accountability that I am thinking of quitting. I have 80 students. Next year my teaching load is going up to 100+. Even in the nice teaching situation we have here, with so many [teachers] working together, I have often felt low morale because of the time that paperwork is taking from the kids. Now I just feel burned out. I don't think I can keep up."*

For reasons like these, the great majority of team members in an educational system usually turn to doing what each can within the precincts of a classroom. But improving education by trying to take care of one's own corner of the education world is like trying to cool a very warm house by fidgeting with the nearest window. If some people are trying to cool the house by opening windows, others are seeking the same objective by closing them and turning on the fans or turning on and off the air-conditioning units in frustration all day long. Still others are using any number of other approaches that look as if they might work today, this week, or for this unit or assignment. The question is: Will the house be cooled and the students educated as successfully as possible if the entire air-conditioning unit were to be made to work in a smoother, more co-ordinated way? Clearly, what is required is a study of the whole house so that a useful air-conditioning system can be installed, one that will take into account all the relevant elements that need to be considered in order to cool the house effectively with the least amount of energy loss.

We are not, of course, suggesting specific, regimented ways of teaching students, for such an approach would snuff out the individual initiatives of teachers, to say nothing of the creative imagination that good teaching requires. Our point is that in a well-honed education system, everyone should have a sense of everyone else's role, making the expectations for everyone clear. In such a system, there ought to be sufficient time left to encourage teachers and all other stakeholders in education to employ their best talents and skills for the benefit of their students, thereby improving the lives of all people associated with the school enterprise.

We know that most people who work in and are associated with our education systems work hard. But that is not the same as working well enough together to help accomplish the communal goal of educating the next few generations successfully. Indeed, what is needed, to use another metaphor, is to see all educators working more in unison, as if they were all members of an orchestra or a symphony, so that all students are primed to achieve the quality education that ideally should be offered to all students. We believe that if educators and society in general were to agree on how an educational system works smoothly, the education system diagram that features the pedagogical relationship between a teacher and a student can considerably improve the education that tomorrow's adults need today.

*T*he following few chapters for that reason are addressed to all people directly or indirectly connected to education. We have in mind teachers, K–12 administrators, and staff members, legislators, university academicians, law enforcement officers, and the average, taxpaying American citizen. By demonstrating how the schools can function to benefit everyone, we believe it is possible to improve and to deliver quality education to all students.

After thinking about all the professional relationships in education, we remain convinced that the relationship between the teacher and the students in the classroom has to be central to the educational enterprise. If we are to improve the quality of the education delivered to students, this is the most important relationship around which educators and citizens need to restructure our education systems. Everybody else involved in an educational system, from the president of the United States to the regular taxpaying citizen, should see himself or herself as a facilitator and as a helper to this central social relationship.

Although some education scholars who have studied other aspects of the schools may place more emphasis on some other relationship than the teacher-student connection, we are convinced that nothing else is as necessary for the individual student. We make this statement because during the length of the day, teachers, in effect, often play a role comparable to that of substitute parents and counselors to the students. For this reason, all Americans need to understand that the teacher-student classroom relationship is at the core of our communal, social effort to educate the young, since, in practice, teachers are widely expected to treat all students as if the latter were their own progeny.

"The secret of education," Ralph Waldo Emerson said in a commencement address, "lies in respecting the pupil." A way to respect students is in paying as much attention as possible to their individual qualities. K–12 students will someday vote and pay taxes. That should tell us that our society has a vested self-interest in educating all students to the best of their abilities as well as we can today. If teachers fail to teach students how to become the best citizens that they are capable of becoming, we run the risk that they will not have the necessary skills to strengthen their talents to cope with the challenges that life may offer them and the rest of us tomorrow. What we thus need to nourish in students are the skills to analyze and to examine options so that they can learn how to make the best decisions for themselves. This means that we have to teach students how to think about knowledge and how to categorize information so that they will know how to go about learning what is necessary, so that they can make wise decisions in their lives.

Victor had just transferred to our local high school as a sophomore. He had been struggling with math since middle school, and he was even going to morning tutorials before his first class. His grades, however, were not improving, and they were staying at the 70s level. His teacher had many years of experience. Victor's class had twenty-eight students, and enrollment was rising. To prepare for a test, Victor approached his teacher to ask if he could check his work on an algebra problem. After waiting for the teacher, who was explaining similar problems to other students, Victor's teacher looked at Victor's solution and worked out the problem for him again. This took a minute or so. The teacher handed the solved problem back to Victor. Dismayed, Victor said, "But, Mr. D., I didn't want you to work it for me. I wanted you to explain how to do it because I want to learn because I want to go to college." Mr. D. replied, "Oh, I know what you need. You need to take consumer math." [Consumer math is a basic math course geared for minimal math skills.] Luckily Victor told his parents what his teacher had said, and the following morning Victor's parents were in the school. Mr. D.

was not clear about who Victor was; he could not even tell Victor's parents where Victor sat in his third-period math class. His parents were not happy; they spoke to the counselor and had him removed to another algebra class, where Victor's grades progressively improved during the semester.

Since many young people are not being taught how to use the energies of their minds to solve problems, many learn to face life indifferently, or, worse, some even develop a desire to destroy what they see around them. Often they turn to living by seeing what they can get away with instead of learning from their errors, improving both themselves and society by employing their energies for the public good. The needs of individuals, we should know by now, do not wait. Miseducated youngsters soon become miseducated adults. Unable to provide for their own needs and the needs of their families, miseducated citizens will often end up creating problems for themselves and others. Since the realities of American schools do not allow educators to make much headway against crime, violence, drugs, and social apathy, today we have to concede that most of our schools only help students reach some of the education goals they need to achieve.

The idea is to promote ideas that most people embrace hypothetically but few are in positions to implement, mainly because the bureaucratic ways that are often in place keep our education systems from benefiting all students. Our objective is to convince educators and the broader public that only by correctly diagnosing experiences like the ones described above can the current K–12 education pipeline to adulthood be repaired. We are not suggesting that our education systems and the school pipeline need to be completely replaced, as some frustrated educators occasionally feel. But once people understand the reasons our systems of education operate ineffectively, particularly for Hispanic and other minority students, we believe that our schools can be repaired to deliver quality education to all students equitably.

To accomplish this goal, we encourage educators to look at the basic skills that education equally seeks to impart to all students. For that reason, we strongly recommend the print and oral approach to teaching. This simple, straightforward, and effective pedagogy can provide quality education for the young because it focuses student attention on the everyday skills that students progressively receive as they move from kindergarten to the twelfth grade. The content taught and the classroom exercises devised by teachers, as suggested earlier, are less important than the actual skills, though great care has to be given to content, of course, for a useful knowledge base is a necessary foundation for all subsequent learning.

By teaching students how to read well and how to interpret all printed materials and signs, by emphasizing oral communication, and by working to improve critical thinking skills, students learn how to work successfully in the adult world. As Latinos and Latinas who have personally experienced the kindergarten through higher education system for many years, we believe that a print and oral approach will offer the fundamental skills that every child in school can use to pursue higher education, should that become a choice after graduation from high school.

At the elementary level, for example, a child may recognize a corporate sign like the golden arches or the Nike check mark and will respond appropriately. As he or she ascends the school grades, students progressively are taught to discover that corporate symbols represent complex organizations on which studies can be undertaken, including dissertations and books. Making use of the print and oral approach that we recommend would allow teachers great opportunities to teach students according to needs and capabilities, everything, of course, depending on the competence a grade level requires and student interest. The print and oral idea, in short, is to expand student intellect by providing the necessary freedom for teachers to pursue pedagogic goals by developing and exploring the reading and interpreting of that sign leading students to writing and oral skills at their full potential.

Attempting to provide a quality education for minority students is likely the most challenging issue for educators of the twenty-first century. Since demographers agree that the growth in the U.S. population will mainly occur among Hispanics and other minorities, a good part of the future welfare of the United States depends on how well such students are educated today. Demographic projections suggest that if we do not repair the education systems now in place, Americans will share a lower quality of life during the next two or three generations.[5]

Aside from the education pipeline that students follow from kindergarten through twelfth grade, there is broad anxiety regarding shrinking financial and social support for both public and private education. Such developments understandably worry administrators and teachers who daily work in increasingly difficult environments that affect the lives of students. Factors such as larger classes, low wages, and increasing teacher accountability adversely affect student learning. Educators and administrators also worry that students will fail achievement examinations, that low test scores will not reflect the great amount of work that educators do, and that the public will lose more trust and confidence in the schools as the main vehicle for the transmission of American culture. Indeed, the recent political dialogues about school vouchers, the idea of using public school monies for private school education, stems from a loss of confidence in the American public school system of education.

When confronted with the prospect of educational failure, educators turn to showcasing successful programs and students. Such students are then featured by media that predictably often cover education by focus on students who have earned recognition. Highlighting student achievement, of course, is great, so long as such practices do not obscure the fact that for every successful student there are usually nine other youngsters who are learning less well or who may already have failed. Often the dearth of ethnic faces when student achievement is being celebrated speaks for itself. What we have to remember is that students not normally championed before the public in due time also become adults. For this reason, education has to benefit not only or mainly the successful students and programs that the public relations people like to point to, but all students. Disregarding students who receive weak educations that leave them unfit for productive futures harms such students now and society in the long run.

Despite widespread talk of educational reform, few students benefit from the nation's costly education reforms. Too many of today's students largely endure school until they graduate or leave. The education systems now in place serve most of the people whose interests are represented, but it is time to pay attention to the quality of education that traditionally disenfranchised students are continuing to receive. The failure to educate such students tells us that we need to repair our schools today, for the future will not forgive or bypass these students. If we do not prepare such students in our schools, demographers inform us that tomorrow we will regret not having done so.[6]

Chapter 3 | **BUT OUR EDUCATION
SYSTEMS ARE DISTENDED**

*T*he purpose of education is not to weed some students out, not to select only the best students, as some people appear to believe, but to discover the strengths of all students and to educate them using their talents and resources. We make a point of this objective because schools cannot "weed out" or separate out their young people without lowering the future possibilities of all society. Students and schools are the responsibility of all members of society, and accepting the challenge of educating the young means that a civilized society has to provide for all of our students, including disengaged students and the ones who appear determined not to cooperate. If we fail with the latter, society ends up paying for the miseducation of every student not taught how to take care of himself or herself, not to mention how to honestly provide for a family.

For this reason, we need to enjoin all citizens to help tackle the task of properly educating our youth. Everyone who attends school in the United States ought to have a real chance at the American Dream, at becoming a successful citizen. At this juncture, that dream is not a feasible goal for too great a number of our nation's students. Despite considerable talk of accountability, testing, measurement, and other validation efforts, educators cannot be expected to educate students properly because they are not empowered or equipped to accomplish that obligation. By educators we mean not only teachers, who are already pressured enough by all sorts of noneducational constraints and duties, but also administrators, who unfortunately are sometimes not sufficiently aware of the pressures under which teachers labor. The task, then, is how to ease everyone's burden while also providing the type of leadership that ensures a quality education for each student.

American educators and citizens need to rethink the individual roles and duties assigned to administrators, teachers, and community leaders responsible for shaping our education systems. Boredom should no longer be accepted as a student's response to education. An educator who works in a classroom where students are bored should seek and receive help to rekindle the interest of students. Administrators should be selected in part because they specifically know how to help such teachers. Delegating more responsibilities and activities to teachers who are already frustrated by inattentive students will not help. Many piecemeal approaches to education will only worsen relationships that teachers should be allowed to develop and nurture with their students.

The view of many people is that education is the province of educators. But educators are supervised and evaluated by school administrators, who, in turn, are accountable to school boards and state education agencies. The federal government, which controls taxpayer funds used in addition to the resources controlled by state legislatures, also shapes education systems and the kind of education delivered to students. We make a point of listing these players in the education world because in a school district any stakeholder can become a dominant force capable of throwing a school system out of balance, if allowed.

What teachers learn about teaching at colleges and universities is usually a separate endeavor from the educational realities that teachers encounter when they are hired by school districts. Invariably schoolteachers find out that what they learned at their higher education institutions requires adjustment to the needs, philosophies, and views of supervisors and other education personnel who hire, evaluate, and to varying degrees shape the schools and the careers of teachers. Enmeshed in regulatory requirements and accountability requisites, many initially well-intentioned instructors become disillusioned, and most eventually opt to do what they can to teach youngsters who spend a semester or two in their classrooms.

Despite the enormously rich educational resources of the United States at the local, state, and federal levels, proper assessment of what students have actually learned depends on correctly interpreting their academic records. Many teachers simply assume that if a student is enrolled by a counselor in a particular class, then the student must be ready to perform certain tasks. But most counselors are overworked because they have too many students whose progress they are required to monitor. Also, when the fit between a student and a class is not right, students and teachers in most cases adjust, though lately issues like school safety and drug prevention programs and discipline have necessarily turned teaching in most parts of the country almost into a secondary activity. Educators for these reasons endeavor to do the best they can under trying circumstances, and although there is a widespread sense that other developments are needed to improve the quality of the education delivered, how education can be advanced has remained vague.

The print and oral emphasis of our approach is designed to help all students, especially disaffected youngsters of any race and income level who have been turned off by education. The challenge is to turn around such students and to change their way of looking at learning by emphasizing reading materials and the critical thinking skills required to interpret all print and oral symbols and signs.

One of my colleagues began a language and culture club geared toward the Mexican American students, since the school was heavily Chicano. At her first meeting, she was relating the glory of the history of the Aztecs, ending with the coming of the conquistador Hernando Cortéz. When she displayed a few posters of the amazing pyramids built by the Aztecs in Mexico, she called them architectural wonders and related how the Aztecs were great mathematicians and astrologers. She then informed the students that this was the race from which they came and talked of the pride they needed to embrace because they were of Mexican lineage and race. At this point, she noticed that one male high school junior was crying copious and unabashed tears. She went over to him, thinking he might be ill. "What's wrong, Antonio?" "Miss, in all the years I have been in school, no one has told me a story like this or explained to me where I came from." "Surely you have studied the Aztecs before?" "No, we usually skip over Mexico in our classes."

Now that we know that educational neglect and the absence of positive media images have not helped to encourage growing minority students, all people who work within our schools need to help create a twenty-first century that will be different from the education avenues afforded minorities throughout the twentieth century. As Americans we have not historically understood that if our country is to remain competitive in the global economy, we have no choice but to educate all students better. Allowing certain groups of people to respond indifferently to education while we provide for the educational welfare of only our best students, we are learning, weakens our entire society. For weak education affects even the most successful people among us, unnecessarily burdening everyone.

Every year many educators, politicians, and other well-intentioned people generously attempt to improve education from kindergarten through the twelfth grade. Year in and year out a good number of experts and regular citizens devote thousands of hours working in the schools and in our communities at the regional, state, and national levels endeavoring to improve education for the students and for all personnel connected to our country's enormous education enterprise. And every semester, many of these education patrons become disenchanted and frustrated with the schools and with educators, largely because few efforts result in permanent improvements that can be confidently itemized.

People who follow developments and trends in the pedagogy of education know that much of the last quarter of the twentieth century was spent "reforming" education, either by emphasizing remedial studies, higher-level or advanced placement instruction, or other changes intended to yield better results. Some schools in various parts of the United States, of course, have been reformed and improved.[1] But what direly needs serious attention that is long overdue is the education of America's minority students and the infrastructure of the education systems where educators work every day of the school year.

Our view is that our current education systems seldom allow the stakeholders to operate as teams that successfully deliver the kind of instruction that students need. For this reason we believe that if we do not pay attention to the systems in which our educators work, the twenty-first century promises to offer the same kind of piecemeal, frustrating approach to education reform that we have experienced during the past twenty-five years. We believe that we need to examine how our education systems currently operate and what they could be doing not only for the students but for our educators and for American society.

Education systems in the United States and elsewhere in the world are unfortunately driven by many more factors besides the often articulated purpose of educating students. As schools have grown and expanded to assume responsibility for more and more societal and ideological needs, the main task of educating youngsters has been eclipsed, marginalized, reduced. Other needs of society, such as discipline and school safety, to name two recent and serious concerns, have displaced education. These newer necessities have considerably supplanted the mission to educate students. Discipline and school safety, to be sure, are required for education, but if the emphasis on discipline displaces the idea of engaging the minds of students, even well-behaved youngsters are going to dissipate their energies in any number of other ways.[2]

Adan had been in the United States four years and, now in middle school, he was the leader of a gang. Why a gang, I asked. They are my friends, he said, we help and protect each other. We do not do bad things. But you fight in school, I replied. Why do you fight? That always gets you in trouble. I fight because I protect others, and if I do not, others will come and beat me up. Why not use those energies to study and to educate yourself, as your parents told me they expect you to? At that point, Adan looked up at me and his facial expressions turned serious and he said, "Miss, don't misunderstand me. I love to come to school to learn. But what I don't like is coming and knowing I am going to get beat up." Don't fight; tell the teachers, I retorted. "They do not listen to me anymore. You are the first teacher who ever said to me, why do you fight and really want an answer. I will not go to any other teacher anymore because when I go I am not listened to. The principals look at me as one who fights all the time and as a troublemaker. They don't want to hear of the other guys who are bothering me."

We are pleased to say that at this particular school, administrators are now listening to Adan and also paying attention to his friends.

Dissipation of good energies occurs because teachers themselves have also been redirected. Schools, to cite an example that has not received much attention, have now been partly transformed into handmaidens to the school district lawyers and the criminal justice system. Teachers, we believe, should not be asked to function as legal assistants or as clerks for lawyers who have successfully convinced superintendents, principals, and school board members that the worst fate that can befall a school district is a lawsuit. Teachers need to be free to teach students once more. Their job is not to keep records and files on every single meeting or utterance that they have with parents or other professionals regarding their students. Teachers are authority figures, both in and outside of the classroom, and they should be given the type of professional respect and the leeway that they need to prepare their lessons according to the curriculum being used at their schools. As things now exist, many teachers cannot carry out their teaching duties because they have other assigned responsibilities. In such cases, students lose time that teachers would otherwise use to help them.

Litigation, by the way, has historically prompted most of the educational changes that have been made to improve the education of Hispanic and other minority students. Since the United States has become a litigation-happy country, school test cases like *Delgado v. Bastrop Independent School District* (1948) and others have improved K–12 education opportunities in the United States for Latinos and Latinas, but not enough.[3] Educators and administrators have understandably developed anxieties over being held liable for missteps in the education of any one student, but what we believe is an excessive concern with the possibility of lawsuits has altered education at almost all levels. For this reason, detailed records are now required or insisted on in most school districts, and teachers have consequently been recruited to keep careful records of what they do and say to students—all in case they ever have to defend their school district and themselves in court. As the needs of society have changed, in short, the education functions of the schools have been progressively encroached upon, and educators have not been sufficiently aware of such impositions to combat them successfully. If educators had been taught how to resist these other onerous responsibilities incrementally placed on them more effectively, we believe schools today would still be true to their main mission, which, again, is the education of the young and the continual renewal of society that schools ought to produce.[4]

Another relatively new way of dealing with "problem" or "at-risk" students that has mushroomed in the schools is the "alternative education programs." These programs have spread throughout the country in the past ten to twenty years, many under the guise of providing a better environment for students who are there to learn and to increase school security. Alternative education programs are pull-out programs that allow teachers, counselors, and administrators to create special classes for students who are troubled or distracted or who continually interfere with regular classroom teaching, often becoming pupils who require discipline. Such students are either pulled out or encouraged to leave their peer groups based on a great variety of behavior criteria. They are then taught separately, usually in different classrooms or even on different campuses. The intent is to provide them with the kinds of attention that will teach them more effectively, keeping them in school.

In the best instances, such programs work and students do graduate. But in most cases, students sent to these programs become disillusioned because they usually leave their peers elsewhere, making alternative education programs little more than holding tanks. This means that many alternative education classes, in effect, keep students in school for a few more years until the student grows tired of not being successful and quits, becoming another dropout.

Until very recently, the loss of such students is not taken into account in the statistics that school districts yearly release to the media, reports that quantify the number of graduates and allow the students who fail to graduate from high school to be left out of the official record. "That's pretty much isolation," said Billy Jacobs, senior director of the Texas Education Association safe schools division, in a Dallas Morning News article. "There should be other strategies implemented for minor things before removal [of students from their regular classes]." [5] Hence, instead of repairing school systems to educate all students, including the ones not reached by normal pedagogical methods, by turning to alternative education programs, school districts jettison students who need extra help instead of making institutional changes to salvage them. Such programs allow students who do not respond to the regular classroom environment to drop out or to leave school in less visible ways, meaning that alternative programs often serve as exhaust valves where students are seldom challenged or expected to exert themselves enough to earn a return to regular classes. Worse, when students realize that not much is required of them in these classes, they usually stop exerting themselves altogether, telling us that if these classes are to continue, they ought to be monitored very carefully by educators. Otherwise, we are talking of institutionally sanctioned ways of not meeting the needs of students who direly need more education instead of less.

Demographic changes have transformed education to such an extent that the school environment itself today ironically discourages students and even educators themselves from even trying to improve the quality of instruction. Parts of our education systems have changed so much during the past quarter century that in some school programs students have become less important than school district efforts to introduce teacher accountability, better measurement and testing instruments, and a host of other developments periodically promoted as necessary ways to improve education. In some districts, students are now so far from being the first consideration of educators that school personnel hardly consider students as their prime reason for working in education. When students become aware that they are perceived as sources of vexation, often they will become nuisances and troublemakers, since that is the expectation.

In one high school ESL class, two earnest recent immigrants came to ask me to please talk to the principal to get them out of that class because their parents, they said, did not bring them to the United States, at great sacrifice, to fool with education. They considered the ESL class a serious one, since it was here that English was taught.

I asked them what they thought the problem was. To my surprise, it was not that their teacher was not bilingual, making bridging to English more comfortable, but that they were not being taught how to help themselves learn. There were not even any English and Spanish dictionaries, and the teacher never gave them any homework, such as learning English vocabulary words or their spelling. The students had become exasperated and had taken to misbehaving in class.

I went to the principal, who felt his hands were tied. There were no qualified ESL teachers available. Those two particular students left the class and agreed to be placed in an alternative English class for low-performing students. Here they learned English! How distressing that the administrators whose very job in the education pipeline is to provide assistance to the teachers were unwilling or did not want to seek a solution for the very students who needed help the most.

As a result of weak legislative and ineffective school district efforts to improve the schools, many teachers, counselors, and administrators today also feel abandoned. That is why they turn to making what small improvements they can. Educators do what they sensibly can within the restriction and constrictions of the school systems. In bureaucracies, apparently no one is in a good enough position to create or to effect the necessary repairs that our education systems require in order to impact students more positively and comprehensively. Individually and collectively, teachers and administrators feel powerless to effect systemic change, for a number of difficult-to-articulate realities sap their time and energies. There are, indeed, so many kinds of system constraints that constantly require the attention of educators today that properly repairing an education system often seems foolhardy and pointless.

As a consequence, educators and parents are turning to focus attention only or mainly on the education that their own children receive. Local, state, and federal government funding entities have also responded by developing a propensity for approaching education segmentally, that is, awarding funding to the best proposals submitted for consideration, with the hope that one or more of these efforts will somehow turn education around and make our schools what they should be: learning places for students. In the absence of carefully thought-out repair programs for our education systems, local interest coteries have consolidated power and developed an inclination to look out mainly for the interests of their own groups—in effect using public tax monies to carry out mainly their desires, values, and more partial agendas.[6]

Education, though, has to be seen as a societal pipeline that ought to begin in kindergarten. Students then have to be carefully prepared at every grade level. Since all students are shaped by their education and become products of everything they experience at all junctures of the school system, K–12 education needs to work seamlessly, successfully moving students through the grades, eventually delivering them to the desired graduation end. This basic goal is widely known, but in the everyday school setting and given the funding priorities and considerations of our state legislatures and federal government, education stakeholders often fail to act according to this fundamental, shaping purpose.

*I*f we are to improve life opportunities for all students, as the goal has been articulated, we need to repair the weaknesses that now exist in the K–12 education pipeline that ought to lead smoothly into our colleges and universities. Some students, to be sure, are not interested in attending higher education, but students should nonetheless be prepared for college, should they later choose to apply. A quality K–12 education will contribute to making a stronger, better prepared American citizenry. The idea is to provide students with a new sense of education, one that will allow our younger generations to see an altogether different and clearer purpose for sitting in the classrooms of America for thirteen long years. Why do we urge such an approach? Over the past thirty years, books from James Herndon's *The Way It Spozed To Be* (1968) to Jonathan Kozol's *Savage Inequalities* (1991), among other useful studies, have convincingly established the need to reform the public education systems of the United States.[7] In 1997, Executive Director Deborah Wadsworth of the nonprofit Public Agenda summarized the findings of a comprehensive national survey:

> [T]he disconnect between what the professors want and what most parents, teachers, business leaders and students say they need is often staggering. Their prescriptions for the public schools may appear to many Americans to be a type of rarified blindness, given the public concerns about school safety and discipline, and whether high school graduates have even basic skills.[8]

The glaring "disconnect" that the Public Agenda survey found does not exaggerate actual school conditions experienced by a good number of people in many different ways. The reality of American schools is that some students clearly receive successful educations, while others do not—and sometimes even in the same classroom with the same lessons.

Lashandra Jones was a bright African American ninth-grade student of mine who lived in a house managed by her older sister because their mother was mentally challenged. One day while I was explaining a lesson for which the students were being asked to utilize a newspaper, she asked me what an "ad" is. By her questions and her quizzical expressions, I had long suspected that she had almost NO knowledge base from which to draw. During class discussions, she seemed to absorb information on all of the topics that I encouraged students to discuss. On another occasion, she spoke of how she was given a calculator in math class and she had "never seen a calculator like that in my life," so she didn't know how to use it and told the teacher so. This was an advanced placement, or AP, class because she was in a pre-college class, so I suspect the teacher thought she was teasing or trying to be funny or seeking attention, since all of the other students knew how to use the calculator. At any rate, Lashandra received no aid. She was frustrated and eventually flunked her math course. She told me it was because of her inability to use the calculator; she just got "mad" and stopped asking the teacher for help. The next trimester she asked her counselor NOT to put her in AP or college-track math courses. She fared better, she said, because this teacher took the time to show her how to use the materials and she understood her.

Lashandra got pregnant in October. The next time I knew any information about her, she told me she was going to "get the Principal's signature" on a paper because she would be attending an alternative program in school. My heart sank. All I could do at this point was to encourage her to stay in her program by reminding her how hard she had worked in my class to bring up her grades and wish her well. Although I later learned she had been absent in her other classes, she had attended mine dutifully. The principal had been speaking with her often about her truancies during the semester; however, I was not informed of this fact and this upset me enormously. I expected better communication from professionals. There are students for whom one cannot do more after a while, because other students and other school demands pressure us. Still, for the school system to run smoothly, all parties who know a student need to keep each other informed, and not as an afterthought. Lashandra did have her baby and in time obtained her diploma.

How are such stories explained? Teachers and administrators will say that unengaged students tend to fail because they do not try harder and because their parents are not supportive. We also know that some students learn not to try, especially after they have found out that despite efforts there is little help available for them.

Teachers and administrators may say that they are willing to help such students, but students usually know when help is actually available and when it is not. Since we know that some parents fail to help their youngsters because they cannot or do not know how to help, we are left to deduce that, in such cases, their own upbringing and schooling failed them, too. In other instances, parents have no time and little energy left to help. We are not, to be sure, excusing parents from helping their youngsters but simply attempting to explain some realities that need to be recognized so we can look for solutions in other directions.

Perhaps the best place to start to repair an educational system is with the realization that in education every person is specifically charged with carrying out certain duties and type of work. Different views prevail about how different parts of the education systems ought to work, but what the task requires is to consider how the entire educational structure needs to function in order to benefit the students, teachers, and every person who works in a system. Administrators would do well to begin a school year by having in-service meetings and discussions for the needs of their particular schools.

Since tomorrow's citizens are in the K–university education pipeline today, we believe there is little time to experiment educationally with the lives of students. If the current educational practices were yielding satisfactory results, there would be no need for this book. Educators may here and there defend current practices, even when at other times they are likely to express dissatisfaction with the ways the young are taught. But for many years students have been passed from grade to grade — call it "social promotion" or something else — without receiving the necessary skills and preparation required to succeed in the twenty-first century. For that reason, we think it is time to work on repairing our education systems instead of spending time defending them further.

Although we believe that the current emphasis on standardized testing runs roughshod over the cultural mores and sensitivities that different students bring to the educational arena, careful, enlightened testing needs to be pursued. Such testing ought to be calibrated to the testing that instructors devise in their own classes, for tests by instructors are and need to remain an accepted way of monitoring student progress, primarily because no one else is in a position to know the progress of students better. The upshot of the issue is that current standardized test scores and other class performance measures tell us that we need to teach our students more effectively. Indeed, the schools are so overburdened and the resources are so stretched that usually there is little time left to address the kind of problems that we highlight in these chapters. We could also have addressed other trouble areas, but we believe that if the issues emphasized are attended to in the K–12 education pipeline, all students, including Latinos and Latinas, will likely be provided with the type of quality education that will allow more of them to compete academically. When we have taken an active interest in their young lives and problems by emphasizing all symbols in print and how they orally communicate, such students have generally improved their grade performance by at least a full grade.

| WHY STUDENTS DROP OUT

O ften students stop attending classes regularly and stop completing their schoolwork a good while before they finally drop out. These early warning signals should immediately alert educators to the students' loss of interest in school. If such signs are left unaddressed, students are likely to drop out eventually, telling us that the students themselves are quite aware that they have been miseducated, that they are unwilling to continue the charade of pointlessly going to school any longer.

I was asked to teach in the same area as mine as a substitute for a teacher who suddenly had been taken ill. I recognized several students from previous years. When the students saw me at the entrance to their door, they appeared surprised and some lowered their eyes. I was usually fruitful engaging students once class started, but I was unprepared for the lack of depth in understanding the class material and their inability to build on past knowledge. At least half of the class joked in embarrassment that they "had never had this material before." When the period ended, three of my own past students filed past me and made these comments in my ear: "We don't learn anything in this class, Mrs. P." The other teacher, they said, "began to teach well, but she never checks our homework and all our tests are scantrons." "Miss, kids take this class as a joke. We don't study in here."

In different ways, teachers, counselors, principals, and other administrators are told by exiting students in alarming numbers that they cannot take school any longer, that sufficient instructional help for their needs is not available. Confessing that they have felt frustrated by the expectation of taking courses that require them to turn in assignments that have little meaning for them is surely one of the most difficult decisions of their young lives. But disengaging themselves from schoolwork perceived as fruitless and making the public statement of dropping out indict a school district, and there should be no mistaking that fact. Such students at that point in life do not sufficiently think, nor do they want to believe, that without school, earning a living will be harder.[1]

Most dropouts know that the roads and the litany of possibilities for them are not attractive. Options invariably available to dropouts are menial jobs, drugs, drinking, crime, prostitution, pregnancy, unwanted children, and early marriages with difficult economic constraints, insipid work, rejections, and depression. A few students, of course, succeed without graduating, but such cases are increasingly less common. Too many well-intentioned youngsters have traveled those hard paths in life before with little relief, even though most students leaving school hope that their experience will be different.

Yet year after year, roughly more than a half-million Latino and Latina students go down these distressing paths of life.[2] What irritates us and what hurts and will continue to harm them is that most students who leave school make that decision knowing quite well that they are diminishing their own future prospects by doing so. Since such choices do not lead to the lifestyles daily paraded before them on television and in the advertising world, we have to suppose that staying until graduation is clearly more objectionable than leaving.

SOMETHING happens to them, particularly at the middle and high school grades, we are left to deduce. It is not so much that the same negative "something" happens to students, but rather that all sorts of different, negative experiences appear to occur to them. The school curriculum and how it is taught, we soon have to conclude, does not seem to take much of their young lives into account. The teenage years, to be sure, are especially difficult, so a good course of study absolutely has to keep students intellectually engaged and anchored as closely as possible to good family values. If what they study in school does not meet society's needs and if the courses they study do not nourish students' self-esteem, educators and school authorities need to analyze what students are daily experiencing in the schools. Perhaps the following questions should be asked: What makes the sad, difficult prospects that dropouts are likely to face more attractive than what is offered at school? Is school that bad and unattractive? If that is the case, then such schools need to be responsibly repaired, since they are failing to provide the education that students need.

Educators and communities need to consider what dropouts experience in school one, two, or three years before they leave. Clearly what such students are encountering in the classroom is encouraging them to drop out of school instead of staying to study and graduate.

These two questions are important issues to address regarding school dropouts. Although the bleak prospects are evident, students continue leaving school undeterred by them. Either these students are uncommonly tough, or they delude themselves into thinking that their own experiences will be different. Maybe, though, what they experience in middle or high school before dropping out is so discouraging that they would rather take their chances outside of school.

*G*ood schools and educators should offer all students a healthy outlook on life. Students who are nurtured and supported properly by their parents, the community, *and* the teachers and administrators of a school district graduate and move on to college and the better-paying positions of society. The ones who "choose" to leave, however, usually are not sufficiently nurtured by their parents *and* teachers, and their communities generally do not help them much, either. At school, such students tend to receive rather indifferent treatment, and the message that they often receive, from what Mexican American and other minority students tell us, is "Make it if you can. It is your life." Students who drop out, in short, do not see themselves as having a better choice. Even minority students who do graduate and attend college relate surprisingly similar stories:

> *Three different university students, two Mexican Americans and one African American, who came to intern in the schools from three different large Texas cities, had received the same kind of advice. Despite the good grades they received, counselors at their high schools had encouraged each to seek careers in vocational training. "You are good with your hands," one was told. "If you really want to continue studying after high school, there is _____ Junior College that you can attend," the other two were informed. All three students had to resist such counseling and continued studying to secure good grades. Not one of them was told about the process for applying and enrolling into a university, and, despite the fact that their counselors knew they were interested in higher education, none was encouraged to take AP, advanced placement, classes. Luckily, each was fortunate to have one teacher who took enough interest to guide them through the application process.*

As educators we have to recognize dire circumstances that are still being shaped by past discriminatory practices, and we need to correct problems that previous generations of educators have not addressed well enough.

So, what is the pattern? We have found that about a year or two before leaving, student dropouts will gradually distance themselves from school in a variety of discernible ways. Our theory is that psychologically separating themselves from school, their peers, and class activities occurs because the school experience fails to provide the students with the necessary support received by students who continue and graduate. Schools will invariably respond that they are doing everything possible to retain students, but our point is that if this is the case and students still continue to drop out, then clearly school administrators and teachers need to find other, more effective strategies. Continued failure in reducing the number of students dropping out from school is simply not acceptable; it is not an option any more. What works for one school district may not work for another, but that is the nature of an educator's challenge. The job is not finished until pedagogical approaches that succeed in engaging the interests of students retain them.

I first met Ana Benitez and her father, Martin, in the school hallway. Ana had been in the United States for about five years. Martin had brought his family from Mexico for "mejores oportunidades para mis hijos," to secure better opportunities for his sons and daughters. Two years before, when I first met Ana in my ninth-grade Spanish for Native Speakers class, she told me that her dad had made a small room in his house, placed a Spanish-English dictionary there, and declared that the room would be his children's "study room." She was happy about that, and we spoke about the study space. She was pleased.

Next time I saw her, she was driving a car into the high school parking lot. "Mi papa me compró un carrito para la escuela," she happily said of the used car her dad had bought her to attend school. I saw her a few more times during the year, always asking how she was doing in her ESL classes. There had been many teacher personnel changes, and ESL teachers were scarce. I wished I could help her more, but that area belonged to the ESL teacher. I would always encourage the students to try their best, but I knew learning English was difficult without the proper instruction.

I last met her in the hall walking through with her dad. She told me she was "checking out" of school. My mouth dropped open. I asked why. She did not answer, saying she was "going to _____," an alternative learning program. Her dad said in Spanish, "Ma'am, I rise at three in the morning to work at Shipley's doughnuts." He had his white uniform on at the time. "I bought her a car," his eyes watered, "and, now, look—the sacrifices that we make, and now she wants to leave school." He showed me a paper from the school office. "Look at all the absences she has. I have been called only two times. I came both times, but no one was available to speak to me in Spanish about the absences. I punished her, not allowing TV or dances on the weekends. Now she just wants to drop out." I spoke to Ana about the hurt her dad was clearly experiencing, and she verbally promised that she would finish her program and obtain a diploma. I reminded her of the difficulties that women without professions face these days. It was a tough and depressing way to end a school day.

How can schools nurture all students? From the time they are placed in the education pipeline in kindergarten until they graduate, parents want their sons and daughters to exercise their individual skills and talents at the hands of sympathetic teachers. That is why parents will usually take a child to school on the first day: to place the child personally in the protective custody of the teacher, within the safe environment of a school, demonstrating by such action that they are willing to make the necessary sacrifices to keep them attending school. But if educators do not respond appreciatively to such efforts, most Latino and Latina parents will feel slighted and stop going to the schools, cutting short any possible subsequent participation in the school activities of their children.

About the fourth or fifth grade, children in the schools are encouraged to begin to show self-reliance and independence, an emphasis that usually surprises most Latino and Latina parents, especially parents who nurture their elementary-age children a year or two longer than Anglo parents. Most parents are not informed about this expectation. By the time they learn that their children ought to have been taking care of their schoolwork and homework assignments independently, often their sons and daughters have already been reprimanded for not taking consistent care of tasks that measure their self-reliance. The adjective frequently used to describe such students is irresponsible. Involved parents, however, monitor the progress of their children to make sure they are studying appropriately, that is, as educators expect them to do. And since most schools expect personal or individual responsibility in the upper elementary grades or the first year of middle school, students who learn good, independent behavior feel encouraged, while others unfortunately begin to feel rejected at the very moment when their emerging adolescent egos seek acceptance and encouragement. Good, responsible behavior is exhibited when students follow normal grade-level expectations, but as we know, there is also a kind of self-reliance that takes pride in resisting expectations. If not recognized and addressed, this latter type of self-reliance can lead to further problems with authority figures both in school and in society.

School dropouts tend to exhibit the second type of self-reliance. Such students, they have told us themselves, usually begin to believe that they can function alone, that they can succeed without the help of teachers and administrators. Although they know that many students who have left before them have had a difficult time, that knowledge seldom deters them and in fact sometimes ironically even encourages them. Why doesn't knowing what generally happens to other school dropouts deter them? Because, despite the facts, every dropout feels that leaving school will be better for him or for her individually than staying in class. If knowing that life will likely be more difficult does not discourage them, this suggests how unpalatable the school experiences are that they want to leave behind them. At the time they leave, they clearly think it is better to go at life alone rather than to stay in school where they daily have to put up with indifference and the "we don't really care" messages and attitudes communicated to them as they move listlessly from one class to the next.

Do educators send out such signals even though their words say otherwise? We believe that students who choose to drop out hear and sense such messages. And if students pick up such signals, those are the realities and attitudes that the schools cannot continue to disregard.

Teresa, a Mexican American teacher, was speaking to me in my room when Velma, an African American pre-college student came in to give me a paper I had asked her to write. I thanked her and gave her a kiss and a hug. At this point, Teresa made a face and turned away. When the student was out of earshot, she said, "I can't stand her." Yet, when I told Teresa the story about Ana and her father Martin, tears welled up in her eyes. Teachers MUST constantly make an attempt to demonstrate goodwill to everyone, even the students who try our patience. Ethnic students of every type, in particular, from their own words to me, are under considerable strain these days, and they immediately "feel" the sting of all types of prejudices. I have heard about and have seen their lives unfold in school on a daily basis and can say that prejudicial signs and expressions interfere and sometimes outrightly destroy their ability to concentrate and to continue with their schoolwork. Of-

*ten these youngsters have the added problems of economic deprivations
in their home lives. Yet they are expected to attend their classes where
we teachers expect total cooperation and respect, as we should; yet, as
professionals, we frequently fail to sympathize and to understand their
individual circumstances.*

What exactly do dropouts experience before leaving school? In the
minds of such youngsters and in their language, they "have to put up
with" school, which they see as harder to endure than the grim prospects
awaiting them elsewhere. Dropouts find school boring and considerably
more unendurable than the unrewarding jobs opened to them.

Why? Because, according to them, school personnel do not nurture
all students equally, even though most people think so. To be sure, there
are other relevant factors, but we have learned that most students are
willing to remain in school if they have a sense of belonging or if they
have established a personal connection to at least one teacher or a counselor or some other adult in a school. By the time a student has made the
decision to leave school, we have found that the nurturing support that a
student should have been receiving has failed in one grade or more.

*I was called to substitute for a high school ESL teacher recently. ESL
classes in Texas, but also in California and in other parts of the country, typically consist of students who are recent immigrants, who have
been in the United States one or two years and are learning English. I
was teaching for perhaps ten minutes when a group of students hurriedly came into the same room where I was holding class to "work on a
test" handed to them by another regular classroom teacher. They were
allowed to be in the ESL room, supposedly to help each other by discussing their science questions in Spanish among themselves. Their teacher,
they told me, could not explain the test to them, since she does not speak
Spanish.*

*I asked if they needed my help, and they politely said "no," explain-
ing in Spanish that they were going to try to comprehend the questions
themselves, using the English they communally know, to write answers.
I asked if every answer would be the same on each paper, and they said
"yes," that was the manner in which they were to do it. Since this was the
first time I was substituting ESL in this school, I later discovered this
was the common practice among the regular education teachers when
ESL students took exams and required help with their assignments.*

Among the students was a young lady named Eugenia, who walked in five minutes after the testing group did. She stated that she had been in the school's main office. She arrived with a note from the office permitting her entrance into the class, but no explanation regarding her tardiness. As I continued my lesson in phonetic English rules to my original group, she kept looking up, keenly listening. She then started to participate in my group. It was fine to have her so interested, but I carefully reminded her that she should work on her test for the science teacher which she came in to take. However, her interest aroused my curiosity, and I later asked her why she had arrived late. "I received a D-hall (detention), Miss, the first one ever that I've gotten," she told me embarrassed in Spanish. I asked her, in English, how long she had been in this country. "Since January of last year, Miss." I asked two other questions in easy English, but she was unable to understand.

I wondered for what reason a student who possessed obviously nice manners and was just learning to speak English would receive detention. So I asked. She told me that while asking a Spanish-speaking peer for clarification of her teacher's instructions, the teacher had told her to "stop speaking in Spanish." She told him she was asking directions, at which point she said he wrote a detention slip and told her to go to the office to see when after-school D-halls would be assigned. On her way to the office, she saw a Mexican American friend and asked her to translate the reason for her D-hall that was written out on the slip she carried. The detention note said, "This student was speaking in Spanish and said 200 swear or curse words directed at the instructor." I looked at Eugenia incredulously, and another student added that the instructor had stated the reason out loud in English for the whole class to hear as he wrote it down on the slip of paper she was then given.

At this point other students spoke up. "Miss, no es verdad! It is not true!" Another student said "Miss, she didn't even say one word!" Another student said that the teacher immediately began writing when Eugenia tried to explain in broken English what she wanted in speaking in Spanish to the other student.

To confirm what I thought, I asked if the instructor knew any Spanish. "No, Miss," stated one of the students. I wondered if anyone would question the reason Eugenia was in D-hall when she arrived. Would any administrator in D-hall wonder what a young lady barely able to comprehend English could have done that would have placed her there? Left without such support, what should such students do? That day, Eugenia, embarrassed and ashamed, stepped into the D-hall room to serve her time. I saw her in the hall during report card time a couple of

*weeks later and asked how everything was going. "OK, Miss." May I see
your report card, I asked. "Oh, no, Miss, it's not good," she added with
lowered eyes. "I wanted to be a good student when I came here, but now
I might go back to Mexico."*

This incident strongly indicates why some students leave, while others
graduate and continue onward into college and then into the better positions of society.

All kinds of reasons have been advanced to explain why the education
system works more for some students and not for others. As we can see
here, some instructors have no defense and should not be teaching. The
most common explanation is that the proper nurturing home environment is simply missing for students who drop out. The truth is that such
students are often mortified to tell their parents about incidents like these
with their teachers, and parents, in turn, cannot always find translators in
schools that do not reach out to hire bilingual personnel. The result is a
Latino or Latina student who begins to feel embattled, disheartened, and
disillusioned. The importance of a supportive home environment, indeed, is likely the single most important factor that helps educators teach
youngsters. But so is simple sympathy, that is, nurturing and understanding for the different challenges that similar students may face.

We have known for some time that many minority students in particular do not have parents who can afford to be at home to provide the
necessary guidance and support. Students themselves often tell educators that their parents expect them to graduate, even though they likely
know little about how to support their sons and daughters. If a support
structure is missing at school, though, more students will consider dropping out. This means that school professionals have to make extra efforts
to provide all students with support that their parents cannot, especially
since minority students frequently lack the necessary psychological and
family resources to succeed.

Although data and estimates of cited studies vary, largely because
counting methods and dropout rate assessments are different from
school district to school district, roughly 47 percent of Mexican American or Spanish-speaking students leave school before graduating in
Texas, while blacks fare only a little better at an estimated 36 percent
dropout rate. Despite all the reasons adduced, the basic reason is that
minority students are not being sufficiently attended to by the school
systems and society in general. Their education problems are being disregarded, largely because other issues traditionally receive priority in

our schools. This is to say that too great a majority of America's ethnic students are not being properly provided with the same amount of the necessary nurturing, encouragement, and support that students who successfully continue through the education system normally receive.

This failure occurs because at the necessary junctures in their lives when their needs should be carefully addressed, teachers, administrators, and other education stakeholders appear to be too busy taking care of bureaucratic activities that effectively leave students drifting through the halls of education. Sometimes students are left to drift because educators do not know how to support such students and where to begin to make a difference in their young lives. At-risk students are then left without the care and concern usually provided to other students who politically cannot be allowed to fail without raising the ire of parents and a community. We are not, of course, saying that educators do not attempt to help all students, but there is a difference between trying and succeeding at providing a quality education to all students.

Brighter minority students have informed us that they have noticed how schools fail to help their counterparts. When minority students begin to feel that they are not as important in the eyes of some educators as the students whose parents are actively involved in school activities and school board meeting decisions, some of those students begin to move toward the exit. Overcoming this perception is extremely difficult, for it basically means that Hispanic, black, and other minority students have to persevere if they choose to stay in school. Once sensed, such perceptions are difficult to combat, for views like these gnaw at young minority minds, disturbing their psychological environments in school and at home. This kind of felt rejections soon manifest themselves in "I don't care" attitudes, in "I don't like school" statements, and in gangs, drugs, violence, crime, or in a combination of these, any one of which leads to dropping out of school, as Miguel's story shows:

Recently I was helping test middle school students who would be entering high school the following year into a pre-college program. The program profiled students with a GPA of 2.0 to 3.0 but who had the potential to be university students. The idea was to work with this group and "fill in the gaps" to have them on a college track as soon as possible. Each student came in individually for testing and assessment, so I was able to speak to each one. Questions included whether they liked school and what the school might do to develop a better learning environment for them. Most students stated they liked school well enough, especially be-

cause they met so many friends. All stated they would like a better learning environment, and standard responses centered around the statement "because some kids don't speak and act well toward the teachers and many have an 'attitude' with the teachers." A very intense Miguel asked what I taught at the high school. Spanish, I replied, and not only beginning, but Spanish for Native Speakers, which is one of my favorite classes. Intrigued, he asked, "Do you teach about our raza [race], I mean who we are?" Do you mean the early history of Mexico? I asked. "Yes!" he said, his eyes bright with a new alertness. I just don't teach vocabulary and verbs, but about our cultura as well, I answered. Why do you ask? "Well, I've been to school since first grade, and no one has ever spoken to us about Mexico or the early times in Mexico. I expected to hear some things here in middle school history class, but other than saying the Aztecs were a great civilization, nothing else has been discussed. I know that the Aztec people were great because my dad and mom have told me, and when I visit Mexico the pictures I see of them look like me. They were intelligent people, but no one ever tells us about that. Whenever the teachers or our textbooks bring up things about Mexico, it doesn't make me feel good that I'm Mexican American. So I want to get into this program so I can learn better, and I'll do well because it's going to tell me how to get to college. I want to get there [university] because I want to become a teacher and maybe write a textbook that tells kids like me what a great background we come from. What do you think, Miss?" That's a great idea! You can do that! "Yeah, and then the other kids can hear about us, too!" I let him know that he was very wise for realizing these things and encouraged him to stay on track and to write that book because it may yet take awhile for the schools to teach our history properly or at all to our large Mexican American population, that the former Mexican territories have been part of the United States since 1848. That has been time enough, right? I also told him that many people are aware of our plight and many are working to rectify it but that in the meantime he must not give up. I told him to look for history items on his own and to make class reports when possible. That way, he would begin teaching others soon. He was quite happy and said he hoped he'd see me next year at the high school and be in my class.

The history of American public education shows that the schools have not traditionally taken care of the education needs of minority students. Schools have mainly served to provide opportunities for students already capable of exerting themselves. Given the rates at which minority students are failing, though, we believe the schools should be the new center of attention for our education efforts. Since demographers tell us our minority populations will soon make up the majority of America's citizens, we believe it is time to make minority students the main measure by which American education is judged, since the schools have shown that they can serve mainstream white students. People in the American education system, from elementary to the university level, need to recognize the importance of minority students in the future of American life. Acknowledging this reality means that we have to devise ways to educate all citizens properly. Minority students are the ones who particularly need to see that society cares enough about them to outfit them well for the future. The time when minority youngsters could be provided with less attention ought to end, because American society will only hurt itself and our future by continuing to miseducate such students.

As in the twentieth century, we can no longer blame students and or their parents for failing in school. Such responses and rationalizations are not acceptable any more. Justifications of this kind continue to overlook the dropout problem instead of reconfiguring school resources and personnel to address and solve this issue.

We know that educators claim they are doing everything possible, everything that can humanly be done, given school realities today. And they are likely correct, given that budget allocations show that they are still trying to serve the needs of the students whom they have traditionally served in the past. But what needs to be done almost everywhere in the United States is to recognize that the majority of the students have now changed, that many are students of color, and that schools for this reason need to address education issues differently. If the school realities have changed, in short, the education systems need to be repaired and altered.

Denial of the minority dropout problem often is the first automatic, natural response, followed by the assertion that educators *are* enormously busy today. The problem, however, is that most educators are required to be "accountable," that is, they are required first and foremost to document, both for their supervisors and state education agencies, the curriculum they are following and everything that they do or try to do for each of their students. Preparing a useful weekly lesson plan is a necessity, but all kinds of other activities interfere and keep teachers from focusing their best energies on thinking how they can teach their students most effectively. School system administrators should allow teachers space and time enough to teach and to prepare themselves well for teaching their students. After all, that is the central mission of the schools. Teachers should also be hired because they are interested in teaching all students. Their goodwill toward students should be a requisite for employment. If teachers are not trained to be aware of and sensitive to the needs and backgrounds of their students, they should not be in the classroom.

Teachers have not been trained as legal assistants, or as guards, or as report writers. All of the emphasis on accountability, in effect, has to be recognized for what it truly is: time and good energies taken away from the preparation of lessons and classroom teaching. Legal clerking daily frustrates teachers nationwide, because instead of spending their time at school working with students and using their imaginations to prepare engaging class lessons, teachers are left with little time to carry out the main task for which they were hired: to teach. Many people recognize that teachers everywhere in the United States tend to "work overtime," that is, after school, weekends, holidays, and late into the evenings. But there is no extra compensation for this extra work as there is in other employment areas. Teachers have to work extra because during their regular school day, much of their lesson-writing and preparation time has been severely cut into by other activities that have little to do with improving the quality of the teaching. This extra work for which teachers have to make time is not a fair burden, and it is not ethical. Legislators and administrators commiserate with teachers, but commiseration does not ease the extra burden that only more personnel and more financial pay can provide.

Students on the other hand simply have to wait until teachers finish documenting and doing all the extra work that teachers of previous generations never undertook. That is why teachers had more time to teach. But today, teachers hardly have a moment to themselves. They are more like school policemen. And like policemen, they spend a great deal of their time writing very specific reports about accidental misunderstandings, home calls and state-mandated paperwork, all because courts and judges today expect such reports in order to pass judgment on issues that someday might conceivably be brought up—if a school district is sued.

A visitor can walk into any school and notice that students are usually standing around, sitting, or working by themselves. Teachers, though, are extremely busy. When they are not teaching, they are often writing something for a student file or grading papers. Our point is that students are increasingly receiving less teacher attention because teachers have little choice but to spend a large amount of their time performing many tasks that do not directly affect or influence students. Much of their busywork, for it is difficult to call it anything else, will end up filed away in the school or district office — ready to use, should a case ever arise in which such information may be helpful.

This is why teachers are extremely busy these days, but, as we suggest, they are not necessarily busy teaching and working with the students who need the most help. We know, for example, that the honors and gifted and talented students are more capable of taking care of themselves, given the fact that they are made to feel comfortable enough in school to secure the grades that will be needed to succeed in college. Students who are not in advanced placement or honors courses also need to be challenged, and this is why teachers need to make extra efforts with such students. By making these statements, of course, we are not minimizing honors and gifted and talented students. What we propose is that teacher activities be examined to see how they directly affect all students. If teachers have their hands full of tasks unrelated to teaching, why not consider enlisting, for example, the brighter students to help other students? The idea, in other words, is to set up the school so that quality education is available not only to the best students but to all the other students who often feel disenfranchised by our education systems.

For these reasons, we believe that the energies of educators need to be better focused on all students, minority and majority, for our country's future citizenry need the kind of nurturing during the school years that produces a quality educated public. Students inclined to leave school should not be allowed simply to walk away when they are sixteen or seventeen before they graduate. At that age, they do not know what they are doing, regardless of what they say and how maturely they can behave.

We believe that students tend to leave behind further education because the current school cultures gradually encourage them to exit. This means that high-risk students need to be made to feel that they are important citizens in the cultures that most schools create. Visitors have only to look at the students in a school environment to see the disaffected, uninvolved youngsters who essentially seek the company of other students like themselves because their schools have excluded them. Schools should not be holding tanks, places, or prisons where youths "do time." We do not need guards, or task masters, or people who like imposing their official roles on the young. What is needed are caring teachers, administrators, and district system leaders who understand that students go through different stages as they make their way through the education pipeline and who can successfully work to keep the students engaged in learning. Teachers need to be provided with the time and the working space to nurture students who will eventually become educated citizens. Each district seriously needs to study how their teachers spend their days in order to provide them with the flexibility they need to address the education needs of their students.

If we are to reverse the unacceptable school dropout rates that we have seen during the last quarter-century in America, we need to realize that dropouts do not choose to leave school for harder roads out of their own volition. That decision simply makes no sense. We should acknowledge that such students are unintentionally but nonetheless effectively pushed in that direction, many little by little since kindergarten and the first grade. One day these students discover a strange fact: that school is harder and more difficult to live in than the hard outside world where they know they will have to fight to survive. And that should not be the case. Life in school should never be psychologically harder to endure than the outside world.

In order to keep students who are now dropping out in large numbers, we need to examine what we are doing to all students in our schools every day.

The curricula we teach are not more important than our students, yet that is exactly the message that most students unfortunately receive daily. We need to remember that the curriculum exists *for* the students; if the curriculum does not engage their interests, we should change what they study to secure and invite their interests. That is how everything is sold and promoted in the world outside of school.

As educators, we need to be flexible and resilient enough to work with students until they respond as they should. We cannot allow students to drift, to walk away and not return, for we know that all students at one point or another lose interest. Growing up these days is a very difficult endeavor, for all sorts of images and ideas assault the senses of the young. Little teaches them how to respond and how to counteract such phenomena. Students see and know much more about the world that youngsters used to discover later. This is one reason students need more attention than before, for there are too many personal and social influences from kindergarten through the twelfth grade today that pull students away from school and from graduation.

For the student of color or the white student who often does not enjoy the necessary home support and family budget, school should offer a consolation and the necessary sanctuary that nurtures the hope for a better future. For such students, the school should not be a difficult place that calls their presence and efforts to learn into constant question. Why should students stay in a school environment when they do not personally see that they are going to be any better off for enduring an educational setting that fails to make them feel good about themselves and their experiences?

As parents, teachers, administrators, and university faculty members, we cannot do much for minority students until we truly understand how our schools are affecting them now. Only when we have diagnosed the problems of school dropouts correctly can we hope to reverse the current situation. To prevent dropout, we need to engage education stakeholders in all areas of society who can advance an open dialogue—parents, teachers, administrators, politicians, and, of course, the students themselves—to identify issues correctly in our schools before proposing solutions.

We personally know the psychological challenges faced by minority students because we went through the American school system ourselves and attended with peers who had the same type of experiences. We know firsthand what our youngsters mean when they tell us they do not feel comfortable and safe in the schools. We have been at community meetings where students have told us they feel "inferior" and uncomfortable at the high school and at meetings where threats of fights and other violent behavior by gang members have been made. Minority students feel bad about being disregarded and, in effect, being "told" by the way that other students, teachers and administrators behave that they do not count for much. The adult world does not expect minority students to amount to much, and students of color see and hear this message almost everywhere they turn, including the media, which represents them negatively. It is enormously difficult for these students to ignore and to get past this communicated communal assessment, for such messages drown out all of the other well-intentioned lessons that good, committed teachers, administrators, and other educators try to impart.

But getting past such messages is exactly what most minority students have to do to survive and succeed. Society constantly tells minority people in many ways that we are not valued members. Educational and cultural programs specifically designed to build and create esteem are woefully lacking in many parts of the country but especially in areas where many minority students live. Every time the issue of helping minority students is brought up, there are always political forces that respond by saying that minorities want special treatment. Since the dire reality under which many minorities daily live is not psychologically healthy, special treatment is exactly what people of color who have endured past inequities deserve. What that special treatment amounts to is nothing more than taking a hard, honest look at what schools offer such students and then finding the personnel and the resources to address problems. Using good energies to deny and to deflect criticisms intended to be constructive is not what such proposals should elicit.

That is why many dropouts in effect attempt to show adults that they do not need school. What students who drop out of school really say is that since they have not received the necessary adult support, they prefer to go at life alone. Due to the lack of support, they believe that they can succeed, though life shows otherwise. Statistics show the legions of unsuccessful stories. If we are as conscientious and as caring as many of us say, we would not allow the constant educational carnage of the school dropout problem to continue unabated.

The school dropout problem should be recognized for the crisis it is. Throughout the nation there is a need to examine the education infrastructures, individually in the classrooms and collectively on the boards of education, if we are to change the culture and the environments that now exist in most schools in America. The terrible dropout problem is shameful by any standard, and it should not be allowed to remain a back-burner issue while educators talk about other areas of education. Once students fail to graduate, most have a difficult time becoming productive members of society, contributing to the development of healthy communities. Indeed, supporting adults who have not been properly taught to care for their social, economic, and personal needs taxes the rest of us unduly. That is why there is so much crime and why prison overcrowding requires attention in this country. When it comes to the real education of our youth, we are failing, despite much research and technological advancement.

We have to remember anew that our youngsters are human beings who need to be shown *how* to become considerate, sensitive adults. If we do not teach and show them that human beings should be compassionate and kind toward each other, they will not endeavor to be conscientious human beings. That is why we need to repair our education systems—to serve not only the needs of all students but of American society itself. The realities that we now have in the schools are simply not producing the society that we need. A better alternative would be to teach all students to take care of their own needs so that the United States can be a proud land of diverse people able to provide for themselves and their families honestly, making every person a contributing member of society. Without proper schooling now, students cannot become the self-sustaining citizens that we want to see tomorrow.

Chapter 5 | **A MEXICAN AMERICAN MOTHER
WHO WILL NOT VISIT SCHOOL**

Acolleague who teaches in a Texas school invited a Mexican American mother to visit her class to see how the mother's youngest son was doing. The totally unexpected, matter-of-fact response from the mother in Spanish was

> *No, yo ya no voy a la escuela. No he ido hace casi veinte años, aunque cada rato mandan invitaciones. No voy porque la última vez que fui me dió mucha lástima. Allí tienen nuestros niños como regados; ni les prestan atención. No más los tienen allí todo el día, haciendo nada.*
>
> That is:
>
> No, I don't visit the school any more. I haven't gone for about twenty years, despite the invitations that they [school officials] often send. I don't go because the last time I went it was very sad and painful. They have our children there thrown aside; they don't even pay attention to them. All they do is to have them there all day, doing nothing.

The teacher was distressed to hear such sentiments expressed with so much disillusionment, yet the mother's words support statements we have made throughout this book. Like that mother, we are haunted by stories of disenchantment and signs that we also see in the faces of our Latino and Latina students. These are all signals that dramatize the extent to which our schools continue to fail to educate Latino and Latina children day in and day out throughout the United States.

So, why don't Mexican Americans and other Hispanics protest educational ill treatment that the mother knows about and that keeps her away from school, like other American parents normally would? Why don't people of color protest and let other Americans know that we are dissatisfied? Why don't we seek redress in the courts, since this is the main way that minority populations have historically brought about social change in America?[1] We suspect this is because the treatment that our minority populations have historically received in the United States has discouraged them to such an extent that they do not see much hope in ever changing the schools. The great majority have simply gotten used to receiving bad and mediocre educations for generations. Change will have to emerge from the school leaders themselves, for many Hispanic parents do not even know how to begin to advise their children about attending college.[2]

State and federal courts in California and Texas ruled in the late 1940s that school districts could not segregate Hispanic students in separate facilities or classes.[3] Until then, most Mexican American students were limited to schools that offered mainly vocational programs. The 1950 U.S. Census revealed that most of their parents had little to no formal education. We make an issue of the history of school discrimination not to be confrontational or to create discomfort, as some readers may think, but to show how and why Mexican Americans and other minority people continue to feel left out of American education.

Such a legacy should tell us that we now need to offer quality education to minority students. Clearly, equal access for some minority students to some of the better schools has not been enough. If the great majority of students of color continue to be left on their own within the classrooms, if they are still being ignored, as this Mexican American mother says, and if academic expectations remain low, most of America's minority students are never going to be academically competitive. Such students are not being socially nourished or properly educated from kindergarten through the twelfth grade. And since this is the case, unless extraordinarily different measures are taken, Hispanic, African American, and Native American students are not going to be educated well enough to be admitted into the better colleges and universities.

Encouragement is central to education. If children are not encouraged by the adults in their lives, we are convinced that they will begin to cause problems both for themselves and for others just at the point when they should be interested in becoming serious students, that is, during the middle school years. During these years, most teenagers are just beginning to formulate ideas about their future careers. These are widely considered the difficult years for every teen. To enter these years feeling ambiguous or disliking the very adults they need to go to for guidance and encouragement within the educational system is troubling.

Traditional education has not been designed with minority people in mind, and the problem is that educators simply have not wanted to acknowledge this fact. And because we have generally avoided recognizing this reality, we have not undertaken successful efforts to change that history and reality. At this point, then, we believe that we can either start to provide quality education for all students, or we can continue to try to educate minority students who have already been substantially discouraged by the time they begin their teenage years.

Every year, for example, we hear three or four stories about Latina mothers who have gone to visit the schools to talk to school officials and who have been turned away for one reason or another. Usually it is because school counselors, teachers, or administrators are too busy taking care of other business, or no one can translate from English to Spanish, or the proper person who needs to discuss an issue is simply not available. These are not out-of-the-ordinary cases but regular, normal, everyday occurrences that schools have failed to provide for and that school districts do not address year after year, despite numerous complaints that usually stop short of embarrassing the members of the school boards. But perhaps that is exactly what is required, since nothing else appears to work.

Our position is that the schools cannot afford to alienate people of color from education any longer. A simple, straightforward comment like the one made by this Mexican American mother suggests reams about unaddressed conditions that tell us why minority parents keep away from school. In turn, well-intentioned teachers and administrators then remain puzzled about why minority communities remain apathetic toward education. Educators need to understand that the United States, as a society, has not wanted to address an education legacy that minority people cannot easily forget and mainstream America would rather not remember.

Many minority people have now written off the U.S. form of education for reasons like the one this Mexican American mother provides. Despite these realities, we need to emphasize, Latinos and Latinas have traditionally esteemed and valued education, showing great respect for educators. But even though equal access to the schools has been guaranteed, the type of experiences that Latino and Latina children report and that parents see and encounter when they actually visit the schools has not changed.

I had a student teacher in a bilingual setting for a few weeks one semester. She and I were at recess observing some students when she said, "Mrs. Portales, I very much enjoy seeing how you speak and interact with your students." I'm glad you do, I returned. I hope you are learn-

ing well. "Oh, yes," she said, "I'm glad I was able to observe someone else and see how it's properly done." What do you mean, I asked. "Well, in my last situation in a bilingual classroom, that first-grade teacher, in my opinion, wasn't very thoughtful. She was rather rough with the children. One day for an ESL lesson, she was separating the students for a game in the classroom. This teacher had been in town for many years, and she knew practically all of the children and their families. The students were to line up single file. She then would come and touch each one on the shoulder, informing the student what part of the classroom they were to stand at. Whenever she came to a Mexican child, she would say, in Spanish, "No, you're Mexican—you are not going to understand well—you go stand over there. The other children were Mexican Americans, so she effectively separated the two. I didn't think that was proper. I felt just awful sensing that the children from Mexico were actually feeling different." I felt especially bad that she explained the rules in English but made no attempt to linguistically bridge the rules to the Mexican students.

If teachers, whether ethnic minority or Anglo, do not make more ethical and diligent efforts to provide equally for the educational and emotional needs of youngsters with other cultural backgrounds, the different separations that currently exist are likely to worsen, helping no one and threatening the stability that American society needs in order to cultivate a productive citizenry.

By disregarding, ignoring, and behaviorally excluding some children from promising futures, we leave youngsters to the lures of delinquency. We know, for example, that many prisoners began by being delinquents and by neglecting their education. And most of the other minority people not in jail cannot be said to be as well off as mainstream Americans who have usually received the advantages that education has afforded them. But blaming the victims for their condition and for the ways that society normally selects its future leaders is not the answer. Blame does not excuse or justify inequities paid for by everyone.

We should not, in short, encourage or promote the stereotype of the "ugly American" that historically has raised ill will for us in some parts of the world. All the players in an education system need to take time to learn about people who have been traditionally bypassed or ignored and the reasons for such neglect. There are many education players with varied views in the world today, and no educational institution at any level can exclude perspectives that influence our communal lives. Provocative books like Derrick Bell's *Faces at the Bottom of the Well* (1992) and Cornell West's *Race Matters* (1993) leave little doubt that racism still needs to be addressed, say what opponents will about victimization, political correctness, and people who are characterized as doing little to help themselves.[4] Racism is a virulent disease that spreads contempt for other people nationally and internationally, and educators need to recognize racist signals both in and out of the classroom. For racism spawns hatred, divisiveness, self-righteousness, and class and tribal pride instead of the good human values and virtues that education and the schools exist to promote. Race and ethnic concerns usually lie in that culturally taboo area that everybody recognizes but that few people are willing to address because these issues cause considerable discomfort. And well might racial matters unsettle us, since what is questioned and brought to the fore is very much our own personal comfort and the stability of the status quo.

One Saturday morning, as we were about to enter a local hardware store, I met an African American woman colleague and we began to talk about the state of things at the university for minority people. The white lady with whom my friend had arrived interrupted us to tell her that some very nice brass desk lamps were being marked down drastically. When both of them went over and picked two lamps apiece, I decided to buy two, too. None of the six boxes had the marked-down prices, so an impromptu line formed. While all three of us quickly made a line, boxes akimbo, my friend and I resumed our conversation and waited for the salesman to mark the sales price on the outside of the boxes with his black magic marker. I noticed the salesclerk wrote $5.00 on the two boxes of the white woman and $15.00 on each of the two boxes my African American friend had. My friend was talking and turning toward me, so she did not see the prices he wrote down. Aloud, I asked him why he had marked the first lady's for $5.00 and my black friend's for $15.00. The salesclerk, a fairly mature-looking university student, I now noticed, smiled and said, "Oh, I don't know what I was thinking." Raising my voice, I said, "Don't tell me that! You know perfectly well what you just did!" He blinked and fluttered his eyes, trying with his hands to signal me to keep my voice down. But in the same tone I said, "I should report you to the manager. You are lucky I am only embarrassing you right here in front of all of these people who happen to be hearing me. I can't believe you would charge that lady $5.00 and the other one $15.00 for the same lamps." Still trying to wave aside the *whole incident, he quickly crossed out the $15.00, marked $5.00 on my black friend's boxes, and then he marked $5.00 on mine.*

We think it is definitely time to call public attention to outrageous racial practices instead of pretending or ignoring them, as my friend politely did. Over many years and generations these are the social behaviors that are exactly responsible for creating the very inequalities that are so visible among people of different races everywhere in the United States and elsewhere throughout the world. Many people, however, refuse to see that in many parts of our country whites tend to help and advance other whites while being indifferent to minority people. As a consequence, too many people believe and want to believe that certain realities continue because they are the cumulative result of merit, character, and superior intelligence and abilities. Many want to believe that the positions held by minority citizens were given to them by affirmative action policies, not by their own hard work, intelligence, and efforts to maintain themselves in such positions. Others want to believe that the advantages that some people enjoy are the result of laws, public policies, and social practices that have created a status quo sustained by long-standing mores and values that keep minority citizens from being helped educationally and socioeconomically. But the U.S. Constitution simply does not function according to such perceptions, since equal opportunity is central to American society.

Chapter 6

*T*HE TRIBAL MENTALITY
AND FAVORITISM

*Racism has always been all around us, but I raised
my children as if it did not exist. I have pretended
all my life that racism is not really there, and that
has allowed us to live. Otherwise, well, otherwise,
can you imagine what life would be like if we had
told our children about racism?*

MRS. G., CENTRAL TEXAS, 1996

*P*retending that racism has not existed has allowed
many Native, African, Asian, and Mexican Ameri-
cans like Mrs. G. to downplay discrimination. Racism has traditionally
kept many ethnic minority Americans, particularly those who cannot
visibly pass for mainstream white Americans, from enjoying better lives.
For that reason, living as if American life is driven mainly by the ideal
standards of the U.S. Constitution is a point of view that some ethnic
people can embrace, while others simply cannot. It is not that the latter
choose not to, but rather that daily life tells them otherwise, as many
incidents presented in this book demonstrate. We could have selected
some success stories, but if that were the general case, Hispanic and
other minority students would not be having the kinds of problems with
education that most of these students experience.

Educated or not, people seek psychological comfort, and to avoid
permanent discontent, many minority citizens choose to ignore discrimination, feigning indifference, for rectifying the status quo requires personal and communal resources that have not traditionally found ready
support in the larger population. Simply acknowledging that racism
makes people uneasy because it questions racial and ethnic relationships
without improving them should not be socially acceptable. Indeed, we
have learned that as individuals and as a nation, most of us would rather
avoid the matter of race. We prefer to hope that time and future genera-

tions will somehow correct past inequities. That is why racism continues to exist. People would rather not talk about unpleasant realities for which useful solutions are scarce, leaving minority people to work out individual accommodations and adjustments.

Racism continues to exist in people who attribute persistent economic, political, and social inequities to the failure of ethnic Americans to improve their lives, generation after generation. Unwilling or reluctant to see people as products of social and economic systems that preferentially advantage whites, people often blame victims of racism themselves for their own condition. Discussing the subject from multiple perspectives, as examined by many scholars and observers, has not yet brought about desirable changes. Whether acknowledgment is willing or grudging, the truth is that indifference and widespread neglect still separate otherwise good American citizens.[1]

Ralph Ellison wrote about the psychological difficulties of being black in *Invisible Man* (1947). More than a half-century later, when asked, most people of color still speak about being ignored, due primarily to race and skin color. We were standing, for instance, in line in a cafeteria in Texas, and because we were having difficulty deciding what to order, we asked two African American ladies behind us to go ahead. The younger one thanked us immediately and went ahead. The older one hesitated and then followed her friend. A few minutes later, she turned back to us and said, "We have lived here all our lives, and this is the first time that anyone has ever asked me to go ahead in a line."

The issue is not so much that people of color are invisible, as Ellison satirically posited, but that people who are not white are simply too visible. This is not something we "make up" or "refuse to let go of," as we have been told. It is that race and color continue to matter in countless negative ways, striking people of color who feel the sting early in life. One four-year-old African American child who was frolicking with her favorite white teacher in the school playground one day suddenly grabbed the teacher's arms, looked into her face, and demandingly said, "Turn black, turn black," as if by willing it, the teacher would be like her. They hugged, not wanting to let go of each other.

Color blindness ought to be examined in light of the Jim Crow laws and the segregation history that effectively led to the racial problems that we have inherited from the past.[2] "Driving while Black," or "DWB," for example, is a recent manifestation that has secured media attention for a long-standing practice. The custom singles out African Americans, Hispanics, and other people of color for driving in white neighborhoods.

Law officers and/or white residents appear to assume, almost automatically it seems, that some kind of underhanded activity is going on. Then, too, ignoring the visibly different person can be a quiet but traditionally highly effective way of demonstrating rejection or outlier status, as Ellison and a host of other ethnic writers have shown.

The unease with which some people of some races approach others is an unfortunate fact of life that needs to be imaginatively addressed by educators in the classroom since it exists in the world outside. Some people reject others solely or primarily on race and skin color features, others on other grounds or for different reasons. Rejection or the inability to feel comfortable with people from other races or ethnicities is a powerful factor because it leaves people separated and apart. Surmounting age-old biases and prejudices requires a conscious desire and an educated effort; reducing racism is no easy task.[3] Not until President Bill Clinton's 1997 summer initiative called attention to the national need to improve race relations, an effort that now appears strangely dated and almost forgotten, did world government leaders take note of the need to eradicate racism.

But simply pointing to the continued existence of racism at that historical juncture, whether subtle or overt, we have now seen, was not enough. We need to look for successful examples in the people around us who have bravely endeavored to avoid the stereotypical likes and dislikes that all members of society absorb from the values and mores that shape our views, often unconsciously. We ought to champion and to emulate the people who treat everybody equally and fairly, in spite of race, color, gender, religion, or disability.

[The following story was written by Lori, a university student.] *As a person fascinated by Mexican culture, I have always had a hard time understanding the reluctance of American society to accept Hispanics. I grew up in a small town south of Houston and have always been around Mexican Americans. I grew up thinking they were just like me. Unfortunately not everyone thinks this way.*

When I was in the eighth grade I started taking Spanish in school. It was very difficult for me at first. I could not pronounce anything correctly, and the sentence structure seemed so foreign. Then one day it just clicked, and the more I knew, the more I wanted to know. Not only the language, but everything about the culture intrigued me. El Día de los Muertos, Cinco de Mayo, and quinceañeras offered fascinating occasions to me. I kept taking Spanish for two more years. I wanted to become bilingual.

My freshman year of high school I met a boy named Nathan Dávila. He was so cute. I flirted with him and did whatever I could to get him to notice me. It did not take long (I was very determined) until he was my boyfriend. I was ecstatic. However, my mother was not so pleased. When I told her, she freaked out and made me break up with him. She is very old-fashioned and does not think people of different races should date. I was devastated. Not only had I lost a boyfriend whom I adored, but also I had been made vividly aware of the social injustices occurring in the United States and in my own home.

I tried to obey my parents' wishes for a while. Nathan moved away and I have never seen him since. I soon started dating another Mexican American boy. This time I did not tell my mother. Instead I kept it a secret and only saw him on rare occasions. It was terrible; I hated lying. It did not work out, and my mom found out eventually anyway. The whole ordeal left me feeling very disheartened and confused. I could not understand my parents' way of thinking. How could I, having been raised by them, have such different views than they do?

I am still struggling with the answer to that question. Maybe it is because people's values in Hispanic culture make more sense to me than those of my own culture. For example, nursing homes are very common in the United States. When our parents and grandparents are too old to take care of themselves, most people do not think twice about putting them in nursing homes. I think this is a hideous thing to do to someone you love. I cannot stand the thought of someone in my family being in such a place. In Hispanic culture, this is unheard of. They have respect and love for their families that are considerably more important to them than a convenient lifestyle.

I know that my mom was doing the best she could and that she cannot help the way she was raised. This is why I think education is most important. The more educated people are, the more likely they are to be open to new ideas and beliefs. If my mother had been more educated, I do not think she would have her thoughts and feelings about interracial dating.

A central goal for all education, one that is not sufficiently pursued, would be to sensitize all students to the similarities and differences among people. A balance needs to be struck between what unites all of us and the qualities that make us different—but which should not separate us. Educators consciously need to work on creating an appreciation for people who do not look like "us," without patronizing or looking down on any person.

Special efforts need to be made to appreciate and to understand people who are unlike us, and this goal should be genuinely taught and discussed in our schools as one of the more important parts of a curriculum. Without recognizing this social need, we cannot call a person who has graduated and who has studied in higher education or a professional school truly educated. This endeavor is not as difficult as some people may at first believe. A genuine appreciation for others will cost time, effort, attention, and constant, dedicated work, since few of us have been taught how to spend our good energies engaged in thinking and learning about people who are different. Yet this is exactly the kind of effort that our society cannot do without at this time in our history. The last thirty-plus years of desegregation have shown us that most people will choose to bypass opportunities to attain an understanding and appreciation for people who are different, mainly because most people appear to be unaware of how the experiences of other people can enrich our own lives.

This is one of the central goals that an education should achieve, part of what all colleges of education need to teach to younger teachers. Such an attitude and point of view, we have learned, will not happen automatically. Communicating views that help bring about changes in the attitudes of students toward other people from kindergarten to an upper-level university education is now a social necessity, even though some influential people may trivialize or otherwise deflect the idea. People who have not learned or who have not been taught to appreciate others who are not like them, we want to emphasize this point, cannot be said to be educated. Such people may be experts in an area appreciated by society, but if they lack true empathy and the sensitivity necessary to comprehend what living in the shoes or the skin of another person is like, we have to conclude that they are insensitive and finally uneducated people. Such people do not respect other human beings, nor do they want or care to make the effort to learn about others because such efforts require time and energies, and they have already committed themselves to other, more important tasks, improving the lives of the other people they daily see when they travel, where they work or vacation.

Certain verities and some very basic human considerations tend to get lost when people disagree and grow apart from each other. These basic principles need periodic assertion to remind us of a balanced education. For what is an educated person if not an individual characterized by the willingness to listen and to act to improve the human lot?

People who disagree with each other still have to live together in some proximity. We all need to find ways that allow groups with different views to advance themselves, even though we may disagree with their politics or perspectives. Instead of living in a world where we continue to victimize others by imposing uncharitable burdens on people who are intellectually, socially, and economically less fortunate than we are, educated persons seek to improve the general lot. By doing so, American society and the world are made better.

The great words of the First Amendment to the Constitution warrant attention:

> Congress shall make no law respecting an establishment of religion, or prohibiting the free exercise thereof; or abridging the freedom of speech, or of the press; or the right of the people peaceably to assemble, and to petition the Government for a redress of grievances.

People can assemble in our country because the First Amendment, as interpreted by the Supreme Court, allows us to meet to exercise the great privilege of "freedom of speech," so long as expression eschews violence.

What happens, however, when we have two or more contending perspectives that express contrary viewpoints? Traditionally, reason, common sense, the public good, and or the rule of law have usually prevailed in democratic countries. The idea of "freedom of speech" or free expression has implicitly meant that sensible positions and views will prevail, largely because it is assumed that untoward views will be seen and rejected as views that no honest, taxpaying, responsible citizen would reasonably embrace.

But within our lifetime, as we know, "freedom of speech" has evolved to mean not necessarily responsible free expression, but the freedom to say anything that people feel like expressing without regard for the viewpoints of others. Since Americans have the constitutionally protected right to say what we think and feel, many of us believe that we can indeed say whatever we want, regardless of who is hurt or detrimentally affected. Some people call this type of free speech "hate speech," pejoratively labeling expressions meant to be emotionally incendiary.

The basic proposition of the Constitution is that we can believe what we want so long as our beliefs do not impinge, restrict, or deny the rights and privileges of others. When we insist that others subscribe to our beliefs, we are oppressively and unfairly imposing our views on others, sensible and correct as our views may appear to us by our standards. By doing so, we are essentially denying people their constitutionally protected rights, and what we hold legally sacrosanct in this great country are indeed the rights of the individual against the charges and burdens that can be imposed by larger groups of people.

In America and in many parts of the world these days, many people are not content simply with disagreeing any more. People are moving past civil disagreements, and nowadays too many of us are forcing, wanting to require, agreement from people who disagree or who tend to disagree with our views. This general movement toward forced agreement is terribly unethical because people who are convinced that they are right are often not easily deterred from intimidating, threatening, and even coercing other less fortunate people from embracing positions that the latter would otherwise avoid. When people feel pressured to conform or when they are in effect forced to embrace views and ways of life that abridge our freedoms, contentiousness rises, quarreling erupts, often ending in shouting, discord, and sometimes even violence. When quarreling becomes the order of the day, public discourse is forced to take place in a difficult-to-resolve environment, the arena of human disrespect.

Many public debates and television programs now highlight the extent to which human disrespect has grown. We are not teaching people to be considerate and respectful of others any more. In fact, we are encouraging people to make decisions based on our tribes, based on what we think is good for the groups to which we belong. Anger, violence, distrust, and discontent are more the order of the day, as the media stories amply document.[4]

Why, we need to ask, should our good sense of ourselves be based on the impositions or the psychological shackles that we can successfully place on less fortunate people? We ask the question because it seems to us that too many people are increasingly depending on the misfortunes and the tribulations of other people to assure their own personal and social comfort. Everyone understandably wishes to be comfortable, but too many of us are not paying sufficient attention to the people who are being direly affected or inconvenienced, so long as we profit or please ourselves.

We have to be careful that our own desire for personal comfort does not displace a higher priority, that is, our concern for other people, our traditional responsibility and desire to protect people who are less able to defend themselves. Having things as we would have them can insidiously lead even the most educated people to disrespect people because their viewpoints are different. When such attitudes develop without being addressed, disagreements enter a different plane. In this different world, we become blind to injustices and inequities, throwing out the old verities of truth, justice, and liberty, the very foundations on which American society and the Constitution are anchored.

Yet these truths are not the only verities that need to be reasserted, taught to every generation, and insisted upon by everyone. Because of the natural desire to have things our way, we tend to forget about some basic common human decencies and considerations that all of us need to embrace — even when we strongly disagree with people who see things differently.

We need, for example, to remind ourselves constantly to show the kind of respect for all people and cultures that makes a marked difference in the manner in which we comport ourselves. For all of us live and feel as we do only because we have been born in a certain time, in a certain place, of certain parents, under certain conditions and considerations. Those of us who are naturally comfortable with our place in society have pride of place and pride of self, mainly because these elements of ourselves have been developed and encouraged by the people who raised us as well as the residents who live around us. Who among us does not think we deserve better, despite the benefits and the privileges we already enjoy?

We lived and taught in south Texas for two years. The first year we were there, I taught a bilingual first-grade class, and many of my students lived in the nearby colonias, or Rio Grande border-area neighborhoods. It is important to know that the students from las colonias are more in need of bilingual education than other Mexican American students who have been born and who have lived in Texas, in the Southwest, or in other areas of the United States for a number of generations. I make this clarification because many educators are not aware of differences among Latinos that exist and that should be considered when curricula and activities are being planned and prepared for different students.

The colonias are substandard minimal housing sites largely constructed by more recent immigrants from Mexico, though a good number of colonias have now existed for thirty to forty years. Most of the dwellings have no running water inside, no indoor plumbing, and some lack even electricity. The houses are literally shacks made almost entirely from plywood and or sheetrock.

I had taken over the class at mid-term after this particular class had gone through seven to eight substitute teachers, a fact that was especially deplorable since the students were first-graders. I found their books scattered about, and no organized curriculum had been achieved when I first entered the classroom. However, by the end of my first month with them, we had established reading groups and orderly classes, and the students were responding as first-graders.

One day the speech teacher came to my door with one of my students who I knew resided in a colonia. Miffed, she stated that he was not cooperating and that he was lying and "fooling" with her. I had not experienced such behavior from that particular little boy. I knew him as loving and appreciative of everything we did in class. He was an avid learner and quick to begin and to finish his lessons. I spoke to him in front of the speech teacher by my open classroom door. She proceeded to explain the problem as one where my student was not being forthright with her. She had showed him a picture of a standard bathroom wash basin and had asked him its name in English. He did not know. She told him this item was found in the place where his mom gave him a bath at night in his house and that he could state the name in Spanish for her if he wished. He said he did not have one where he took a bath. "You have one in your house," she repeated. "No, I don't" he replied. This went on for a few minutes, when, frustrated, she brought him to me to be disciplined, since he was clearly "trying her" and "pulling her leg," as she said. Emilio, I said, where does Mami give you a bath at night? By the faucet outside, he said. Do you have a bathroom inside your house? "No, we go to the restroom in a little house outside the house." Have you ever seen an item like the one in the picture the teacher showed you? "Yes, in school." Then why did you tell her you had never seen one? "Because she said it was like the one I have in my house, but we don't have one in our house, only in school."

The look of astonishment on the face of this upper-middle-class lady who had lived and taught in the Rio Grande Valley for over twenty-five years without apparently being aware of the plight of some of her own students was simply overwhelming to me. As I think back on these events, I believe I would have found this story incredible myself if I had not seen this exchange take place before me.[5]

In our own way, almost every one of us makes the necessary accommodations, rightfully congratulating ourselves on our achievements and the adjustments we make. The world is a difficult place, but why make it tougher on people who belong to other groups or tribes because they are clearly different and because they also feel good about their differences?

People in the general population might be unaware, but teachers, especially, need to be acutely aware. The best teaching, we believe, is accomplished when our understanding naturally brings about nurturing. Such nurturing enables a teacher to empower students, allowing the confidence that the teacher possesses in discussing an issue to be transferred to the students. Our sense of what the world might be depends not on ignoring or burdening others who are less fortunate, who are not yet like the authority figures that we represent as teachers, but who, despite cultural differences, may someday live in the same socioeconomic environments enjoyed by most middle-class Americans. Cultural differences, in fact, offer and provide the United States with considerable enrichment, if we would only learn to invest our time and our lives more productively finding out about the lives of the people around us who need us. The idea is not to spend all of our time on the regular task of sustaining and extending what we have, but in learning more about the very people around us who are quite willing to help us shape tomorrow.

The respect for self and others that we are talking about requires us to develop and to nurture the kind of sensitivity that we would like to see and, indeed, expect in other people. Being sensitive to the needs and the desires of others will allow us to begin to understand them, for, as we know, it is easier not to make the effort to understand. We can simply say, "I just don't understand how those people think," and continue to disregard them. We suspect that if we had lived through their experiences, we might know why they think and act as they do. If we but make the effort, we believe that we are all capable of beginning to understand how other people see life. Given a people, their culture, and their history, understanding is appreciably brought closer, but to accomplish this goal, we have to make the effort to suspend our prejudices and biases and to reassess issues. Learning to appreciate what other people labor against in the struggles of their daily lives can offer us quite a different experience. Isabel, one of our students, wrote the following short essay.

When I was in the seventh grade, I had to prove who I was to my friends. They didn't believe that I was born in the U.S. They thought I was born in Mexico. So I took my birth certificate to school to "prove" I was from the U.S. Now I wonder why I did that. They were not bad people who made fun of me for who I was. They were my friends. This did not change anything between us, nor was I treated any better or worse for being Mexican American. So why did I feel the need to prove myself?

Many Mexican Americans have difficulty being accepted by Mexican as well as American people. This was said best by Edward James Olmos in the movie "Selena" (1997). He said that it was difficult being Mexican American. You have to prove how Mexican you are to the Mexicans and how American you are to the Americans, often both at the same time.

So why do we feel like we have to prove ourselves to anyone? I believe that people just want to "fit in." For me this meant that I could be just as good as all the white people, if they realized that I was an American. I did not want to be seen as being less than them just for being Mexican. After this experience, I realized that if I let people's opinion direct my life, then I'm letting people mold me into what they want me to be. People need to be in charge of their own lives and to be proud of who they are and where they came from. They need to stop trying to please all the people around them who try to change who they are.

Nobody likes being the "oddball." Everyone wants to be liked by everyone, to be as smart or as pretty as the next person. Having to prove yourself should not be anyone's major concern. I believe that if someone has confidence in who and what they are, they do not have anything to prove to anyone else. Just trying their best in school, at work, and in life should be enough for them and everyone else. Mexican Americans have always tried to prove who they are to the white people of this country. We try to live like them and to act like them. And many Mexicans see this as a disloyalty to Mexico. We need to realize that we are Mexican Americans, which means that we are two cultures in one. We are Mexicans and Americans at the same time. We are proud of who we are, and everyone needs to realize that we, as Mexican Americans, deserve to be our own people.

What we are talking about in effect is integrity, that is, having the personal honesty to give all people—particularly people of a different race, color, and culture—the time, the space, and the very attention to which we feel entitled ourselves. For if we ethically seek impartial and fair treatment for ourselves, we should be willing to provide that to everyone else. This type of thinking should allow us, as educators, to transfer the learning we have acquired in an equitable way to all students.

If we were guided by basic, humane considerations, we doubt that we would spend as much time as we do forcing and imposing our views on others and that others would spend as much time and effort understandably resisting such domineering and constraining tactics. Our views may indeed be the best ones possible and the most sensible; but if they are, let other people hear and examine them for themselves. From the returns, from how people respond, we will see whether our views are as useful and helpful as we think they are. Let us see if our perspectives create converts. The common aim ought to be to empower and to increase the self-esteem of all people, including the ones with whom we regularly invest our time and efforts. The purpose should not be to impose perspectives that keep others psychologically shackled from contributing what everyone can toward making the world a better place.

We have done that long enough in the history of the world, and civilization continues to pay an inordinate price for the ethnic and national rivalries that unfortunately shape history in too many parts of the world today. Look at any of the troubled spots anywhere on the globe, and we will find ethnic and tribal rivalries at the root of the problem.

Too many people for too long have flayed at each other either blatantly or surreptitiously, but we are now at the stage in the world's civilization where we can say that we are beginning to recognize ourselves both as victims and as instigators of many of our self-inflicted problems. The past is not necessarily the fault of one group or the other. What is at fault is the way that we have not made the educated effort to understand the practices and the legacies under which we unnecessarily labor. We have all been conditioned to see people who are not like us as lesser human beings, as those who belong to other tribes or groups of people.

Edna Dominguez' parents were driving her to one of the two largest universities in central Texas from El Paso where the family resides. Her father wanted Edna to stay home and to attend the University of Texas–El Paso, but Edna wanted to leave home for a flagship campus. They had been traveling all day after leaving El Paso about eight that morning. They had taken their time and had made several stops, delaying them. It was about eight in the evening, and they decided to find a motel in a small town about an hour and a half away from their campus destination, which they decided they wanted to see for the first time the next morning. When they drove into the grounds of the motel they picked, they saw that the lights that had been on outside the office and in the office were suddenly turned off. Edna's dad did not like that, and he was about to drive away, but Edna said they were tired and should stay. So Edna and her father parked the car, and Edna walked up to the office and knocked. No one answered, but Edna could see the outlines of a man and a woman sitting in the office behind the counter. Edna knocked again and again. Still no answer. When she knocked one more time, the man's voice from the inside said, "We're all full. We don't put people like you up." Edna's father wanted to turn back and drive back to El Paso, he said, where people are not like these people. But Edna convinced him to go to another motel. She had made the decision to attend one of the state's top public universities, and she said she was determined to stay.

Enduring discouraging experiences like these, to be sure, is part of the standard fare for some minority people, but such events should not be occurring anywhere in this country in the twenty-first century. In society we all depend on each other, and we are involved in each other's lives, as most of us have been progressively discovering for some time.

| CRIME AND PROPERLY
FUNDED SCHOOLS

*D*espite the millions of dollars appropriated for education by the federal and state governments, almost everywhere we look today education falls short of meeting the academic and social needs of students. Education should both equip students to be academically competitive and teach them how to be great U.S. citizens who respect the laws and who know how to behave maturely. Although there are a good number of success stories that could be featured and which school districts often use to promote their programs and activities, there are still too many instances, periodically reported in the media, that show that education in one of the world's leading civilized nations continues to fail large numbers of students at the elementary, secondary, and higher education levels. A 2002 article in the *Houston Chronicle* underscores Texas spending priorities:

> By 2000, spending on higher education grew to $4.5 billion. Meanwhile, the state's budget for prisons had risen to $2.7 billion. In that period, the amount spent on colleges and universities grew by 47 percent, compared with a 346 percent increase on corrections." Texas state Senator John Whitmire, D-Houston, vice chairman of the criminal justice committee, said he "believed the Texas Legislature needed to evaluate the way it allocated dollars to criminal justice and education." "Most members of the Legislature say they are pro-education, but what they put in their campaign brochures and cite in their rhetoric is that they are tough on crime," he said. "We have to see the relationship between crime and education and find the right balance." [1]

In the early years of the twenty-first century, several alternatives present themselves. We can continue to fund education at current levels, supporting the metaphorical leaky education pipeline systems that continue to allow students to drop out of school. Or we can become serious about our perennially expressed desire to support education and begin to repair the education systems that are usually last among the items funded by legislators. Repairing education means that we have to determine how much money is seriously needed to upgrade the parts of the educational pipeline that are not properly educating more American youngsters. Currently, for example, Texas ranks thirtieth among the fifty states in the amount that its legislature spends on each student in higher education and forty-sixth in the amount of tuition and fees charged to resident undergraduate students. Almost everywhere else education remains a back-burner issue, though no one would think so to hear the rhetoric of politicians election after election.

Why educate youths more effectively? Because, as a society, we have little choice, even though most people do not realize how irresponsible we are when we fail to educate the young. Funding for education is as simple and as serious as making education our top priority—not the economy, prisons, space programs, corporate America, defense, or anything else. By investing properly in the education of our young people, we move toward offering quality lives to more of our citizens today and tomorrow. If we educate the young as we need to, almost everything else begins to take care of itself because the schools will be producing people who can handle problems as they arise appropriately. Not to educate our youngsters properly cheats them out of their possible lives, making the future of American society more difficult for them and for everyone else who has to deal with less than their full potential. We have or should have, in effect, a vested interest in preparing the young for a future that daily unfolds before them. Indeed, every time a position opens up, we see the quality of the education of the people who apply or who badly desire to qualify.

The needs of people, young and old, indeed, emerge from our very successes. Americans have been very successful both in this country and throughout the world imbuing people with the desire to own and to dispose of consumer products that will make them feel good and promote American goods. Our nephew, for example, would like a Corvette. Our neighbor's married daughter desires a summer home by the beach, and farther down the street, another youngster wants to take a trip to New York to see the new fashions this season. All of us have wants, realistic or not, and our wants are multiple and ever-changing. We have all been taught, whether we admit it or not, to be consumers of items that extend and enhance our lives. We have learned and are constantly encouraged to want luxuries that will make us look or feel better in the eyes of others around us.

But we do not sufficiently teach all of our students how they can better secure what the advertising world teaches them to desire. Education is the key, and educators need to remind students at every level how essential it is, difficult or unattractive as that may appear to the students themselves:

By the time he reached my classroom, Abel was an academically struggling fourth-grader beset by many after-school discipline slips. He was a nice enough Mexican American youngster who kept to his own. He did not give me any difficulties, but his attendance record was dismal. By the end of the first six-week period, he already had a number of visits from the attendance officer. One morning, his mother brought him to school forty minutes into the period. The school had called her at work because he was absent. Looking disheveled by what must have been a tug-of-war at home to get her fourth-grader into the car, half-apologetically and obviously frustrated she said she could not afford the time from work to bring him. He was not interested in school and did not want to attend school. Later that day, after classes, Abel stopped by my room. Looking down at the floor, he said he felt bad about making his mother cry. I asked him if he had something better to do at home instead of attending school. "No, I get bored at home since everyone is in school." He told me his father had left the family when he was four years old, and he lived with his mom, smaller sister, and brother in an old trailer. His mother was "trying to get a husband," but boyfriends hit her, so "she doesn't want a husband any more." He also said that he had two uncles who used to help his mom with the bills, but they were now in jail. They were his mother's brothers, and they went once a month to visit them. He looked forward to those visits. He told me he had spoken to his uncles various times. They were dropouts and without money; they "got into drugs" and were caught and sentenced. They advised him to get good grades and to stay in school.

"You know, Miss, jail isn't so bad. My uncles told me they can play checkers in there, get food without having to pay for it, and sleep." I couldn't help wondering how many other students had heard this view of jail, how many times they had openly discussed the issue among themselves. I wondered whether anyone in our school would have thought to bring up the subject, let alone have a discussion about jail with the students. Another teacher and I decided to mention the issue at our next faculty meeting. The reaction was mixed, with some educators saying that the topic was so negative that it disgusted them. They were not about to bring up the issue, since people might "think the wrong way."

Perhaps, a few retorted, but the idea would be to make students think about the reality of what incarceration means. Jail, at any rate, did not appear that bad to Abel, my fourth-grader, so we had a talk.

Stories like this one tell us that we need to discuss options with our youngsters. We do not spend enough time asking them to see the kind of careful steps that are required as they progress through the school years to secure the better things that American society offers.

This is one of the main reasons we have little choice but to invest resources in education as a society. Although we have shown in the last half of the twentieth century that we would rather spend our financial resources on other needs, we have to finance education properly to ensure the type of success that will reward the desires that we have encouraged. Investing money in education is much like filling our tanks with gasoline—if we expect to arrive at our destinations in good spirits, we have little choice.

Investing in education allows us to learn how we should best teach youths to learn so that they can also begin to move in directions that will contribute to the healthy well-being of society. Without proper education, without proper funding, without proper gasoline for the trip, the future will be strewn with wrecked lives that for one reason or another failed to materialize, failed to develop a person's full potential. Without proper education that allows for time and the means to examine alternatives available for doing what people desire, ideas will not occur to society's members as easily, because people will not have been taught *how* to work toward feasible goals safely and in good repair, always ready to help the people who, in turn, will follow us. Without a proper education, we will not readily recognize options, and we will likely move away from the dream of civilization, which is providing for the needs of all members. Exploring options, however, requires that we spend time in education, which translates into the patience required of people who want to succeed at doing what is required in order to carry out responsibilities to our youths and civilization.

There are, we know, proper and less advisable ways of doing things. What we generally see around us are the products of our less useful ways of funding education. Education is exactly that: the art of learning how to teach best so that everyone associated with a particular task accomplishes and enjoys the process as much as possible. The process of how education is accomplished, to be sure, needs looking at if we are to make the journey more attractive for the students and for all of the people associated with education.

Somebody, however, has to pay for the trip, particularly for the students and for the members of society who cannot provide for their own education. Since the young and how they do in the schools today will shape our communal future tomorrow, we all have a vested interest in contributing toward education, for the interests of society at large obliges all of us to pay the bill. Otherwise, we are sure to face larger problems as a society in the future. There is, indeed, only one way to look at the school situation today: teachers who are providing the education and the students being educated are either being adequately provisioned for the future, or they are not.

People may disagree, but we believe the reason there are so many problems today is that the educations received by our own citizens, including the current forty- to sixty-five-year-old group of people, have been inadequate for the needs of society. If people had been properly educated to respect others in previous generations, we would have considerably fewer problems today. For good leadership seeks to lessen the problems and to smooth out the paths as much as possible, keeping problems to a minimum. If we spent more time as a society addressing problems before issues turn into crises, fewer people would be in jail, and we would have less graft, dishonesty, corruption, and selfishness. We would then be engaged in producing more law-respecting citizens.

Education should teach us how to take the needs and desires of others into account. Very few people have been taught to take into serious consideration the perspectives of other people. At most we all share a nominal attention to the needs of others. Ethics, which are extremely important, should direct us to help people who cannot provide better for themselves. For too many people, ethics are sugar-coating: good, if possible, but not especially binding.

That in part is why education has to be funded better. We cannot afford to continue to educate our young people as we have been educating everyone in this country during the past thirty years. If we do, education will only continue to worsen.

We need to become convinced that educating the young is, in the scheme of all the things that are important to a society, of paramount importance. For if we love our sons and daughters, we need to realize that we have to educate everyone around them, too. Why? Because our sons and daughters will necessarily have to live and work with all of the other members of society. Everyone else, because of the ubiquity of the media, now has the same desires and the same wants that have been encouraged in most children, and this state of affairs amply suggests why we need quality education not only for our leading citizens but for everyone.

A whole litany of facts, to be sure, could be pointed to in support of the contention that education can be improved in most parts of the United States. But such a list is not necessary. We think most people are well aware that public education needs improvement. Fewer people are now entering the teaching professions because the schools actually scare young people, some college students have informed us.

An instance or two underscores the point. The Federal Bureau of Investigation, for example, reports that at least seven bank robberies are reported on any given day in the United States. The FBI's National Crime Information Center (NCIC), a computerized index of criminal justice information, is so busy that in 2002 it "set a new record for transactions processed on a single day, with 3,295,587." In 2002, it averaged 2.8 million transactions per day. Such facts illustrate why we have so many people involved in crime prevention and surveillance—the police, security officers, and criminal justice personnel. Security-minded people do deter people from committing crimes, and they increase the number of people caught committing crimes, but curbing crime without providing viable, desirable alternatives does not address the perceived attractiveness of criminal activity well enough.[2]

The crime problem is directly connected to the kind of educations that people receive and do not receive, since many schools are failing to teach the young how to respect other people and their property. We are not teaching students to respect and to appreciate other citizens well enough. Respect, to be sure, has to be taught and learned, for the human impulse appears to be selfishness, to seek to gratify ourselves first, apparently even at the expense of others. Most crimes point out this sorry tendency. People who commit crimes are out satisfying themselves first, and the victims usually happen to be the people who were in the way of the criminal.

But improper educations do not affect only people left without educations. Such a state of affairs victimizes all of us. For none of us are capable of rising to our full potential in a crime environment, and that is why many of us spend our days not discovering what we can do to help ourselves and others but essentially flaying at each other and protecting ourselves from other people. That is what our elementary teachers, if we remember, tried to keep us from doing, from fighting with each other. And for the most part, they succeeded; but as we grow older, we revert to our nonproductive, acrimonious ways, and the schools do not counter this behavior enough. So, we need to be constantly reminded that there are better ways to live, better ways to go about doing what we would rather do tomorrow—if we were better educated today.

*S*ince education is too widely failing to instill the young with the proper, respectful ways of treating other people, we should consider what that means. It is not that minority students are simply dropping out of school, as educators and newspapers constantly lament. The issue that needs to be acknowledged and successfully addressed is that throughout the country, mainstream middle-class white citizens proportionally tend to have better support services that promote their success, while people of color largely remain without sufficient help. This means that day in and day out educators and society in general tend to work more comfortably with students who are expected to replace them in the future, helping them to overcome problems that universally beset most teenagers. This is not to say that all educators fall into this category. Many, we thankfully acknowledge, are generous, selfless educators who work tirelessly for all students. But in America, the institutional inclination is to help majority students more than minority students. This tendency allows the former to weather the troubles, to be less affected by their disillusionments, providing them with more advantages than students of color usually enjoy as both groups trudge through the schools supposedly toward better futures. That is why on the whole white students tend to stay in school, why they usually are more successful, and why they generally earn more and better college degrees than their minority counterparts.

Minority students are implicitly left behind or expected by the schools to more or less make it more on their own. And, indeed, most people of color who do succeed, when asked, will say that they worked and achieved success because they were willing to work through the obstacles in order to reach their objectives. Minorities tend to receive fewer words of encouragement and less institutional and social support to help them actualize their full academic potential, and we can personally testify to this fact, which is confirmed by what many minority students continue to tell us. From personal experience, we know that there is little in the regular everyday school environment that makes minority students feel that the future depends on them. In fact, what is absorbed in the schools very clearly by many Hispanic, black, and other ethnic minority students is that our own cultures and ancestral backgrounds are expendable and can be left out of the curriculum.[3] If minority students make a place for themselves in America's future, that is great, but American society, the message is, does not count or rest on whether minority people are successful. That is not a good message to send to our minority populations at a time when the greatest proportion of Americans born in some areas are projected to be Latinos and Latinas.

What minority students learn at school is that it is really up to them to cut a place for themselves within a future that clearly even appears to promise to exclude them. Surmounting this challenge is daunting, for, although such a challenge may occasionally spur the minority students with more spunk to compete harder, this prospect severely tends to dishearten most black, Hispanic, and other less-regarded students. By the time they are in middle school, most minority students are quite aware that it is going to be very difficult to stay in school to graduate, because constantly before them is the idea, in many ways reiterated daily at school, that their futures are not likely to lead anywhere. What they unfortunately pick up in the current school atmosphere—even though they may not hear the message in so many words—are professional adults basically saying, "If you want to succeed at school or anything, that is up to you. If you do, more power to you, but keep in mind that we do not expect much from students like you." How do young people feel if this is the message heard most of their lives? Like thumbing their noses at the teachers and administrators, right? That is what happens, what students themselves have related to us.

Our point is that all adults ought to care, and their caring should be genuine and should be credibly communicated, especially by adults in our educational institutions. Better human relations should not be the responsibility of the students, since most of them have never seen that, nor do they know better. The majority of them need enormous amounts of proper guidance to counter the multiple numbers of discouraging obstacles that they daily face in their lives both in school and outside of the classroom.[4]

White students, on the contrary, know that the future depends on them because the idea is continually reinforced by almost everything that teachers and their parents do and say. Some of these students, as we know, choose not to accept these opportunities and may also turn to drugs, crime, and other avenues of the underground economy to sustain themselves, but the point is that help for them is easier to secure if they show the desire and disposition to try again. This is to say that for such students there is generally that great, secure, safety net supporting most of the educational flaying, experimenting, and testing of social and institutional boundaries and parameters that such students traditionally test—so long as it is possible to save or reconstitute them at the end.

So, although both white and minority students find the going quite difficult in junior high and high school, the reason that more minority students tend to drop out of school is that minority students are constantly being told in subtle, and unfortunately sometimes in not-so-subtle ways, that their perseverance in school ultimately is likely to make little difference.

In the face of such wonderful and encouraging prospects, can we blame students for junking school, where they feel they float purposelessly, and for seeking satisfaction elsewhere when shorter-term and more attractive goals periodically appear on their horizons?

Nancy Kelly, a first-year math teacher whose room is in the hallway, was talking with an African American student. Her door had opened with a loud bang, so I stepped outside into the hall to see what was happening. Nancy was standing outside her door with a tense student. She had a stressed look on her face, and said, "One of my students . . . " At that, the student interrupted and said, "She says I had a beeper in the room but I didn't!" Nancy stated, "Someone had a beeper and it went off. It was either him or another boy." At that I gently touched Andy's hand and said, "Patience, now." He again said, "It wasn't me, Miss!" His muscles were so tense I felt I was touching concrete. I held his arm and said, "Hold on, we'll solve this." I then put my hand on his back and directed him toward my room. I felt his muscles relaxing. At that point, the school security guard came by and took Andy and the other boy, who was Anglo, aside and into my empty room to frisk them. He did so for close to ten minutes, and then told them to go back into their room. They had nothing. Before he returned to his room, Andy came over to my desk, gave me a big hug, and said, completely unprompted, "I'm sorry about the noise, Miss. Thank you," and left. He went back and completed the rest of the period in his math class. I wondered about the nature of his math lessons the rest of that semester. Later we discovered there were two beepers in the classroom, each belonging to Anglo boys.

*F*unding education properly was to serve as the last of these chapters on repairing our education systems, but these thoughts cannot be left without discussing the unfortunate but rather pervasive connection between education and crime. Recently we were among a group of Hispanic educators who met with two highly influential legislators. At one point in our talks, one of the legislators informed the group that, as elsewhere, when Texas voters have a choice between approving funds to support education and reducing crime, crime wins every single time.

We left the meeting thinking about this grim fact and awoke the next day still talking about and mulling over the statement that the politician had made about crime. Throughout the day we went about our business, wondering what would induce a responsible population of citizens to elevate crime prevention over the funding of education.

On the surface, anyone can see that safety is of paramount importance, for without freedom from crime and violence, a society cannot adequately carry out its public good activities. However, the reduction of crime, gang violence, and general disrespect for laws is also fundamentally a matter of education, basically a matter of recognizing that proper social relationships that assure law and order have broken down. As we see it, American society experiences rampant crime and violence largely because we have consistently failed to educate our citizens about the necessity of establishing psychologically healthy relationships with everyone else.

We have allowed people to go through the schools without sufficiently making sure that we have informed them in ways they understand that society functions better not by pursuing only personal gain and by looking out for opportunities to victimize others but by helping others. This failure to educate people about the essential, fundamental values associated with having communities that nourish all of us has led to untold human waste and enormous losses that breed criminal activities. Surely, we believe, it would be better to appropriate money to educate people about how we can create better, more satisfactory human relationships, substantially reducing the attractions that induce people to lead lives of crime and violence. But the question persisted: Why do the majority of citizens believe that crime and violence have to be better funded than the needs of education?

The following morning, as we read the newspaper, we began to see in an altogether different way why voters would rather use tax money to prevent crime and violence than to support education. When we look at our local newspapers and television newscasts and, indeed, most media throughout the country, we will find that most of the stories that make the headlines between the advertisements concern crime, violence, and lawsuits. Education issues, on the one hand, tend to receive marginal attention unless they are initiatives that call for more money. When they address these issues, reporters usually write bland and rather perfunctory informational pieces that seldom raise interest. Crime and violence, on the other hand, are transformed into featured articles almost every time, clearly the top priority of the media. Television and other news media, in short, highlight the most noteworthy crimes or violent acts committed every day. Education matters rarely receive that kind of priority coverage. Education issues almost always are used as news fillers, as items that help round out the news of the day, generally toward the end of the news reports so that a picture or two of a few local students can be shown partially to balance the negative news on crime and violence.

Is it, then, any wonder that voters would rather see their tax dollars going toward "fighting crime," as the politicians say so well? Whoever heard of funding and supporting education so that teachers can also "fight ignorance," assuring a better citizenry?

Perhaps the best way to bring this chapter on crime and funding to a synthesis is to relay an event that occurred on our large state university campus. With considerable effort and help from many quarters, a group of African American students organized a campus conference to discuss a wide variety of timely issues. The big event went very smoothly according to plans for two whole days. After the conference ended, and around two in the morning of the last day, the campus police were called to report a drive-by shooting. What made the news the next day was not that the two-day conference was very successful. Indeed, the news reports said nothing about what the educators who comprised the panel presentations had said or anything that the participants discovered or may have learned. Rather, the drive-by shooting took the headlines, and the conference was only mentioned as a campus event where the shooting occurred.

But that is the way journalism functions in society, some people will say. Yes, the public's safety is first. But why disregard the particulars of an educational and timely conference so completely? The message constantly sent out to people everywhere is that learning and engaging in educational activities are only pastime activities, that they are not particularly important events in the lives of communities. What is clearly more important is violence, destruction, and all the untoward things daily addressed in the newspapers, television, radio, and the Internet. Is this the message and legacy that we want to leave our young people?

As teachers, administrators, education board members, legislators, and peace-loving, taxpaying American citizens, we should all want to invest more of our hard-earned resources in educating students. After all, they are our neighbors, and either they will help provide for America's future better or they will not be equipped to improve society.

When we first arrived in town with one of the largest universities in the United States in our backyard, I told my third-grade students that the material I was going to teach them would later help them to get to the university. "What's that?" they asked. You know, the university, the big school in town. To my surprise, there was no sense of recognition until I said, "You know where the McDonald's is, right? It's the big school across the street." Several students said, "Oh, that's the place where my mom and dad work, Mrs. Portales." Yes, I said, immediately realizing that the only association they had with the university, unlike others of their age in my elementary school, was that they knew the campus as the place where their moms and dads worked as custodians. As an educator, this was a tremendously sad realization. Many of these students had lived in town all of their lives, and most had older brothers and sisters who were now in middle school and at the high school. Yet they had not connected the "big building" that their parents cleaned for students and faculty to a place of knowledge and advancement for themselves. We quickly remedied that, and I ended by telling them that I hoped they would continue to strive to make good grades in school every day so that one day they can enroll as students at the university after they graduate.

PART II | *H*OW TO REPAIR AN
EDUCATION SYSTEM

	*T*EACHERS, ADMINISTRATORS,
	BOARD MEMBERS, STATE EDUCATION
Chapter 8	AGENCIES, LEGISLATORS, AND
	TAXPAYERS: WHICH IS THE MOST
	IMPORTANT GROUP?

*I*dentifying the influence of the many groups of professionals and individuals in an education system that shape the curricula that teachers deliver to students is no easy feat. Effectively coordinating the contributions and the suggestions of people connected to education is difficult, yet that is exactly the nature of the challenge today. If we are to provide a quality education to every student, we need to recognize that how people feel about the schools largely depends on the nature of the interactions that they have had with members of a school system. Indeed, whether recognized or not, most us see through the lenses of the experiences that we often bring to the opportunities that we may have to "reform" or to restructure education. That is why constructing a teaching environment that allows students to learn better too often proves a nearly unattainable goal. This second section of our book is structured around the assertion that events that occur both inside and outside of the classroom directly and indirectly impact the climate and the nature of the relationships that classroom teachers establish with their students.

Although many educators claim to understand that learning is the result of how teachers interface with students, few schools operate according to that principle in their day-to-day activities. If teachers instructing students within the classrooms is widely regarded as the ideal center of the educational enterprise, then everyone else associated with education consciously ought to work to support and to advance this most important of pedagogical relationships. We want to make an issue of this fundamental, anchoring relationship because too many people connected to education today—particularly central office administrative staff members—do not fully appear to understand, or they have forgotten, the nature of their roles in relation to the main obligation and the goal of the schools. The goal of everyone who is not a classroom teacher ought to be to help the hired instructors teach the students. If education stakeholders who are not classroom instructors do not completely understand this basic fact, no amount of excellent work anywhere else in a school district is going to matter much. To achieve the central mission of the schools, then, the actual learning of the students has to be directly affected by the teaching that teachers impart to the students.

Many people with specific assigned responsibilities within other parts of an education system pay lip service to the relationship between teachers and students, or they carry out their roles in ways that continually demonstrate that they do not care much for this central relationship. Instead of promoting and facilitating work for the teachers and the students, too many people who are not in the classrooms teaching students, though often well-meaning, unfortunately end up obstructing and making the teaching of youngsters more difficult than the task naturally already is. Currently, for example, the amount of paperwork required of our teachers during their teaching hours is likely the single most stressful requirement. The amount of after-school paperwork and meetings is so dangerously close to overwhelming that many good teachers continually consider and talk about leaving the profession.

Take note, for instance, of any school parking lot after 5 P.M. on any given day, including weekends in some schools. Those parked cars do not belong to the students. They belong to teachers trying to meet state and school district paperwork requirements. They are also not earning overtime pay, as many other people do when they have to work past their regular forty-hour weeks. Some people, to be sure, will respond that teachers have their summers off, but few citizens know that teachers are not paid for the months that they are off during the summer. This means that their nine- or ten-month salaries have to stretch to cover the summer months when they are off, or they have to work elsewhere during summers to support their families. Even then, our point was to say that teachers' cars parked at the schools after hours means that such teachers are usually working to complete the day's paperwork, not preparing for tomorrow's classes. Tomorrow's classes will probably be left for the next morning, for the occupants of those same cars will likely drive in two and sometimes even three hours before classes start. This tremendous expenditure of teaching energy should be an issue of great concern to all taxpaying citizens, it seems to us, but especially to top administrators who should be working on minimizing state and local district paperwork that saps the energies of overworked teaching personnel.

These observations lead us to ask: So, how should an education system function? The relationships can be easily explained, and that is why citizens generally do not have difficulty understanding how schools within an education district ought to work in theory. The perennial problems within the schools, however, occur in securing the agreement of all of the important players in a school district to establish the healthy, necessary linkages that will bring about quality education. That is where school districts fail and fall short. The purpose of a school district, to be sure, is to provide a quality education to all students, and that is the real test for the leaders of any education system.

It is common knowledge, for example, that the fundamental authorization that empowers a public school system derives from the parents of the students and other voters who elect the state representatives, senators, and governor. By their election, these officials are charged with the responsibility of appointing or selecting leaders for the state education agencies that, in turn, establish the standards and guidelines for educating the youngsters of a state. At the local level, parents and other citizens usually also elect school board members who are then accountable for the K–12 education in a school district. In many districts, the board is entrusted to hire a knowledgeable superintendent, an educator who should then select, dismiss, or keep the district administrators, who will help the superintendent carefully select the principals for the schools in an education system. The principals in turn appoint responsible assistant principals and counselors, and, finally, the principals also hire the most essential people in the entire educational structure: the classroom teachers.

Teachers, indeed, are the most important employees in a school district. But often their importance is not sufficiently recognized. Many people believe that the most important people in a school district are the members of the board of education and the superintendent. Everybody else is seen as being subordinate to this hierarchical chain of command that begins at the local school district level. Since teachers are generally hired after everyone else is in place, many people in our schools throughout the country appear to believe that it is the professionals in education who are outside of the classrooms who are actually the most important stakeholders. But that is not true. This belief likely prevails because, except for the elected board members, administrators and other nonteaching personnel often earn more than the regular classroom teachers. But if teachers and school district personnel subscribe to such a view, then that misperception helps explain the sad operating reality that, in effect, adversely affects students—adversely because in school systems where teachers and others believe that administrators are more important to the teaching mission, teachers often are required to be more concerned with how their superiors assess their work than with the quality of the teaching that they actually deliver to the students.

These statements may surprise some educators, but we make them so that teachers and administrators can examine the nature of the professional relationships that they have established over the years. Administrators do assess the quality of teaching by periodically observing how teachers measure up against standard criteria. Even then, we believe that many of the problems that we have in education today stem from faulty education relationships that do not clearly allow instructional personnel to devote their best energies to teaching their students. We believe teaching is the most important part of the job of teachers. When central school district personnel do not correctly value the importance of the teacher in educating students due to other factors and realities that weaken or shorten instructional time, the students and their teachers lose interest, making academic achievement less important. What educators need to remember is that the academic accomplishments of their students represent the quality of the education being delivered, and if emphasis is placed on excellence in learning, the teachers and the schools are soon going to develop reputations for delivering quality educations.

In the best schools, teachers and students are at the center of the educational enterprise. Since students are the reason for the existence of the schools, and teachers are the people who either deliver or fail to deliver the information that students need to learn to master their subjects, what daily occurs in the classroom shapes how a whole system is seen and assessed. Everyone else, from the principals to the superintendent to the members of the board of education, state agencies, legislators, and governor, should therefore exist to help classroom teachers. The role of all the people who work outside of the classroom is to facilitate the learning that occurs inside a class, smoothing out the paths so that teachers can focus their best efforts and attention not on controlling students, but on delivering quality education to all of them.

Many of the problems that we have in education today occur because most people in positions of more authority and power outside of the classroom do not appear to realize clearly enough that their roles should always be ancillary to the work of teachers. This state of affairs exists partly because educators outside of the classroom generally are responsible for more duties or supervise professional personnel other than teachers. Since teachers are then placed in positions in which they have to account to superiors who often have not been in the classroom for years, or never were, classroom instructors consequently end up being seen as less important and influential. Our challenge, then, is to explain how, despite this traditional division of labor, schools can work better when the relationships that teachers establish with their students are made central.

If everyone in society and in a school system carried out his or her role, and if everyone took care of the responsibilities of that role—instead of encroaching into the duties and tasks of other people in the educational hierarchy—there is no doubt that teachers would be able to focus their best energies on actually teaching students. Teachers would then progressively improve the professional training they received in the universities, and their expertise would continue to grow as their experience accrued. As it is, teachers often spend their best hours taking care of business that does not directly benefit the education of their students. Counselors too do everything but counsel students; the very word that describes their profession today is often lost in a sea of documents they oversee and student schedules for which they are held accountable. Stacks of papers line their desks, not to mention the tasks awaiting them on their computer files, all minimizing and cutting into their student counseling duties, which should be their main concern. Principals are so stretched by their many obligations that caring, responsible ones literally almost live in their schools. Would corporate America's CEOs dedicate half as much of their lives for a principal's salary? One student teacher was struck by how different the teaching profession is today from how she remembered it:

> I'm not sure how elementary school became so fast-paced. When I was in first or second grade, it was not like this. I do not remember as a student feeling rushed or my teacher having behavior problems in the classroom. I'm sure I didn't realize how some of that occurred. But why is it so prevalent today? It bothers me that teachers can hardly find time to fit in lessons for every subject. By the end of the day, teachers are frazzled and exhausted.

These are serious problems, the consequences of which are not fully understood by the legislators, school district administrators, and most citizens. Indeed, it would behoove all school districts in the United States to examine whether their educators and the people in their education systems are working as a team to improve the education of their students. The challenge of smoothing out problems in a school district initially can appear quite complicated, because different people see the education system from their various points of view. But we believe that if everyone were to agree that teachers and students should be at the center of all educational activity, as the diagram at the end of Chapter 9 demonstrates, everyone involved in delivering education would soon contribute to the school system's capacity to produce quality education to all of its students.

When we first arrived in Texas from the Bay Area of California, I was ecstatic thinking about how neat it would be to teach in a state that, because of its longer border with Mexico, would probably have the best bilingual programs in the country. Excitedly, I began teaching in Texas in a bilingual third grade in a small town immediately outside the Houston area where the school district's population had a large Hispanic component. This particular district did have bilingual education, but only up to third grade in its elementary schools, and a fledgling ESL/migrant program in the high school. When I asked who headed the program, I was told no one, really. The program was "run out of" the central office, and it was under the charge of an administrator who headed other programs as well. When I met the lady in charge, I found out she had no training in either bilingual education or ESL and that she coordinated the education principally of Latino students in more than five area schools. The other bilingual teachers, all of whom were Mexican Americans, each served in schools with at least two grades of bilingual K–3, along with a migrant high school program. I realized that it would be a good idea to ask for a director of some sort, as we at least had in California. At mid-year, after one of our meetings, I approached the bilingual teachers with this idea. I did not want them to feel pushed aside or slighted by the fact that it would be me who would propose the idea to administration. To my surprise, they were not terribly enthusiastic or excited at my words; rather, they were withdrawn and sheepish in their answers, which amounted to no more than a "go ahead and try it." Slightly puzzled, I decided that it was enough of a signal from them to forge ahead.

I communicated my intentions to my principal, and she immediately said, "Go ahead — see what they say." I made an appointment at the school district's central office with the administrator in charge. She was very cordial. She informed me that one of the reasons the bilingual program had no one to head it was that there were no administrators who spoke Spanish. No administrators who speak Spanish in Texas!

I exclaimed to myself. Besides, she added, there was really no need for Spanish-speaking administrators, since bilingual parents did not come to school to inquire about their children. At open houses, very few attended. I stated that I found that strange, since education is considered very important in most Latino homes—next in importance only to religion, in the family sphere. As we continued, she stated several times that she was going to be late to her next meeting, suggesting that I was delaying her. However, I had made an appointment, and I kept up my inquiry since I felt I finally had her undivided attention.

Did the district ever send out announcements inviting parents to open house in Spanish? I asked. Not really, she answered—the bilingual teachers, however, tell their students to invite their parents. But there IS a flyer sent out in English inviting everyone, correct? Yes was the reply. Would you mind if I conducted and headed such a meeting based more on an informational format for the bilingual parents? I felt such a need because of some statements the parents had made to me in phone conversations when I called to report on the status and progress of their children. Most parents began or ended the phone talk with the statement, "I've never had anyone call me from school before to tell me ANYTHING about my child."

I told her I would very much like to invite the administration, including the superintendent, to attend such a meeting. Not only would the administration hear firsthand (since we would translate) any problems or concerns, but the bilingual parents would see how the administration was trying to help more effectively. She fumbled for words but ultimately had no reason or cause not to accept. I felt a tension in her voice as we continued and thought to reassure her that at this meeting we bilingual teachers would translate so that she and her colleagues would all understand. I told her it would merely be a first step in bringing parents to the threshold in establishing a home-school relationship. We left in a friendly tone.

My visionary principal was happy when I told her of the meeting, promised to be there, and told me to use any paper I needed to send notices to parents or any other item I thought she could help with.

The night of the meeting, all bilingual teachers came, but they did not want to translate. I was to do that. Many parents came, and very few administrators. Only my principal and one administrator from another school showed up. I was depressed and amazed. Perhaps our superintendent would arrive? I queried my principal. I had received no reply from him, but I felt that was due to a busy schedule. Most likely, the administrative lady with whom I had spoken would remind him. After twenty minutes of waiting on the superintendent, who never came, we began. The woman administrator in charge of bilingual education seemed nervous. All of the teachers greeted her warmly, as if to make sure she felt comfortable.

After preliminary introductions were made in both languages, we proceeded. The meeting went well. We teachers mostly addressed issues of school rules and curriculum, and we talked about our purpose in using bilingual education to help their children. As the minutes passed, parents continued to enter the cafeteria—some obviously just having left work, since they arrived in their work clothes. I couldn't help but notice the look of surprise on the face of the administrative coordinator.

The day after, my principal thanked me for the meeting and said the administration was awed at the number of people who kept coming in, some bringing their whole families. It was the first time she had seen, as a group, the students and parents served by their bilingual education program. The bilingual teachers also had spoken to me of their surprise at having so many people attend. I felt gratified and told my principal I hoped it was only the beginning of a good thing. Having such a meeting was a normal course of events for me. I had taught in both New York State and in California, and that was the way business had been conducted there. This process kept lines of communication open and well-oiled in the schools where I had taught before.

Before this parent meeting, I frequently had seen the lady in charge of bilingual education. She often came to visit around in the schools, since she was also in charge of other programs. She would always make it a point to stop by our bilingual classes, if only to say hello. Weeks passed by. I stopped my principal one day and asked if I could please have some extra construction paper for my class from the school's supply, for I had called the central office a few times, asking for them under the bilingual code, as we were supposed to, but had, so far, received none. By the way, did she know if our bilingual administrator was ill? I had asked my other colleagues, and no one had seen her around our school, which was unusual. She didn't think so, but why didn't I call her. I did so but was told on three different occasions that she was at a meeting.

One day, I saw her coming in the side door of my particular classroom area. I ran and stopped her, asking how she was and if she had received my messages about the supplies I needed. This was a different lady who met my question. Her body language was one of almost anger and almost shock that I should even be stopping her, let alone asking for supplies.

Mrs. . . . is anything wrong? Have I upset you? Rita, came the reply, from now on, you do not call my office. Have everything you need go through your principal written on a memo from her desk and write no more notes in Spanish to the students' parents, unless they are OK'd by my office. With that, she hurriedly walked away.

After school, I asked my principal for any explanation. I told her I felt like quitting right on the spot and not doing anything at all for our bilingual program. Mrs. Portales, she stated, you can go ahead and quit, but if I were to die tomorrow, just as surely as I'm sitting here today, there will be another body in this chair. You have been doing an outstanding job. If you quit, think of who will take over in your classroom. The administrative coordinator is very upset at your having had such a successful meeting. She cannot relate to the Mexican Americans, particularly the migrant workers in our area, and she is beside herself that you were able to "pull in" so many people. That has never happened in our district. Was she afraid? I asked. And, if so, of what? No, she was just simply dismayed at its success. But that is just such a thing as we were taught should happen between home and school, I said. Mrs. Portales, understand carefully, continued my principal. Mexicans are not well thought of in this area by some people. You and I are here to educate all students, but not everyone is. Don't worry about your supplies. I'll give you all you need. You are a leader who can do her job well. You have proven that Latino parents will come when they are invited and encouraged. Pay no attention to those who make your job difficult. Now go and teach well.

How glad I was to have that principal enter my life just when I thought that I should quit! How many other people with good intentions have been driven away or totally disillusioned from their missions and career objectives by similar behavior from hired administrators who should know better?

Chapter 9 | *T*HE K–12 SCHOOL DISTRICT TEAM

*I*f quality education is the goal of a school district, then the teacher-student classroom relationship necessarily must be at the center of all educational activity in the schools. We assert this main anchoring education principle not to take the "side" of teachers, as some top administrators may incorrectly interpret our effort, but to begin to show how the carefully orchestrated efforts of a unified school team can be made to work to benefit students, considerably improving the standing of both teachers and administrators in communities across the United States. Again, teachers need to be seen and treated as the most important employees in a school district, not because administrators and other education stakeholders are less important, but simply because schools are judged on the quality of the education that their students achieve. For the quality of the education delivered is finally always based on the nature of the effort and the amount of time that teachers are provided to devote to the learning that their students absorb.

Administrators, school board members, and state education agencies lead and are held accountable for how school systems actually function, but it is the teachers who daily work in the classrooms delivering education to students, making all of the educators above them either look good and professional or not. The issue is not that people ought to choose to side either with teachers or the administration or with other school stakeholders, as these areas of responsibility have been traditionally defined. Rather, every American needs to know that if quality education to the young is to be dispensed, learning can only happen in the classrooms where teachers directly interface with the students on a daily or frequent basis. For this fundamental reason, everyone else mainly serves to facilitate, to encourage, and to promote the interactive relationship that good and great teachers work to develop with their students.

If a child's mind is engaged by a teacher's approach to the material, learning occurs. True learning, indeed, should be an enjoyable, fun experience; and gradually discovering how things work or how they can work better is central to a quality education. The nature of the interaction between the teacher and the student is the point of contact where learning can occur, and a whole school district either succeeds or fails as a result of the efforts and the quality of the teachers' contact with students. Since administrators lead and are charged with supervising and evaluating teachers, all school activities very clearly ought to function smoothly and well. For this reason, keeping the learning activities of the teacher-student relationship at the center of the educational enterprise is first and foremost. Everything else in the infrastructure of a school system needs to be designed to support teachers and students.

Earlier we used the metaphor of a baseball team. We said that the central activity in a baseball game is the agreement that goes on between the pitcher and the catcher. The game does not begin until the batter is standing in the batter's box and the pitcher hurls the ball. At this point, everybody else on the field, including the coaches and the owners as well as the other team members in the dugout, sit and watch, waiting to see if all of those practice sessions and their strategies work well enough together to win the game. Like pitchers, teachers deliver instruction or they do not. Their responsibility and goal is to educate the youngsters in their care, but everyone else has to help them accomplish this purpose. Many people recognize this objective, but some professional education team members are not sufficiently attuned to their part in helping teachers and not the other way around; that is, teachers are not in the classroom to help administrators or the board of education or education state agencies.

Education systems, as they currently exist in too many places, are not always successful in delivering the material that needs to be conveyed to students because even though the official rhetoric is to serve the student, functionally that is not the main goal. In such schools, too many other activities interfere with this essential, interactive task. Often, teaching is only one of the duties that teachers are required to do, along with supervising the lunch hour, helping to load students on and off buses, and watching the halls for students skipping class, among other duties. These extracurricular activities should not be burdens assigned to teachers, since such work takes them away from preparing and delivering instruction to their students.

To make education systems function more effectively, the following recognized healthy professional relationships require wide implementation. Principals need to select teachers carefully. Principals themselves should be cautiously chosen by the school district administrators, who should look for knowledgeable, fair individuals who enjoy teaching and who understand that teaching is at the core of all educational efforts. Principals, in turn, should not be overburdened by their supervisors, impeding their own supervisory relationships with teachers and students. Committed school district administrators should be selected by a trusted superintendent, who in some districts is elected by voters or more commonly is hired by a local board of education elected by citizens and parents because such candidates have previously shown an interest in the best education possible for all students and not just a certain group of students. Parents and other citizens should also elect responsible state legislators who know that their duty is to provide proper funding for the schools and to design effective state agencies that establish and monitor pluralistic requirements and guidelines for all school districts. Such systemic criteria, when observed from the citizens to the legislature, ultimately affect the teacher-student classroom relationship. For what goes on daily in the classroom, to be sure, is always the best measure of how all of these relationships in an education system either work or fail to work effectively.

The diagram in this chapter summarizes the previous paragraph by showing the nature of the necessary team relationships that place the teacher and student relationship at the center of an education system. To improve the educational experience for every student in a teacher's classroom, educators and concerned citizens have to help teachers in any way they can from the various positions available in our school districts.

How to Use a Team Approach to Repair Our K – 12 Education Systems

Basic working principle: <u>When the **Classroom Teacher and Student Relationship**</u> <u>is the central concern of a school district education system, educators better</u> <u>understand their different team roles, making student learning more effective,</u> <u>producing quality education</u>

Residents and Parents <u>advocate and make education a top state and national priority</u>

↓

Voters <u>elect</u> state and federal lawmakers willing to support <u>this education mandate</u>

↓

State lawmakers provide <u>proper funding</u> and <u>create effective</u> Education Agencies

↓

Education Agencies <u>establish and monitor</u> Requirements and Performance Measures

↓

- **Providing <u>accountability</u> & <u>support</u> for Teacher & Student Relationships**

↑

School Principal <u>carefully hires</u> classroom teachers capable of working with Students

↑

School District Administrators select <u>enlightened</u> and <u>fair</u> Principals who know that quality education is based on the relationships that Teachers establish with Students

↑

Superintendent selects District Administrators who <u>trust</u> the judgment of Principals

↑

Board of Education members hire a <u>respected</u> & <u>knowledgeable</u> Superintendent who knows how to hire District Administrators willing to help Principals and Teachers

↑

Voters (Residents/Parents) <u>elect</u> Board of Education members interested in educating every single child in their school district

Chapter 10

TEACHERS AND STUDENTS IN THE CLASSROOM

*W*hat is the nature of the recommended relationship between teachers and students? In *Emile* (1762), Jean-Jacques Rousseau expressed the belief that a carefully selected mentor should ideally instruct only one pupil at a time, but public and private school budgets today require teachers simultaneously to teach as many students as legislators and supervisors deem reasonable. Budgets, to be sure, often establish most of the parameters for education, but our view is that the education of the young deserves the highest priority in any enlightened society. Why? Because the social and economic future welfare of a society largely depends on how well the young are educated in the schools, as we earlier said. Administrators, we believe, should strive to allow and to encourage teachers to use their best energies to develop an enthusiasm and an appreciation for continuing to learn the subject or subjects they teach. Since learning ought to be both an enjoyable and serious experience instead of a chore, students who dislike a discipline they are taking or their teachers should not be allowed to continue with instructors who cannot stimulate their curiosity and imagination. Intellectually stimulating the students, after all, is central to teaching.

Too many students in today's schools feel indifferent toward their teachers or do not like them. Also, for a great variety of reasons that ought to be examined by individual school districts, many teachers do not see having a good, healthy relationship with their students as a prerequisite for quality education to occur. Teachers, as we have stated, are not often provided with enough time to work on improving their teacher-student ties. These circumstances help explain why many mentor-pupil relationships ironically end up being detrimental instead of helpful to the education of youngsters. Some teachers, particularly new ones, daily suffer from not knowing how to approach and work with students in positive, constructive ways. This is especially the case when teachers themselves have not been properly shown how to create a healthy learning atmosphere. Creating such an environment is one of the most important tasks that good teachers shape from the first day they begin teaching. Knowing how or learning how to facilitate student learning is an essential component of teaching. Students' attitudes can be harmed by teachers who communicate indifference, for students who discern lack of interest in them will immediately mirror back that same attitude. In such cases, students usually reciprocate by showing indifference not only to their teachers but to everyone else around them, often baffling many well-intentioned educators.

In *Maggie's American Dream: The Life and Times of a Black Family* (1988), psychiatrist James P. Comer writes the following assessment about the recent history of the American education process:

> One of the reasons that school staffs are ill prepared for children outside of the average expected, or mainstream, experience is that educational reform in the 1930s and 1940s focused on academic standards and content rather than on child development and relationship issues. "Sputnik" in the fifties, or interest in high technology, exacerbated the problem. All of the educational reform talk and reports of the past few years ignore child development and relationship issues. And yet when you ask school teachers and administrators what is wrong they say "A lack of respect, discipline, and motivation"—all relationship issues. When you ask high school students why they didn't do well in school, or left, the most often heard complaint is: "The teachers don't care"—a relationship issue. The question I most often hear from school staff about parents is: "How do you get parents to participate in the school program?"—an issue suggesting we have to work out a proper relationship.[1]

Academic standards and the emphasis on content are no doubt important, but when these components of education become the one and only purpose of education, then all the students who are not in the top 2, 5, and 10 percent of their classes understandably feel significantly less important. It is difficult to encourage students who may develop later to enter the top echelons of their classes when such students have been effectively discouraged from challenging themselves academically by categorizing percentages.

In schools where such practices are in place, the nature of the relationships that education systems need to establish and promote between students and teachers are significantly diminished, for both educators and students soon see such a desired relationship as unimportant and inconsequential. Students are either classified as bright or not, and once they are placed in one cohort or the other, it is difficult for students in the latter group to move into the former category, since their grades and school records follow them. Instead of always connecting students to their school files, students should yearly be allowed and encouraged to develop healthy, educational relationships with their new instructors, since the nature of the professional connection that students establish with their teachers is central to their education. Professional ties that develop between pupils and their mentors should be shaped to improve student learning, but such relationships have been progressively slighted over the years. Due to the large class sizes, today some teachers do not even know who their students are, and many instructors will even admit that they do not have time to learn who their students are.

A high school teacher friend of ours, for instance, taught so well that he was sought out by students. His discipline was not an easy one, yet his classes were engaging and fun, and a high percentage of his students received good grades and successfully passed state-mandated tests. Because he was an excellent teacher, as the years passed the size of his class increased while he was progressively asked to teach the more rigorous courses in his discipline. When he asked school supervisors to reduce his workload, the reply was, But Mr. X, you are so good at what you do! Our responsible friend who loved his profession went to see a medical doctor who advised him not to put so much pressure on himself because he might suffer a stroke. When he responded that he had all of these teaching obligations, the doctor said that perhaps he ought to consider retiring. After working another year and a half, and seeing that he was not going to be provided with any relief, he decided to retire, as the doctor advised. This was a senseless loss of a good teacher who left the profession due to increasing pressures created by working in an environment that was unresponsive to class size increases.

So long as students learn what they are going to be tested on, then everybody assumes that education is occurring as it should.[2]

But educators who know better are aware that it is important to know who your students are because doing so tells us how they have grown, where they have been spending their growing-up years, what they have had to cope with in their pasts, and what they will be struggling with while they are in a particular class. We secure a glimpse of habits at home, for example, from marketing research showing that Hispanics tend to watch more television than non-Hispanics and that Latino and Latina TV viewers tend to be younger than the general U.S. viewing population.

> Hispanics watch more television than the population at large, accord-
> ing to a new study of viewing habits. Nationwide, Hispanics spent
> 58.6 hours a week in front of the set last season, 4.4 hours more than
> non-Hispanics, reported Stacey Lynn Koerner, senior vice president
> at ad-buyer Initiative Media. The six major English-language net-
> works don't benefit proportionally from this large Hispanic turnout,
> however. Research indicates that nearly 50 percent of the viewing
> done by Latinos is of Spanish-language programs.[3]

Such findings might mean any number of things that researchers have yet to discover. Being able to interpret such trends, like creating and maintaining a proper learning classroom atmosphere, can be the happy result of knowing and understanding cultural habits. Conversely, an inability or reluctance to use such knowledge about our students can lead educators to fail to secure their attention effectively. Overcrowded classes and testing pressures on the teachers, to be sure, have also not helped, but, such obstacles aside, the main teaching challenge remains establishing some kind of personal relationship with each and every student. Every individual wants to feel and to know that her or his performance in class matters and is being closely followed by the teacher.

A gesture of goodwill or of a nurturing nature can be the single most effective component that produces effective teaching. Such signals from teachers are of particular importance to all types of minority and ethnic students who so often feel uncomfortable in a school setting.

*A new student from Mexico daily brought in a burrito for lunch. Cafe-
teria food was different and more expensive, so his mom prepared lunch
at home. When the class sat down for lunch, my teacher friend noticed
that all eyes were fixed on Alberto as he opened his brown bag. With
downcast eyes, Alberto had been opening his bag and taking a few bites
before quickly returning his leftover burrito into his bag. My creative
teacher friend took the opportunity not only to speak about different
cultures and foods in her social studies class but invited Alberto's mom
in with an interpreter to make burritos for the entire class. The positive*

psychological impact on Alberto as his classmates paid attention to his culture and traditions was visible from that day forth.

Good instructional time with the students is the main reason that teachers are in the classroom. Teaching time spent with students is what teachers ought to be hired for, not to establish or to monitor relationships with parents nor to keep records and reports that will ultimately be filed away and used only if lawsuits or out-of-compliance charges should emerge someday. If we were to ask, for instance, today's minority adults about the nature of the relationships that they had to their teachers when they were in school, we would find surprising responses. Most minority adults report having had no more than two or three teachers who appeared to care for them when they were going through their school grades. These were the teachers they especially liked or may even have loved from kindergarten to their senior year, if they graduated. The ones who did graduate were the more industrious, usually parent-supported students, the ones who generally went on to pursue college educations. If we pursue the issue further and ask them to remember the names of the teachers who encouraged them, most adults tend to remember their favorite teachers, and, like most of us, without too much encouragement they will mention that they have not easily forgotten the names of the teachers who definitely had it out for them or who did not care one hoot, as the slang expression correctly captures that attitude.

The constructive point we wish to extract from this discussion is that good teachers will not settle for, nor will they allow, an indifferent student or a group of apathetic students to sit before them in a classroom. In order to learn, students have to be actively engaged by a teacher who knows how to elicit in positive ways the interest of students both as separate individuals and as members of a class. Teachers have to learn, which means that they have to be taught, how to develop an interest in the welfare of each of their students, whether teachers comfortably "relate" to the individuals students or not. Good teachers also know they should avoid favoritism in class, for nothing discourages students as much as knowing that teachers prefer some students in class while others are visibly only tolerated. Such realities, we know, occur in too many classrooms across America, and these are some of the reasons minority students in particular often report feeling excluded, helping to explain why some remain unresponsive to classroom activities.

We know that many teachers, administrators, and educators may take issue with these and other observations that we are making, but we speak both as educators and as parents who have talked to many other educators and students over the years. We have learned that students, like the teachers themselves, need to know that the people around them, including their administrators and school district personnel are working for and with them in good faith.

What we have seen is that minority students become disaffected and discouraged and not due only to an "attitude" problem, as some rumors run. Rather, when attitude problems are supposedly exhibited, what is being encountered is usually student apathy. Such a stance is the result of having teachers who have, perhaps inadvertently, communicated messages that effectively say that they do not especially care if students pass or fail. Students should not feel that teachers are interested in them only or mainly because they want their students to score well on academically important national and state-mandated tests.[4] Students are naturally interested in teachers as people, as adults who ought to care enough about them to teach them what they need to know to be successful citizens later in life. If the signals students receive, regardless of whatever else teachers say, simply indicate that students better learn the material, students often soon exhibit behavior that says, "I am not interested because you don't really care about me, so why should I care about helping or pleasing you?"

If we have many students feeling and acting out such a belief without being attended to, then the school district and the educators of that school have a serious problem. For if education is to succeed, students have to be continually primed and encouraged to learn; they have to be constantly engaged in creative ways that draw out their best talents and sharpen their skills. This is why we have spent time discussing the importance of whether students like or love their teachers. When students personally like or admire their teachers, learning becomes an exciting experience in which they want to participate every day. In a very real way, students want to please not only themselves and their parents, but their teachers as well. We are convinced that when schools have problems energizing students, it is usually because somewhere in their past, such students have been turned off or discouraged by some experience or careless remark made by some adult who was not sensitive enough with a young person. Nothing is sadder than to see students who have been turned off from the excitement and enjoyment that true learning offers, for such pleasure provides students with a purpose in school for pursuing a quality education that can do wonders for their young lives.

The way to repair such practices, of course, is not to waste time finding out who are the offending educators but rather to diagnose the behavior of such students and then to devise strategies that will effectively counter teachers' indifference or hostility or whatever other emotions they spend most of their class time communicating in one way or another. Once assessed correctly, efforts should be made to change how students are deflecting opportunities for education, for that is exactly what the challenge of education is, difficult or impossible as it may seem. To change students from what they are when they walk into a classroom to what society needs them to become as good citizens is one of the main tasks of a good teacher. The idea is to make the effort, to meet the challenge and to reinvigorate students who have been discouraged from learning somewhere along the K–16 path. In this effort, the teacher knows or should make it her or his business to find out what is the best way to proceed. Everybody else in our school systems should be on heightened awareness to help the teacher in whatever manner possible, especially by not obstructing or misusing the energies of an instructor to carry out other tasks that do not directly and immediately benefit both the teacher and the student.

*T*here are effective ways to fix anything, and the pedagogical challenge is how exactly to repair such big, seemingly insurmountable problems in K–12 education so that students become qualified to pursue higher education, should they choose to. Most people who address the task stay within the elementary, middle school, high school, or college level, knowing that each one of these areas has sufficient issues to keep people engaged for several lifetimes. Education is an arena perfectly suited for the saying "Anything really worth doing is worth doing again and again." Educators' constant efforts to reinvent or redesign the world of education would be significantly enhanced if some of the following principles were to guide the challenge of repairing the school systems to improve the education delivered to all students.

The great secret to understanding education is that the most important relationship in the entire educational system is the one between the teacher and the student. This is true not only at the kindergarten level but all the way to the Ph.D. When all administrators and education reformers understand and keep this central fact clearly before everything else, many of the other school problems will be reduced or disappear altogether, including teacher and administrative stress and burnout.[5]

Educational reformers who do not understand this truth or anchoring reality should know that nothing that they do by way of improving education is going to help much if the relationship required between a teacher and the students is not given the necessary attention and support. Again, in education, almost everything in the daily life of the student depends on the extent to which a teacher is allowed to establish and develop a healthy mentor-pupil relationship with the students. That professional tie or connection, more than anything else, shapes how teachers feel about teaching and how the students respond to the material they are expected to learn. School district administrators need to see this relationship as paramount when they plan the events of every school year calendar. Given the diverse student bodies in today's classrooms, teachers need time within their schedules to serve individual students as well as the entire class.[6]

One can, of course, envision all kinds of futuristic and, one assumes, technological ways of delivering knowledge and learning to students, but until some truly affordable educational system is devised that better replaces the interactive chemistry provided by good teachers, the ongoing, dynamic opportunities afforded by having an instructor teaching students in a classroom is the best way to deliver instruction. Part of the challenge, of course, is to prepare teachers so that they themselves are sufficiently excited by the intellectual give and take available in classroom settings.[7]

Having expressed what in some education circles may sound trite, actually implementing a sound and healthy teacher and student relationship would bring about a true revolution in education. Experienced teachers may smile because they know that many forces outside of the classroom militate against setting up education systems that revolve around teachers and students. Yet if top administrators and legislators were to pay attention to what teachers actually need to make the schools better, we are convinced that the jobs and the pressures of everyone associated with education would be considerably improved.

It was library day for my bilingual first-graders. They walked into the library quietly and in the orderly fashion that I had instructed them to their assigned tables. The librarian, who knew no Spanish, began to address my class. Very quickly the students began looking at each other, losing interest in the adult speaking to them. Pardon me, I said. Would you mind if I translate what you are saying to them? She was in fact stating new rules they were to follow in the library from now on. Well, she hesitated, I guess. This IS a bilingual class, I explained, and only three students know some English. OK, she said.

I began translating to the children at the same moment that the principal of the school stepped into the library to set down a box of books. When she heard my Spanish, she looked up at me with a look of horror. I certainly took notice, but proceeded. After the translation, my students had a great library visit, carefully signing their book cards on the new forms and placing the cards and the new pencils in their proper places. At the end of classes that day, I approached the principal in her office and asked to speak with her. Mrs. Smith, you are aware that I have a bilingual class, I began. Of course, Rita. Well by the look you gave me in the library I thought perhaps there might have been a misunderstanding or that I had acted in some manner incorrectly. She looked up from her desk, face muscles quite ready to say something explosive, I thought, when she stopped as if in thoughtful retrospect and slowly said, No, Mrs. Portales, you know what you are doing. Keep doing what you are doing. We in this valley do not yet want to see bilingual education for what it is worth, and it's time we start teaching them correctly. Continue what you are doing. Mrs. Smith turned out to be one of the best principals for whom I have worked.

But listening and allowing teachers to be true to their training and instincts usually is less normal in education these days. Today, most of the other people connected to education who are not classroom teachers in an education system are unfortunately seen as more important. The job of the teacher is to work to meet and to satisfy the duties and the requirements that educators are expected to carry out for their supervisors, administrators, parents, and state and federal government agencies. Such tasks, to be sure, require an enormous expenditure of time and human energy, both of which translate into subtracting teacher time from the nature of the relationship that teachers could be offering students.

People who work outside of the actual classroom will likely say at this point that we have taken the side of the teachers and that this book will make all supervisors, administrators, parents, and state and federal government educators look like the ogres that, of course, they are not. Our point is that the people outside of the classroom are essential and important, but we need to understand that without a good working relationship between the teacher and the student, no school system can be repaired successfully.

Again, perhaps the best way to communicate what is necessary in the daily business of education and what is ancillary and complementary is to compare the schools to the better-known world of sports. Teachers cannot educate their students properly if they are not helped by all the people outside of the classroom who facilitate and who carry out all the other kinds of work and activities that must be done. Taking care of these duties leaves the teacher free to concentrate on the kind and the quality of the teaching experience that she or he can deliver to every student.

In football, baseball, soccer, or any other sport, a great number of people are involved in facilitating the game for the players who go out on the playing field to show their mettle. On the day of a sporting event, the real excitement occurs when the spectators learn who has the best team and who the best players are. In professional sports, of course, big money is associated with these momentous encounters, so the intensity surrounding a game sometimes can create enormous pressures for the players, their families, and a good number of the people directly associated with them, to say little of the excitement that fans experience. What works considerably better in the sports industry than in the world of education is that observers seem to know, from the players themselves to the individual fans who may even watch a game on television, what the nature of the players' involvement is. The sports world, like education, is enormously complex, and although countless predictable and unexpected problems arise, as in all complex endeavors, everyone nevertheless knows that the people and the conventions are in place to take care of whatever exigencies or issues arise.

Education has a history as long as sports, if we recall the ancient Greek games. But education has not yet learned how to take care of the mix formed when the business side meets the human relations issues that constantly arise in the teaching of our young. In part, we are not clear on how the business of education connects to the issue of raising young people properly because, while we continually refer to the "education system," we have not sufficiently clarified what an actual system of education has to accomplish for the primary intended beneficiaries of education, namely, the students.

Since the prime objective of education is to educate the young, then *everything* done in the field of education should be attempted principally to improve the quality of the education that students receive. This may sound like too obvious a point, but we write this because simply too many distractions in the schools today keep people from seeing this basic, fundamental objective. People easily lose sight of the fact that schools are there to educate youngsters and not to control them or to contain them or to "straighten them out" or for any number of other purposes. There are, of course, other social benefits of education, but if educating youths is not the main goal, then we need to say that the personnel involved in an education system do not properly understand their place, and their role should be clarified as soon as possible.

I once attended a conference of bilingual educators in a nearby large city. At this meeting, one lecturer, a Mexican American lady administrator/educator, related an idea that she had, along with some overhead prints that she had prepared to communicate her views about a method that she had developed that was producing very favorable responses in her bilingual students. Their report card grades had risen, and after a few weeks their English improved quickly and steadily. It was obvious this was the first time that she was going to share her ideas with an audience. She did not have all of the overheads she used in the program, but she would be willing to send them to those of us who wanted "to try the program," if we gave her our addresses. A list was begun and passed around for people to sign their names and addresses. She was saying that she wanted to know if her ideas would work as well with our students, when an older male administrator asked her if she had considered putting out her ideas with a large publisher, that certainly she was in for some money when she did so. If he were she, he said, he would definitely NOT give out even one of her overheads. She looked befuddled, surprised, and then said, Of course!!! She asked that the list be stopped and said that she would not be sharing her information. When she did have her program published, several asked her, could she send us notice? Well, you'll just have to look at the teachers' stores and magazines that come into your schools to see when it does arrive. We never heard word again.

The prime deliverer of knowledge or education to the student is the classroom teacher. That is why the relationship between the teacher and the student is crucial in the business of education. How the teacher interacts with each student is likely the best measure of the effectiveness of the entire system of education. The objective of the school system is continually to enhance the relationship between the teacher and the student. For this reason, the point of contact between the teacher and the student needs as much support as possible. This link or association is not just another piece or part of the education system, as it tends to be these days in too many school districts throughout the United States. It is, rather, the most important point of interaction in the entire school system. If primacy is not given to this relationship, then all of the other activities aimed at supposedly helping students, in effect, end up detracting from educating students.

A friend and teacher in a South Texas middle school tells us that she overheard one teacher within a group in the school conference room saying, "Why should we get together to plan how to teach a bunch of little Mexicans who have no goals, no discipline, and no parents who want to support them?" That teacher had been calling parents and had not been able to reach them for one reason or another. We recommend that instead of emphasizing the negative characteristics under which students obviously labor, that instead of resorting to the cross word or to a stinging remark that a student will never forget, why not do what our friend Mrs. Bartlett did? In speaking through a teaching assistant who spoke Spanish, on his first day of class she looked at an intimidated Eugenio with a smile and said, "Please tell him that I can see that he is a very talented young man and that he will be a very good student in my class." Eugenio saw her smiling when she spoke to him, and he knew that the teacher was saying something good. That young man went successfully through the rest of his middle school grades, graduated from high school, and enrolled in and graduated from college. Like other Mexican Americans who have become successful, he credits that one moment in his life with providing him with the necessary incentive. Today he is a superintendent of a public school district.

| # *U*NDERSTANDING AND EDUCATING ALL STUDENTS

A few summers ago considerable construction went on at the local high school. What adults thought and talked about were the higher taxes brought on by the new construction. Almost every adult we spoke to hoped that the school would be safer and better and that the extra taxes would translate into improved educational opportunities for the students. Although some citizens had been reluctant to vote for the school bond to support the new building, later most people were pleased that neighborhood property values rose, that our tax dollars were visibly being used to provide for the young, since most school districts have to wait for years to build better buildings to accommodate increasing enrollment.

But what did the teenage students see? Aside from the emotions usually raised by the start of the football season, youngsters were generally excited about the new facilities, but most did not expect much change in their everyday lives. What the majority likely expected was another "boring" year before them, to use their word, another humdrum experience at the school, eclipsing the new school facilities. Such a response, to be sure, is often teenage posing, but there is an issue here, and the question adults need to ask is: Why is school generally seen as more of the same by students? Why is school just what it was like last year and most of the previous years, even though every year in school is obviously different? If schools are supposedly improving academically and test scores are going up, as some educators and studies tend to claim almost yearly, shouldn't the actual teaching and students' responses to better educational experiences show that difference? Why do so many students feel discontent in the schools when learning ought to be an exciting experience? Is learning, in short, being approached creatively and with imagination?

For minority students, who now comprise a little less than half of the nation's high school students, we can visually see that school is a disappointing experience that they have to struggle with simply to endure. Visit some schools and classrooms and we can see what that Mexican American mother we highlighted earlier meant when she said she saw Mexican American students visibly marginalized by the schools. Such circumstances ought to explain why surveys and school records yearly show that nearly one out of every two minority students does not graduate from high school. Of the ones who do graduate, about two-thirds will attend community college, and then usually for anywhere from four to six years, instead of the two years that students are supposed to spend at this level as freshmen and sophomores.[1] These statistics alone also help to explain why not enough students of color are showing up at the better higher education institutions, in keeping with the minority population increases that Texas and the Southwest are experiencing.[2] Since school districts and responsible taxpayers do not want to be known for failing to educate *any* of our students, most people should agree that statistics of this kind are simply not ethically acceptable.

Education programs that change and excite the minds of students, teachers, counselors, and administrators have to be created. Every single student ought to be educated so that he or she is properly prepared to attend college, should the student decide to do so. That choice is not available to most of our minority high school students today, largely because they have not been properly educated from kindergarten so that they can later decide about going to college. By their junior and senior years of high school, they have a long academic achievement record, and usually what their school records show is that they were simply "passed" with D's and C's, mediocre grades that, of course, deter them from applying and being accepted into the more competitive U.S. colleges and universities.

When minority students are first informed about college along with other students, whether during the elementary or middle school years, most of them are usually not equipped, either by background or family support, to sustain themselves through the school years that loom before them. If they are fortunate and reach their senior year, based on whatever support they have been fortunate enough to receive, that is usually too late a juncture to consider going to college. Nurturing parents, to be sure, sustain students from kindergarten through the school years until they become seniors. But when parents are absent or unsupportive or when they do not know enough about higher education, as is the case with most Latino and Latina parents, learning how college admissions procedures work can be daunting. Often, minority students are simply left unattended, unadvised, as it were, especially during the adolescent and most difficult years of grades six, seven, and eight, leaving them very unprepared for taking the courses in high school that they will need to apply and successfully enroll in an academically competitive college or university.

Can teachers engage the interests of students who express the sentiment that school is boring? Students who are bored by school usually tie their dissatisfaction to how they feel about reading, writing, and doing homework assignments for which they see no purpose and to how they individually and collectively feel about their teachers. All of these issues are intimately connected for students, and since they have usually not been taught to think critically, often they do not analyze their situation and end up expressing boredom.

Generally, students tend to feel one of four ways toward their teachers and schoolwork, the latter actualizing itself most noticeably in their attitudes toward reading. Most educated people either love or like to read, though some people in this category dislike reading and others may even hate it. Nonetheless, those who do not enjoy reading know they have to read, if only to stay current in their fields.

As scholars and teachers, most of us tend and prefer to address people who love or who at least like to read, that is, colleagues, students, and audiences who generally are well disposed toward reading. Because we are so inclined, we expect people to enjoy sitting down with a book or a publication to read, which is to say that through little fault of our own, most of us end up avoiding and disregarding people who do not share our views and who do not look for materials and occasions to read. By the time we are adults, we expect people who dislike or who may even hate to read to have been filtered out by the education pipeline or to have eliminated themselves as they have made their way through the school system. Among this group we have people who prefer not to read and people who do not read because they have not been adequately taught to appreciate that effort or who have been traumatized by some early reading experiences.

In most cases, we believe minority students do not attend college because they have not been sufficiently prepared to read correctly, and this has occurred because they have not had the benefit of the necessary resources for the effort. For too many minority students, reading is not a significant part of their lives. In their case, reading is unhappily connected to bad or inconsequential memories of school, and because school has not been a positive experience, reading is associated with a period in their lives often seen more as mental abuse than as the cultural empowerment experience that schooling should offer.

We suspect that many Hispanics, blacks, Native Americans, and other minorities do not read more because our cultures are not adequately represented in our reading experiences, though happily that is changing. Historically, ethnic minority groups have empowered themselves not through the printed word but in other ways, and that is because quality educations have been difficult to secure and simply not readily available for minority populations. In our daily lives, too many other attractions and pressing needs successfully compete against school, that comparatively joyless experience communicated by printed words found in dry, inert books. For people from poor and working-class backgrounds, reading is a luxury seldom enjoyed because the reading, as well as the fun of thinking and talking about what is read, has not been sufficiently taught in the schools, so reading is not a skill that is enthusiastically pursued.

Instead of enjoying the pleasurable experience of a good read, too many minority youths for this and other reasons come to dislike reading. At most they tolerate and endure the teachers who encourage them to read.[3] Our view is that minority students need to be more effectively engaged by print symbols that communicate meaning. Because they tend to receive less attention at the elementary, middle, and high school levels, most minority students tend to be nominally educated, as the schools implicitly require of them.[4] Since they too are focused on more pressing personal and family needs while also enticed by the consumerism that besets almost everyone in the United States today, and because they usually lack helpful parental support, most minority students flee, at almost every opportunity, into whatever pastime, escape, or entertainment is available. Reading, which invariably is difficult to accomplish in homes not equipped for that sedentary task, progressively becomes an unpalatable, unattractive reminder of school—the very activity that repeatedly underscores the message that they are not as good as the college-bound students. Reading and therefore anything associated with reading progressively becomes something to avoid. Since the schools, in effect, psychologically leave such students to wander about on their own, even though they are physically required to attend classes, reading becomes just one more bothersome exercise that they associate with the boring, imprisoning experience that school is for many minority students who understandably feel unwanted.

Why is it readily apparent that many more white students and fewer minority pupils love or like reading? We suspect because even though all students are ostensibly encouraged to enjoy reading, white students have more attractive reading environments and have been more effectively supported, cajoled, and mentally engaged by teachers and parents with promises of rosier futures since the elementary grades. The nature of the mental engagement and the subsequent reward is the difference. Minority students hear the same teacher and perhaps even the same parental messages, but their school and home lives are less likely to lend themselves to reading and to discussing the materials that they are supposed to be learning in school. When these students look at their parents' livelihoods and stations in life, they often feel that the future will not belong to them, despite their parents' telling them that they do not want them to inherit their jobs and low pay. Working to secure good grades in school is not going to matter greatly for them in their actual lives, several students have informed us, explaining why participating in a print-oriented culture is not an imperative in their young lives.

Reading is seen as enough of an imposition by many teenagers, and the imposition is not effectively surmounted or offset by the enjoyment of that exercise nor by the promise of a better tomorrow for minority students. Through the empowerment that sustained support of reading provides year after year, on the other hand, Anglo students successfully compete for places for themselves similar to those of their parents. This is why schools tend to work better for white students and less so for minority people, continuing social networks that make it consistently difficult for minority students. So, although the message is the same, implicitly minority students tend to be discouraged from the type of social success that good reading habits can promote.

What can be done? As teachers, scholars, and educated citizens, we need to assess our specific strengths to see what we can individually use or refashion to help minority students with reading obstacles. Nobody knows our disciplines and areas of competence better than the teachers themselves, so few people can tell educators what can and might be done to exert our influence individually and communally. If we focus attention on improving the reading skills of students, each teacher can personally implement an idea or two that would particularly help two or three minority students who can use more sympathetic direction.

In literature, for example, we have roughly three types of writers.

There are writers whose work tells a reader, "Meet me on my turf, and only the best readers will understand me." Then we have the work of writers who in effect say, "I will do everything I can to help you understand my work." A third group takes a stand between these two positions, saying, "I want readers to understand, and I will help and show them how to understand, but readers still have to make an effort to meet me on my own turf." Teachers, too, often approach students very much in these three ways. We have teachers who approach students by saying something like, "I mainly have commerce with the best students, with the students who are willing to meet me on my turf." We also have teachers who endeavor to understand where students actually live their mental lives. Teachers ought to employ a combination of these approaches, that is, make efforts to understand students and show them the expectations, then work to meet students on the common turf that their discipline inhabits.

Igniting or reigniting their love for learning is another effort that conscientious teachers ought to attempt, since students are naturally curious and should want to learn. How, for instance, can teachers create a new excitement for learning good English?

A good, sensitive instructor interested in building or in enhancing the self-esteem and confidence of students might ask individuals to use Spanish or black English as a vehicle for learning how standard, conventional English works. Although this area of learning and teaching is now fraught with politically correct advice and counter-advice, students know that they have to learn how to communicate competently both in writing and speaking if they are professionally going to impress other people. The idea, however, is not to reject the language or languages that students daily use and feel comfortable with, but to employ that knowledge to expand their learning and interests in the disciplines they need to master. In class, for example, confident teachers can imaginatively learn about words that Hispanic and African American students may have that derive from slang or street talk situations to create the type of student interest that will lead to the learning of good, standard, conventionally used written and oral English.

If a student knows Spanish or speaks some Spanish, or if he or she uses black English or likes to use rap terms and expressions, such languages can be creatively used to teach the type of English that educated people are expected to communicate in to graduate and secure some of the better jobs that society offers. We know that the cultural politics of teaching good English in some parts of the country may be more difficult than in other places, but as minority educators, we tell our students that we all have to follow the rules for conventional English, even though we may not individually or collectively like the conventions. Although no one person made the rules for what is regarded as good, conventional oral or written English, most people know when understandable English is being used. When language is not used or written correctly or acceptably, people know. The objective is to teach students the difference so they are empowered to choose what words and languages they want to use for different occasions.

Once students see that reading is a multifaceted experience, they will soon also realize that English, math, science, geography, or any other subject for that matter is worth learning. The idea, then, is to teach them the acceptable conventions. When we were taught how to play chess or basketball, for instance, most of us responded positively to good teaching. The goal, as we see it, is not to punish and to ridicule students for the ways they communicate, but to encourage them to see education as a great learning experiment where mistakes will be made. Learning, indeed, is exactly that, finding out what works and what is regarded as acceptable for an educated person and what is not. The endeavor then becomes fun: seeing who can learn the most about any subject, so that students can later creatively apply that knowledge in their own lives. That, by the way, is one of the best ways to begin to promote the development of students who may later even become experts in specialized areas.

By beginning with the basic information on a subject, a student may someday become an acclaimed scientist or a known researcher who can pay the bills, raise a family, and generally learn to take care of himself or herself as a respectable member of the community. A good education moves a student in that direction, but it is difficult to accomplish such purposes when educators themselves joke as one did:

One year I was working in another elementary school by the Texas coast, and many Vietnamese people were settling into the nearby towns because it was known as a shrimp area. Most began their new lives in the United States living in a trailer or a shrimp boat as their first home. These students came into the area, filling our schools. Relations between the local fishermen and the newly arrived immigrants were tense. At that time the individual who headed the school's instructional division was from East Texas, near the Louisiana border. His family, as a matter of fact, had once owned a large plantation, he announced to a group of teachers as we sat hurriedly eating our lunches, since we had other duties waiting. One day I was testing for the ESL program and was visiting a middle school. I was waiting for the list of children whom I was to test. This administrator came into the foyer of the school, where I was waiting, and, picking up the local paper whose headlines echoed the new immigrants' settlement locations in our area, he began reading the stories. Quite unabashedly and nonchalantly, as sometimes one is wont to do when one reads a newspaper, he turned to his friend, the principal of the school, and said, "Well, John, it looks like we'll have to be getting out our white hoods."

That was twenty years ago, some people may say, after the war with Vietnam. But on Easter Sunday in 2001, we were traveling on a Texas road heading east of Houston, when we saw a bus with three white-hooded and robed Klansmen beside it hailing passing cars. It was about two in the afternoon, and Klan members were very publicly waving at everyone traveling through that bright, otherwise cheerful day. Why hasn't education made more of a difference in our communities and in the lives of all Americans during the past twenty years? We think society has not made outlawing racism a top priority.

| *T*HE FOUR K-16 CULTURES

*I*n the United States, students have to learn how to negotiate at least four separate school cultures as they make their way from kindergarten to graduation and on to college. We say four, although the community college level may arguably constitute a fifth culture. Then, of course, there are other variations, depending on whether we are thinking about a public or private school education. Nevertheless, assuming that students study from kindergarten through the grades that lead to college graduation, it is sensible to know about the four school cultures for youngsters. At the elementary level, children are socialized and primed or prepared for the later grades. During the middle school years, the knowledge base is extended for preteens and early teenagers, an activity that is extended and either results in a quality education for teenagers in high school or not. Finally, at the college or university level, young adults are encouraged to reach their full potential so that individually they and all members of society can benefit from the education students received at all school levels.

We believe that as students move through the school grades they are either provided with a quality education or they are not. This desideratum, as we argue, depends on whether teachers, parents, administrators, and the legislature pursue and provide for that goal. We also believe that kindergarten and first grade are among the most important grades, for these are among the best years to introduce children to the fun that all learning should be. It is here that children are first exposed to the fundamentals of learning on which they will progressively practice improving their skills and talents as they move up the grades.

We want to emphasize the word practice, because progressive mastery is what school exercises should be designed to achieve. In school, students ought to be shown how information can be accessed and how it should be organized to facilitate retention. To accomplish that objective, the best teachers have traditionally depended on devising learning exercises that allow students to flex their mental muscles on materials that teachers believe are significant and important. Testing is a teacher's way of checking to see what students have actually learned, given what a teacher has attempted to show them. So class lessons and exercises created to enhance the lessons deemed important are central to the teaching enterprise, and the point is that the better prepared children are in kindergarten and first grade, the more likely they are to attain a quality education.[1]

A quality education, to be sure, requires that the second-, third-, fourth-, and fifth-grade teachers, as well as the teachers in the middle school years and in high school, all continue to provide quality educational lessons and experiences for their students. If any teacher in these grades fails to provide very good lessons for students, that means that a whole class or group of students endure and will suffer what we have to call a bad school year. And nine months with a teacher whom a student does not like can feel like an eternity.

Bad school years over which students have little control are very difficult to make up and virtually impossible to forget. The challenge, however, is that somehow students themselves have to become aware that their educations have been shortchanged, and then they have to develop the desire to try to make up for the education and the information that they did not learn. These two extra steps do not ordinarily occur in the lives of such students most of the time, but many Hispanic and other minority students experience bad school years frequently enough that they miss those two steps and fail to capitalize sufficiently on their educational opportunities.[2]

Scholarly experts have studied each of the four school levels, and if we are to repair school systems, it would behoove all of us to study their work further. But teachers in the classrooms can also provide us with considerable information about the cultural complexities found in each cluster of grades. Part of the challenge is that, having negotiated the K-12 expectations or the K-college trajectory, most adults tend to forget the anxieties and difficulties that each one of us encountered when we first faced a set of grades and contemplated moving into the next school culture level.

The one constant that we hope most readers will agree with is that there are four very different and distinct school cultures at the elementary, middle school, high school, and college levels. Each of these grade groups—kindergarten to fifth, sixth to eighth, ninth grade to the senior level, and the four years of college—has a different culture with very different expectations and requires quite altered behaviors from the students. Successfully meeting the demands of each group of grades is therefore not an easy task. The higher the cluster of grades, the harder it is for people of color, for apparently minority students grow increasingly uncomfortable as they move up an uncertain educational ladder that successively offers disturbingly unclear goals.

At the elementary level, teachers generally love to teach "the little ones," as educators tend to characterize five- to ten-year-old children. The goals at this level are to socialize these youngest of students and to teach them good reading and writing skills as well as basic math, science, English, and the arts. Elementary teachers usually like to work closely with their students, supervising and teaching them on a one-to-one basis whenever possible.

Around the fifth grade or so, teachers begin to emphasize student responsibility, that is, students are expected, and parents are usually informed, that the members of the class have to take responsibility for their school assignments and homework. When the parents reinforce what teachers expect, students are expected to respond. But when parents or other adults in a child's home life are not available to work with the teacher and school officials, problems frequently develop. Sometimes all a student needs is to forget to finish an assigned lesson or to fail to bring in two or three homework assignments. At that point, raising a student's grades to a passing level becomes almost insurmountable. Try, for example, factoring in two or three zeroes along with nine or ten passing grades during a six-week term, and anyone will shortly see that once a student falls behind it is very difficult to recover enough to pass. In keeping with our print curriculum, teaching grade averaging to students early on proves a useful visual aid for them in understanding the meaning of good grades.

What school performance rewards in many cases is therefore not so much merit, as most people like to think, but student consistency. Students have to show up daily at school, and then they have to carry out all of the expected assignments and classwork in order to be rewarded with an A or B grade. Failure to attend school consistently and to carry out the assignments warrants a punishing grade, and most students who cannot fully control the circumstances of their lives generally end up punished for these inconsistencies. In fact, school rewards consistency: consistent attendance, consistently higher grades, and consistent reliability. These are the exact attributes that many minority students simply cannot count on because they have no or little control over conditions of their lives.

This is very much what the middle school years wind up doing to the eleven- to thirteen-year-old cohort of students. Sixth, seventh, and eighth grades are especially trying years for students who previously sailed through elementary school and who suddenly are expected to measure up and to be personally responsible enough to learn on their own and to take care of their school assignments. These are also the years when peer pressure increases and students' hormones are changing, so the formerly lovable "little ones" now arrive at school variously prepared to assert their identities and individuality and to show teachers and peer-friends that they are young adults with views and opinions that matter. Teachers tend to agree that teaching at the middle school level is more challenging or taxing than teaching at the elementary level or in high school, for in the preteen years, students are in that in-between stage when problems frequently arise with little warning. Students who drop out or who will not graduate usually begin to exhibit that inclination sometime during the middle school years, particularly during the seventh and eighth grades.

Students who make it into the ninth grade or freshman year of high school are usually fourteen or fifteen years old, and by that time, teachers expect them to be completely responsible for all the work in the courses for which the counselors enroll them. Counselors are very important in the high school environment; based on the academic records and the grades that students have previously attained, courses are selected that appear appropriate for certain types of students. Some students are clearly seen as "college material," and others may, in fact, be told that they are not likely to go to college, given their lackluster K–8 grade performance.

We cannot protest too strongly against such practices. It is absolutely damaging to a young person to tell him or her that it does not look like they are headed for college, especially if that student is a minority one. Indeed, the challenge of teachers and counselors is to encourage students and to place them in courses that will allow them to grow to meet their full potential, not to stifle, sideline, or otherwise discourage their interests, articulated or not. At this age, again, some students, particularly minority ones, are likely to feel excluded, and they will begin to move toward dropping out, becoming pregnant, or running into other predictable difficulties that may then force them to leave school.

Here and there high school teachers will work closely with students to provide the most help that is possible for such students, but many educators simply expect students to take care of their own schoolwork and to turn in assignments and classroom exercises when these materials are due, often without talking to them or extending them much time or attention. In a less caring environment, failure to finish lessons, homework, and school assignments when due is reflected in the grades a student receives. Since students are treated as separate, independent young persons by the teachers and the school system, high school can be a particularly difficult time for students who did not develop good, responsible study habits at the middle school level.

Students who do graduate, of course, can either choose to enter college or the workforce. As in the case of the previous three school cultures, attending college or the university is an altogether different experience, too. Here professors may take an interest in students, but a great many college instructors expect students to show up in their classes with an interest in the course material. Aside from the required college curriculum, college professors and instructors act on the assumption that students sign up for their classes because they are interested in the materials addressed in a course.

All of which is to say that the four cultures that exist between kindergarten and graduation from college challenge students differently at every grade and at every set of group levels. Such a path in the education of a student is therefore not as seamless as it may appear to people who have journeyed successfully through a school system without being stymied or handicapped by poverty, parents who cannot speak English, lack of acceptable school clothes, useful academic support, or any number of other drawbacks that students do not like to acknowledge or mention. Indeed, most students like to minimize differences that dramatize social and economic inequities, hoping, rather, to be seen and accepted as being as good as the most popular or the most affluent or the most gifted students in a class.

When moving from grade to grade, students provided with the proper support and encouragement usually experience a smooth road that easily connects the different grade clusters. But if we recall our own individual school experiences, most adults will remember that changing from the fifth grade to the sixth or to the seventh grade required some difficult adjustments. And jumping from the eighth grade to that freshman year of high school was a highly anxious moment in most of our lives. Negotiating these separate school cultures today is an even more trying affair, for the complex psychological worlds that many students inhabit are perilous and difficult. Minority students may face greater challenges, particularly if they are conscious of being without some perceived necessities such as good clothes, a nice home, reliable transportation, and other amenities. Having made it through the challenges of elementary, middle, and high school, in short, does not necessarily mean that students have mastered the social environment or the academic essentials that they will need for college or that they will receive the necessary advice and encouragement from peers, counselors, parents, and other adults.

Counselors at the middle and high school levels have important roles. Like other students, many students of color organize their academic courses based solely on their counselors' guidance.

Anita came to this country in the sixth grade. Four years later in high school, she was speaking and writing perfect English. Her report card in the tenth grade, first semester, was a perfect A, and all her courses were regular, non-ESL classes. Why are you not in any AP classes? I asked. What are AP classes? she responded. I found she had met with her counselor at the beginning of the year, but she had not been told anything about such classes. When I inquired, her counselor told me that Anita was still "officially" classified as an ESL student. ESL students are not placed in AP classes in that school district.

We find such professional behavior unconscionable, for policies that unfairly hold back students should be changed to encourage deserving students.

PART III | A PRINT AND ORAL APPROACH

| 𝓔MPHASIZING ALL PRINT
AND ORAL SKILLS

Children and young adults learn in a great variety of ways, not all of which are addressed pedagogically in the schools. Some ways of learning actually distract, interfere and even counter other more organized ways of learning that teachers invent and design. That is why educators need to identify both the areas of learning in which students need to succeed and the best methods to deliver knowledge and information. For if children are not progressively taught how to learn, how to use and how to access knowledge by every teacher assigned to them from kindergarten through college, none of the other efforts that school districts undertake to "improve education" will matter much. If students are not taught how to learn and how to make use of the ideas, knowledge, and information to which they are exposed in school, the schools will continue to fail our students.

Within the constraints of the curricula and the policies that school districts follow, currently there are no national across-the-board practices or pedagogical methods that educators employ to improve the academic performance and the achievement of students. We have found, mainly by listening closely to students, many of whom are minorities, that most have never been told what their courses are supposed to help them accomplish, either in class or later when they leave school and become adults. Given the multiplicity of learning and teaching methods and techniques devised by educators over the years, we want to propose a more comprehensive, overarching print and oral pedagogy that reinforces existing curricula in every single grade. We are proposing this approach because in our classes we have seen that such a curricular blueprint gradually allows students to build their self-esteem by demonstrating day in and day out to their teachers that the knowledge they are acquiring will progressively make them more sophisticated learners as they move from grade to grade from kindergarten to college.

By singling out lessons and processes that actually teach students, from mastering the alphabet to writing a full-fledged college essay, teachers can creatively devise classroom experiences that will usefully show students what learning allows them to accomplish. Since today's culture is primarily visual, one in which images, pictures, and films dominate, educating students about the value and the significance of books and words is an especially difficult endeavor. For this reason, we believe that educators need to develop pedagogical methods that emphasize learning how to read all print symbols available as well as gradually learning how to speak to different audiences to secure and to maintain attention. We are not interested in promoting a particular set curriculum that all teachers can follow. Rather, we believe that the best way to teach all students is to outline a print and oral approach that allows teachers to use their best instructional skills to unfurl the talents of students by building on what students have learned in the previous grades they have passed. Given national and state testing requirements, teachers sensibly need to teach the subject areas that students are required to know to pass such examinations, and by continuing to develop their teaching skills we know that teachers can help students enormously, achieving what everyone desires: a quality education.

When considering education curricula, E. D. Hirsch observed that educators can historically be divided into two camps: the "content-neutral curriculum of [Jean-Jacques] Rousseau and [John] Dewey" and the "narrowly specified curriculum of Plato."[1] In order not to encroach on the academic freedom of teachers, administrators, and school districts responsible for determining the content of the curricula for which their students are accountable in national, state, and grade-level tests, we have decided mainly to emphasize a print and oral approach. Learning the skills associated with these two areas particularly well, we believe, will allow students to employ and to access whatever knowledge they will subsequently need in our information society. Since educators follow both instructional camps, our interest is in emphasizing the learning skills, the tools that students can use to learn more successfully and with a clearer purpose visibly before them.

Students often hear the admonition to stay in school to secure something called an "education," but they are seldom specifically informed in ways they can understand what an education is. They are also seldom told or shown how they might someday use the knowledge that teachers spend so much of their time trying to inculcate in them. Because the great majority of students spend many days of their youth in the schools trying to learn what they are told, it may surprise educators to learn that most students do not ever figure out how all of the learning they are expected to absorb as they move through the school grades is finally supposed to coalesce in their heads to help them realize a future in which they contribute toward the public good.

From parents and teachers they ubiquitously hear that going to school to learn is good for them, that learning will help them into college and eventually secure better employment. But what exactly their roles are in achieving that much-desired goal of learning too often remain vague and unclear, mainly because the purpose of education is not adequately articulated in ways that students can understand. Students are not often told, in so many words, that it is up to all individuals to make something of their education in order to support themselves later, after the formal school years are over. Subjects like math, English, and science, studied for years in school, are supposed to help a person cumulatively qualify for some employment position that will allow him or her to earn a living and raise and maintain a family, if desired. School, in short, is supposed to help our younger generations contribute to the general welfare, to the public good of society.

Indeed, if we ask students, most of them will say that no teacher or adult person of authority ever spent much time telling them how some of what they learn in class can prepare them for life once they leave school. As most of us surmise, someone probably did inform them, but likely they were not psychologically ready to understand when that message was delivered. So, as far as they are concerned, no one informed them in ways that they meaningfully remember that the more they learn about the subjects that teachers placed before them, the more resources they will later have. This is a reservoir of knowledge and information that their skills and talents are later supposed to draw from to help them construct a place for themselves in society as adults.

For students who fail to hear, who never figure out the benefits of schooling, and who are not directly instructed about how learning can help them, an education appears to be nothing more than sitting in a classroom and listening to a teacher "drone on" (their language) about biology, mathematics, social studies, or another subject. They are amply aware that they are expected to learn what is being taught, largely because they will have to pass tests, but why they are being subjected to this process is not fully understood. They know that they are on a road, experiencing some mysterious series of "education" steps that teachers are taking them through, but *where* exactly they are supposed to arrive and, more importantly, *what* they are supposed to do with all of the information that takes such a long process to absorb is a subject that is often not made clear to them.

Many teachers, we need to emphasize, unfortunately do not help students understand the meaning or the importance of the very subjects they teach. Such clarifications, we believe, should be requirements that dedicated teachers spell out to students. Currently, most teachers simply assume that somewhere before they encounter their students, the latter have been explicitly told why dividing fractions, studying algebra, and dissecting a frog are important activities. But when students are asked, we learn they have not. Most students cannot tell other people why subjects like literature, writing, social studies, biology, or algebra warrant or deserve studying. Other than the basic math for which almost everybody can see a good reason, higher mathematics, for example, needs to be explained in ways that engage the thinking of all students. And much the same can be said for most of the other subjects that students are expected to study as they move through the school grades. There are, to be sure, great teachers, unsung heroes, as the cliché has it, who offer certain courses wonderfully, but explaining why a subject is necessary and creating excitement for a course are different accomplishments of a higher order.

The sad fact is that few students are told important points about subjects they are required to take. Sometimes we have found that no one has ever clearly explained the usefulness or the relevance of mysterious processes that are studied so that students will understand why they do certain exercises or activities. Teachers themselves tend to see their work as the challenge of teaching a certain amount of information and material to students, certainly to socialize them into processes known to biologists, mathematicians, or English instructors. But "why" we need to know how these disciplines ask questions about their subject matter often remains assumed and seldom articulated in ways that a sixth- or seventh-grader will understand. The best teachers, of course, do explain why their subjects are important, but too many instructors are so involved with a host of other school activities they simply do not have the time to find out what their students know and what they need to learn, making teaching the uncertain endeavor it is in some schools. Again, administrators are empowered to provide time for their teachers to address the needs of their students, but if teachers are charged with too many other responsibilities, placing the students' learning as their top priority is difficult.

Learning why we study a subject or a discipline is extremely impor-

tant, for if we are not persuaded that a subject or a task warrants attention, few good results can be expected even from the best endeavors. If
teachers cannot show students how the subject they teach is useful in
some way, then what students supposedly learn in school will end up as
wasted time and dissipated teacher and student energies.

Students can use a considerable amount of their energy to try to learn
about binomials and social studies, but they also have to be taught what
binomials can do and why studying society is a necessary challenge that
may translate into possibly helpful contributions to the way people live.
Learning about a discipline by studying that subject is not good enough;
students also have to be taught and they need to learn why a particular
area of study is useful and how they can put to use such learning. The
question for a teacher might be: Why are binomials important? Explain,
and explain clearly, that is, so the students understand. A good mathematics teacher should be able to talk about binomials in a way that his
or her students can see both the theory and the uses for the information
that the teacher writes on the board, the overhead projector, or the computer. If a teacher cannot explain a subject or discipline satisfactorily to
his or her students, that inability begins to explain why some students
fail to be engaged by binomials. The same would be true and necessary
for all other subjects. Good teachers, we know, passionately believe in
what they teach.

Most teachers will state why their subjects are important on the first
day and then mention the purpose and usefulness of their disciplines no
more the rest of the year. Other teachers do not or cannot sufficiently explain why their subjects are important. That means that students will not
know what a discipline is for, which explains why many activities and
class exercises do not make more sense to students. A student's natural
question is: Since I am required or advised to take this subject, what is it
good for? Why should I care about this material? How is it useful to me?
which is to say: How can *I*, as a student, employ this information now,
and how will such knowledge help me later? These are sensible and le-
gitimate questions to ask of any discipline and material placed before
students. Successful teaching encourages students to ask questions like
these, questions that require answers.

Education is what each student makes out of the material studied.
Teachers are paid to teach students roughly between 8 and 4 o'clock.
During that time the minds of the students are supposedly engaged by
a variety of subjects prompted primarily by their texts and surrounding
environment. What they are really learning depends both on the student

and on the teacher, especially since the learning that the student accomplishes continues to accrue as a student progresses through the school grades. Some students who make it to college do not really know how they have accomplished that, but since the school system has granted them a diploma and they are admitted into higher-level learning, such students feel that they have been educated. But, again, an education can only be as good as the use that the student makes of the information delivered in and out of school.

All teachers at every grade level can and should periodically explain and remind students why math, English, kinesiology, and any other subjects that they teach are necessary, important components of a school's curriculum. If teachers cannot do so, perhaps that subject area needs to be reconsidered. Because if teachers do not explain the usefulness and the relevance of the subjects they teach, countering whatever reasons deter them from doing so, students are left either to flounder or to discover for themselves why the material or the class activities in a subject or discipline are good for them. When these are the two options, brighter students may figure things out, but other students, that is, the majority of our future adult American citizens, are not likely ever to figure out why algebra or calculus or chemistry are components of a well-rounded, quality education.[2]

A friend who was the district's migrant coordinator was talking to a group of her school administrators when the topic turned to the district's gifted and talented program. There was no such program for either the migrant or bilingual programs. She said, "We need to address the gifted and talented in the migrant program." Everyone laughed. The Special Education Program director said to her, "Don't you know that only 5 percent of the population is gifted? Your population could never qualify!" My friend retorted, "My students ARE part of the population!" At her retirement party, to which a good number of her former migrant students came, one recent university graduate publicly told her, "Mrs. _____, I want you to know that you made a difference in my life. As I went from one state to another picking crops, I kept remembering your words of encouragement to continue in school. Thank you."

When we find out what a discipline or anything else in life offers us, we either stay committed to the task, continuing to learn the particulars and details of a subject with continued interest and excitement, or we immediately, gradually, or eventually abandon the effort. Many minority students do not make it to college because they are not aware of how the disciplines they are required to take during their middle school years and in high school are important and relevant to their future lives. Too many teachers simply assume that their students already know why the subjects they teach are important. That, however, is not so, particularly for minority students, who often have parents not knowledgeable enough about educational choices to inform them. Without periodically being told by educators or creatively reinforced by how they are required to learn, most students remain unclear about how the knowledge they are supposed to acquire can be useful to them. As a result, somewhere in their educations, usually in the middle grades or in high school, most minority students mistakenly conclude that school is not offering them much and that knowledge of a subject they are not enjoying is not going to help them in the future. At that point, they conclude that college is for other students, for the ones who receive the better grades, for the gifted and talented ones, the ones who, in effect, are the students whom the schools position for success now and later in life.

Is it true that some students are better prepared to succeed than others, even though students have been in the same classrooms? Yes, that outcome can be discerned quite readily from as early as the elementary grades. One can walk into almost any grade in many schools and soon see the students who are visibly being prepared for further study, as well as the students who will be lucky if they graduate from high school. By the end of the third and fourth grade, most students themselves know or sense the ones who are headed for college, who might go to college, and who likely will be excluded from higher education.

Since a print and oral emphasis seeks to make a student understand that all subjects studied are supposed to coalesce within each individual student, we believe this approach to teaching and learning is one of the more useful, efficient ways of educating students. In its simplest form, emphasizing print and oral skills is a K–12 and even a K–16 teaching approach that focuses student attention on all of the print symbols seen everywhere in American society on billboards, newspapers, and signs and on other signs and signals throughout the world. The idea is to teach students both to interpret all things and symbols that are communicated in print and to make them aware that everything they read, think, say, and write can improve how they are seen and assessed for advancement in society. Continually sharpening their print and oral skills encourages students to improve how they write and speak, giving rise to tasks that continually reinforce these over-arching skills in each grade at increasing levels of sophistication.

At the elementary level, for example, let us say the first grade, a lesson in English might be creatively structured to teach students the difference between action and inaction, between the roles of verbs and nouns, for instance. Verbs, students are usually told, are action words, whereas nouns define a person, place, or thing. This is quite an abstract idea for first-graders because even the words used to clarify this basic distinction are likely all Greek to this age level. The challenge for the teacher then becomes one of how to dramatize this concept so first-graders understand it and so their desires to move, look, and touch are naturally brought into an activity that they can learn from and enjoy. Asking first-graders to sit and listen to the difference between a verb and a noun is not likely to meet with much success if teachers are not inventive. All teachers have to be creative; they have to invent or to find ways to communicate ideas engagingly so that the students like being in class while they are actively learning the concepts that are appropriate for their grade levels.

One way, but by no means the only one, is to design an activity to teach first-graders the difference between the verb "walk" and a noun. To walk is the targeted verb. A teacher could write the word walk on the board and state out loud that to walk and walking are verbs. But that verb makes no sense until the word is directed at someone, and who do we have who could show us that? The teacher could make a big issue of the verb walk, a word that does not walk (and just sits there on the board), because the command has not been directed at anyone in particular. What we need, the teacher can demonstrably say, meaning out loud, is for someone in the room who can show the rest of us what it means to walk. We need, in other words, someone to walk across the room. Elementary hands should go up at this point, and that is what good teachers always want in a classroom: active student participation in a class activity. The teacher can then select a student to demonstrate walking, followed by two or three other ones who also want to show the class that they also have learned the concept. The individuals selected to walk would be showing the verb; the students selected to walk would be the nouns. The names of these students might then be written on the board, too. These names are the nouns that have shown us what walking is. Teachers, of course, can be as creative as they want or need to be with a class activity like this one or another one that more inventive teachers might devise.

At the middle and high school levels, teachers are also faced with finding appropriate ways to teach their subjects, all of which would be greatly improved by asking students to work on exercises that improve their interpretative and critical thinking skills. The idea behind the print and oral skills approach is to allow students to show their understanding of all things in print by writing and by talking about how they understand the ideas of a lesson in clear terms to other individuals around them.

Emphasizing print and oral skills is not, of course, the panacea by itself. We are nonetheless fully convinced that if educators focus student attention on interpreting and seeing that students understand all ideas and concepts communicated in print, requiring them to articulate such materials through speech and writing, we believe the education of all K–16 students will improve remarkably.

As Latinos who have long been involved in education as both students and teachers, we have learned that by focusing attention on how we read, think, write, and talk, students can be taught to work simultaneously on improving all four related skills in ways that reinforce each other. Indeed, if we look at educating students by using such an approach carefully, we should see why most students who graduate from high school and enter college are white and not minorities. Aside from the discouragement that most students of color feel from teaching approaches that do not encourage them to master school disciplines, we need to understand that white students are usually more successful in school precisely because they are adequately taught to read, think, write, and talk in closely related ways that do not require the kind of language adjustments that Hispanic and other minority students have to make between the home environment and school. Many studies during the past thirty years have observed as much in a number of ways that it is not necessary to dwell on or enumerate. At this point we are more interested in explaining how education systems can be made to work to serve all students better.[3]

What is "education"? There are many definitions of education, but the best definition we can think of is that education is how an individual student is taught to use the knowledge and the information communicated to him or her in school and in society. Education means that *students have to be taught how to create something* out of the general knowledge base they learn in, say, chemistry. They need to learn how to make something out of the algebra problems and the English assignments on which they work on in school. If all of these exercises do not help a student actualize himself or herself as he or she assumes an adult place in American society, then what ought we to say about the class experiences to which such a student is exposed?

Learning depends on language. Since language is the key to everything that makes an education successful, considerable time and effort should be placed on how words can be made to work for students. If a student understands language as a vehicle for communicating ideas, he or she will soon begin to understand how words shape and create a great number of realities. Sharpening print and oral skills for that reason prepares students for school success so that students learn more effectively.

For years we believed in the basic tenet of the preacher in Ecclesiastes, that there is nothing new under the sun. We now know that the biblical writer of that book was mistaken. If through some miracle the preacher in Ecclesiastes were suddenly to see what is new under the sun since his days, the writer would be overwhelmed by the nature of the new realities and changes that today surround us everywhere. Some defenders, of course, would say that the writer of Ecclesiastes was speaking figuratively, that he wrote to express a general truth. The point is that there are so many new ideas that have materialized since the time of Ecclesiastes that one has only to look out of the nearest window to see a myriad number of developments that the writer of this biblical book never beheld. Any list of examples will quickly illustrate that there are all manner of transportation vehicles, wonderfully landscaped areas, and all sorts of unthinkably fast ways to communicate with others, to point to a few new things under the sun.

In the area of education, all manner of ideas are constantly being devised and invented to help students. Some ideas have proven good and useful, while others have only served to dissipate the time and energies of too many people, including teachers and students. So, how exactly would a new print and oral skills approach produce a quality education where other ideas have not?

A print and oral skills approach can pedagogically be adapted to meet the education needs of students from pre-kindergarten to the university level. This claim may sound too general to be helpful, but nourishing the communication skills of students is central to a quality education. Educators may be skeptical if they are accustomed to academic programs designed to accomplish specific purposes for students, but the idea is generically useful because print and oral skills emphasize the importance of interpreting signs and symbols and being able to communicate using these abstract means, encompassing pre–K student needs to the sophisticated theories of university-level disciplines.

A print and oral approach is the result of studying the particular needs that minority students evince at the high school and college levels. After many years of teaching in K–12 schools and at five universities in New York, California, and Texas, we have found that every semester the perennial issue, in one way or another, focuses around reading and interpreting texts, on thinking and on writing clearly enough to discuss ideas and concepts engagingly. The issue invariably translates into the problem of teaching what to look for in the material being studied and how to write about it, processes that test the nature of the critical thinking skills that students from six to twenty-one have previously learned. The goal is to teach the increasing levels of skill necessary so that students can function well from kindergarten through high school and in college, as well as in society after they graduate.

A print and oral skills emphasis allows teachers to make creative use of the best methods they know or can devise from their training for their own classroom teaching. Stressing the significance of print and oral communication skills naturally leads into teaching critical thinking skills, since one cannot point to or select words without also recognizing how they can be used effectively or misused. As such, assessing the reading, writing, and oral talents of students can revolutionize education, since this way of teaching can provide many disheartened, disenfranchised students with better futures, based on the educational materials that K–12 teachers incrementally offer students.

Several Mexican American students who have been taking yearly state-required tests for four and five years the other day informed us, when we asked, that they did not know several words that tend to appear quite frequently as part of the directions in these tests. Those words are "combine," "paragraph," "sentence," "concise," and "analyze." When we asked them why they did not raise their hands to ask their teachers to explain the meaning of these and other words they did not know, several said that they did not want to interrupt their teachers. One added that interrupting a teacher was a sign of disrespect (which is a correct concept in some countries); another said that he did not want to ask because the teacher might think him "dumb," as one of his friends had been called.

A good friend told us the following story. A delegation of educators sent to Africa was touring a number of countries, and, having completed their business, they were told to wait for an air-conditioned bus that would take them to the airport for the return flight to the United States. The educators waited and waited, but the promised bus failed to appear. At length, a native drove up in a rickety old pickup truck and offered to take them for a fee. Two of the educators jumped at the opportunity, but the other ones looked at each other as if to say, "Come now, are we expected to go in that?" The driver loaded the two educators, and, then, to the amusement and amazement of everyone watching, he packed the pickup by dint of hard work until he loaded the belongings of the entire group on his truck. The two educators went ahead to the airport with the luggage of the group, and, on a second trip, the man picked up the other educators.

As in this story, a print and oral emphasis may not initially look like much to experienced educators, but we are convinced that if the idea is embraced, this approach to education can be the vehicle that allows teachers to empower not only traditionally disenfranchised students but students at all school levels.

PRINT AND ORAL SKILLS: BACKGROUND

The assumptions that have shaped curricular development at the elementary, middle school, high school, and college and university levels during the 1960s, 1970s, 1980s, and 1990s no longer guide practical curricula that engage students. Educators have recognized that for some time, but having tried various approaches during the past thirty years that we will not revisit and not having anything that works more effectively, classroom teachers understandably feel wary of abandoning techniques and materials that partially appear to work for them with some students.

At yearly conferences throughout the country, educators discuss and debate the state of education, and to improve the educations locally provided to students, they keep broaching and trying different approaches. During the latest cycle people are talking about charter schools, a voucher system, and national test standards. Educational change, indeed, has become a way of life for educators, but few approaches survive for more than a few seasons. Colleges of education, in fact, appear to have developed educational change almost as a cottage industry, promoting the latest "hot" approach in education every two or three years. Without referring specifically to previously fashionable trends, researchers have claimed that one approach works better than another and that yet another reform works still better than one tried by a neighboring school district or college. Apparently no single approach works well enough to be adapted by a wide variety of school systems. The indubitable proof of this is that although school district scores change a few points up or down every year, student learning has not noticeably improved. The end result is that we have many approaches being practiced under the educational sun, most accompanied by claims to being the best and the latest.

At the college level, as in every other school grade level, students are not what they used to be. And students are not what they have been in the past because teachers, parents, and educational objectives and goals are not what they used to be, either. As always, the world continues to change, but educators should not be implicitly or explicitly saying that no one appears to know how to prepare students for the needs of the uncertain future. The future, of course, has always been uncertain, and the challenge of education is exactly to prepare students to cope with however the world turns.

*T*he state of K–college education has engaged our interest for many years because we have found that students pursing higher education can only be as good as their previous preparation. For that reason, a curriculum focusing attention on all things in print and on oral communication stands, we believe, the best chance of unifying and advancing the education of all students. With some imagination, most of the following suggestions can be adapted to the situations that virtually all teachers encounter, for teaching students about all print symbols and how to discuss such ideas orally allows educators to mold their basic tenets and pedagogical philosophies to the needs of students at any school level.

In our efforts to devise a useful, basic curriculum, we should ask: What are the common components or elements that cut across all curricula, disciplines, and types of educations? Regardless of educational level, we think such a question eventually ends by saying that all good educations seek to impart confidence in reading, writing, speaking, and thinking critically about a discipline or topic.

To move toward confidence and competence on all of these skills, the next question to ask is: What needs to be emphasized and insisted upon to make all students *understand* what an education is and what an education should do for them?

Since knowledge is conveyed, regardless of technology, whether a paper-and-pencil one or a highly sophisticated advanced medium, the use of words, either as *printed* signals or in their *oral* form, is universal. That is why a successful education needs to start with an appreciation of words, of language.

*A*t the college level, the standard "traditional" curriculum used to assume that eighteen- and nineteen-year-old students were adequately prepared by the high schools,
which, in turn, were satisfactorily prepared by the elementary and junior
high schools. College and university curricula used to be predicated
on the seemingly sensible assumptions that when the number of eigh-
teen- and nineteen-year-old students increased, states would continue
to provide needed budget increases. The idea was that students would
absorb and/or master a set, fixed curriculum determined by a faculty
who looked after the interests of the students.

The bases of these assumptions, educators know, have significantly
changed. However, we are not interested in showing how things were
and how they are today. Our point is that the world is not likely to return
to what some teachers regard as the halcyon years of education. For our
purposes, it is sufficient to say that the world is different today and that
we have to adopt new strategies that are not too complicated and that
will effectively educate members of society at all levels.

If the number of eighteen- and nineteen-year-old students has increased, so has the number of older students, who are now, for a variety
of reasons, seeking higher education degrees. Although student numbers have increased, in the past ten years states throughout the country
have significantly reduced funding for most public colleges and universities. Instead of providing more than half of the higher education
budgets, states now provide less than one-third of the money needed to
sustain most college and university budgets. Much of the new money for
higher education is now paid by the students themselves in the form of
extra fees and higher tuition rates. Due to changes ushered in during the
past thirty years, college-level curricula also have changed. The needs of
students now affect the courses and the course material more than before, and faculty members now recognize that students are less well prepared for college than previously, that there are more part-time students,
and that steps need to be taken at most school levels and in virtually
every class to educate and to prepare students better for successful post-
college careers.

DESCRIPTION OF A PRINT AND ORAL SKILLS PROGRAM

A print and oral skills approach to education should be specifically developed by the faculty members of a school or college to meet the par-

ticular needs of students and society. The purpose of emphasizing print and oral skills is to reawaken student interest in the all-pervasive significance and importance of the printed word and signs and in the oral skills they need by working continually from the first grade to high school graduation and in college on their reading, writing, speaking, and critical thinking skills. Why this particular essential emphasis and not others? Because the proper and effective communication of ideas and issues at all levels of society requires careful honing, continual practice, and constant work.

All people with a stake in education for this reason ought to make a professional commitment to promoting the study of the printed word and signs and to working on improving the oral skills of all students. Yet as education systems are currently constructed, the printed word and oral skills are simply two of the many other tasks that teachers attempt to address among other skills that are sometimes given more or equal emphasis. Our sense is that work on the value of the printed word and on oral skills can be made to encompass all other skills comprehensively, since words and speech are the two basic root forms by which people communicate. At the present time, school and university curricula are not overtly designed to highlight the importance of basic skills that promote writing, reading, and interpreting printed words and signs in their wide variety, nor in successfully communicating ideas orally.

Educators who emphasize Print and Oral Skills, for instance, would focus attention on the study of (1) Printed Words and Signs in all their manifestations, receiving appropriate grade-level instruction, and (2) Oral Skills. These are the two central, overarching areas of the curriculum under which all the other disciplines function.

If education is to receive the kind of new meaning and purpose that will make a difference in the lives of all students, teachers have to examine the current offerings in order to strengthen the curriculum, to underscore the importance of deciphering printed words and signs, and to teach effective speech communication skills.

THE PRINT AND ORAL APPROACH: PURPOSE OF THE PROGRAM

The purpose of the print and oral approach in education is to impart a new kind of *confidence* to all students. This confidence needs to rest not only on a teacher's assessment of students' work, but increasingly on the students' sense that they are now being successfully taught how to interpret and analyze all forms of written language and the signs and symbols that are used to communicate throughout society and the world. Students should also be convinced that the knowledge and skills they acquire are showing them how to express themselves clearly, both orally and in writing.

PRINT AND ORAL SKILLS: RATIONALE FOR THE PROGRAM

Knowledge about how words and signs are created and interpreted in all forms and in the ability to communicate well both orally and in writing are central, enormously needed skills in the education of every student. Students either learn to master these abstract ways of understanding and communicating, or they do not.

Schools, colleges, and universities do not now emphasize the study and acquisition of these necessary skills, and that is why many students do not achieve more success in the work world they encounter following their formal school education. Since most curricula focus more attention on the information being imparted than on how students read, interpret, write, and talk to understand others and to communicate their own ideas and views, this emphasis on the content plays down what students personally make out of the material learned. Content is important, and the level of proficiency grasped in a subject or an area of study needs to be communicated. But how that proficiency is acquired and, in turn, conveyed again is a pedagogical area that teachers and students emphasizing print and oral talents consciously endeavor to bring to the fore. Print and oral exercises are developed by each school or district as needs arise. Automatically assuming that students possess these skills and are working on them in a class or homework assignment is a mistake that undermines most efforts at education. Language in all its ramifications, in short, is central to everything that is essential to the business of education and civilization, and that is what the print and oral curriculum seeks to highlight in ways that engage student attention.

THE PRINT AND ORAL APPROACH: WHAT IT IS/WHAT IT ISN'T

Focusing student attention on printed words and signs and on oral skills does not mean that the school or university curricula should be restructured to highlight language only. Rather, employing a print and oral pedagogy means that instructors and students are engaged in a more concerted effort than before in emphasizing the idea that the process of education fundamentally depends on the ability of students to achieve goals like these:

1. Interpret words and cultural signals in all their ubiquity
2. Create, shape, and manage words and signals themselves
3. Pronounce words correctly and intelligently to different audiences under varying circumstances

If students are to master the content and the accepted conventions of the specific disciplines studied at schools, colleges, and universities, learning how to read all printed material and learning how to talk about a subject require considerable flexibility. This need means that it is open-ended enough to allow faculty members from all disciplines to emphasize the necessary higher-level critical thinking skills at each grade level of a student's schooling. By focusing attention on building and creating the knowledge base for a much-needed educational foundation, teachers can better prepare students for the work world and for careers after graduate and professional school.

Chapter 14

ℬLUEPRINT FOR REINSTATING SOCIAL VALUES AND CIVIC VIRTUES

*T*eachers who employ a print and oral pedagogy in their classrooms are in a great position to emphasize the essential social values and civic virtues that undergird American society, helping to promote academic excellence with this strong supporting structure, too. Excellent print and oral skills foster an academic integrity that creates responsible citizens who possess the kind of good public-serving qualities that healthy societies require, regardless of political persuasion. For that reason, students progressively taught, from the first grade to the senior year in college, to pursue excellent print and oral skills come to endorse and recognize the importance of good citizenship standing. In learning how to respond sensibly to the all-pervasive print and oral signals, which abound everywhere in U.S. culture, they develop a true appreciation for hard work and earned accomplishments, distinguishing, for example, between media hype and the realities that people daily face. When accosted by market-driven television advertisements, hate-talk programs, and other kinds of discombobulating influences in our globally oriented culture, such students will not be easily swayed, since they have been taught how to think and how to scrutinize ideas carefully.

Staying balanced in a milieu that constantly seeks to secure the attention of our senses is a difficult proposition for all Americans these days, but it is particularly hard for young people not prepared by an education. Parents and teachers need to tell children who they are and where their cultural roots emanate from, so that students can exercise the option of developing self-pride in the accomplishments of their ancestors should they desire. That, in turn, encourages individuals to express themselves and to cherish our First Amendment rights. Such freedoms are basic constitutional privileges that have to be taught and learned so that students can develop a positive sense of themselves and of other people in our democracy. For these reasons, we hope teachers as well as all other members of society will agree to work on inculcating the following social values and civic virtues to all students:

1. Require *respect for others* and for the cultural differences that people of different races exhibit in their daily lives and behavior.
2. Develop class assignments and exercises that encourage the use of the *imagination* in students.
3. Focus attention on *interpretation,* on understanding and on the production and creation of reasoned viewpoints and perspectives.
4. Introduce students to *consequential ideas,* that is, ideas that matter, ideas that make a difference in how people see issues and treat people and what people do with their views.
5. Show students how to read, how to write, and how to speak with a *clear purpose,* consciously encouraging students to shape what they say, paying careful attention to how students express and communicate what they think orally and in writing.
6. Promote *sensitivity* and *understanding* toward the feelings and the viewpoints of other people.
7. See *cultural and linguistic diversity* as a rich resource for empowering students who traditionally are disenfranchised.
8. Emphasize personal and professional *integrity* and the useful lessons that can be learned from *honest failures.*
9. Increase opportunities for *student responses* to course materials and life situations.
10. *Usefully spend the class time* of students and faculty, eschewing the waste and dissipation of valuable human energies.
11. Recognize and demonstrate, where appropriate, how all disciplines are *related.*
12. Stimulate *enthusiasm* for learning as much as possible.
13. Communicate that *learning* is *a lifelong enjoyable endeavor.*
14. Productively *channel* and appropriately encourage student *cultural self-pride.*
15. *Reading, discussion,* and *writing* are the *central activities* that lead to a *successful education*—skills that extend the horizons of the minds of students.
16. Encourage the *life of the mind* in all students, an intellectual trait that expands options and contributes to the quality of life that students can enjoy in society.

Since improving print and oral talents and skills is a malleable, pedagogical endeavor, such a curricular emphasis is flexible enough to be communicated in a wide variety of ways in classroom situations from kindergarten to the university level. Because the same basic skills and principles would be taught and reiterated by teachers in many different ways, in keeping with the growing sophistication of students as it increases through the grades, this approach can be adjusted by teachers according to the actual needs of students as they move through the education system.

For instance, if a teacher notices that students are not comfortable enough expressing themselves in, say, the seventh grade, the teacher of a particular discipline can consider assigning oral reports to help students gain the kind of confidence that they are sure to need when addressing audiences in the future. Similarly, if students do not understand the significance of algebraic symbols, a mathematics teacher could devise exercises to teach students the origin of the symbols in math, explaining why they continue to be used, and how knowledge of math symbols can be useful in solving problems today. In such cases, we can see, pedagogical attention would be on developing the necessary critical, oral, and print/reading skills that students require to grasp the subject matter at hand before proceeding to the next grade or level of learning.

Print and oral exercises that periodically reiterate social values like the ones listed above might also be initiated for different grade levels as needed. School systems that have students not sufficiently aware of the civic virtues that American society champions can promote these qualities while teaching reading, writing, oral communication, and critical thinking skills. We are not talking about imposing rigid expectations that would encroach on the civil rights of students but simply proposing that schools work on counteracting student behaviors that do not help society in general and that ride roughshod over the rights and responsibilities of teachers and other members of society. Because other successful teaching methods can also be employed under the umbrella offered by a curriculum that emphasizes print and oral skills, such an approach in effect can serve as a national agenda for school improvement. As such, it can be considered, used as needed, and implemented wherever school districts are interested in providing quality educations to the next generations of U.S. citizens. The desired, larger goal would be to show every student in America how he or she can learn to take care of personal needs, reducing the number of people whom society later has to help financially because the schools did not sufficiently show them how to provide for themselves and their families more successfully.[1]

Certainly different educators using different means can all contribute toward instilling necessary social values and civic virtues in students. The idea, though, is to follow a blueprint like this one or another that closely seeks to instill necessary qualities in all of our schools so that American society consciously chooses to work at creating and producing the type of citizen who appreciates and respects the society that we all need to live in our multicultural world. Not to work at educating students to understand what the United States requires from our students today, indeed, is to be irresponsible and to fail to provide for the needs of our future generations.

Chapter 15
A PRINT AND ORAL APPROACH THAT CHAMPIONS THE IMPORTANCE OF CLAUSES

A print and oral pedagogy considerably enhances a student's writing, and one way to demonstrate this, as an example, is by championing the lowly, unappreciated clause. Effective essays and well-constructed, informative oral presentations are basically built around clusters of words that most writers think with before turning these words into clauses and phrases that capture thoughts and ideas, lest they disappear, lost forever. Motivated by the necessary desire to select well-chosen words to describe concepts and ideas, budding writers can be taught how to write carefully, how to begin with a few empowering words and how to move on to develop larger chunks of rhetoric as needed, making and unmaking sentences and paragraphs, a process unseen by readers, all of which end in a piece of writing designed to impress anyone interested in reading.

The definition of the term tells us that "clauses" are clusters of words containing a subject and a predicate, while phrases are groups of words lacking a subject-predicate combination.[1] Thus, "what you decide" is recognized as a clause, while "running here and there" is a phrase, since the former group of words has a subject and a verb, and the latter string of words does not. Most writing professors pedagogically focus student attention not on the clauses or on the pieces or stuff from which sentences are made, but on writing complete thoughts, on creating whole sentences. Others approach writing by focusing interest on how to write the paragraph, or on expressing that great thesis statement, for example, in riveting ways that will engage reader attention. Still others sensibly underscore how essays can be used to organize ideas so readers can sail by picking up information as *hors d'oeuvres* disappear from trays at parties and receptions. Grammarians tell us that clauses exist in dependent and in independent forms. In their dependent form, clauses lean or depend on their independent brethren to express complete thoughts. Independent clauses, as the name says, can stand alone, self-sufficient by themselves, or as mainstays that explain dependent clauses.

But such clarifications do not easily help students until they are capable of distinguishing what independent and dependent clauses endeavor to accomplish in sentences. One way to teach students about this difference is actually to pull out some sentences for examination, to study word groupings separated by commas, semicolons, and periods so they can see how clauses and phrases or groups of words are either self-contained or not. The dictionary tells us that linguistics helps by telling us that clauses are utterances with certain intonation patterns, which means that most clauses and phrases carry their pronunciations with them, an aspect of word clusters that proves useful once students learn to listen for meaning.

Regardless of the subjects that instructors teach, a main goal in most courses is and should be to work with students to help them write sentences and essays that feature what they have learned, what they know. The time and effort required for such endeavors often weigh on writing professors, but if students are shown how to write effective sentences, we believe the challenge of teaching students how to write better can be enormously rewarding and not the drudgery that most people think. Of course, administrators have to ease off requiring teachers to submit other reports, as we have suggested, because such paperwork heavily interferes with a teacher's prime responsibility—which is to evaluate and to help students improve their written work and oral presentations.

By emphasizing a print and oral approach, we want educators to build on the idea that every word is a concept, since words provide us with good, clear mental pictures that readers ought to see in our minds and listeners ought to hear and understand. Consider the word "cipher," for example. On hearing this word for the first time, most people tend to draw a blank. The dictionary tells us that cipher is "the symbol 0 denoting the absence of all magnitude or quantity: zero. An insignificant individual: nonentity." Cipher is "a method of transforming a text in order to conceal its meaning"; it is "a message in code." As soon as we see this idea, some of us may think of the word "decipher," which, of course, means to "reveal, to convert to intelligible form, to decode, to make out the meaning of something despite indistinctness or obscurity." Such word exercises can work wonders for student learning.

The word "jiffy," we have lately learned, is actually a physics concept. We use the word as in the phrase, "I'll be back in a jiffy," but the actual meaning of the word is "1/100 second—which is the time it takes light to travel 1 centimeter in a vacuum." We suspect there is also a symbol or a way to communicate a jiffy on paper, say in a mathematical formula. But since no one ever taught either one of us how to make that concept meaningful, we have no way of talking about or using the word for anything other than as a slang expression. That, in effect, means that our inability to make effective use of that symbol is our loss.

We like to keep 3 × 5 cards on our desks, for example, to show students how to write better essays. Students often have good ideas, but organizing a paper from a conversation with a student precedes writing because they frequently lose themselves in trying to express their own views. The problem with writing essays tends to revolve around basic questions like How should I start? Can I envision the end of this paper? and What ought to be the in-between matter?

Helping students improve their writing skills turns on understanding where a student is in her or his educational development. Once an instructor determines what a student knows about writing—essentially by paying close attention to the student's remarks about recent papers—a whole series of writing and literacy approaches opens up for the task.[2] Since writing instructors influence papers in a number of ways, we wish to suggest a way to help Hispanic and non-Hispanic students write more impressive sentences.

Students write better sentences when they are clear about why they are writing an essay or other assignment. Some teachers use "quick writes" on a particular teacher-assigned subject as a way to encourage students to employ writing to clarify their views. If teachers follow up and write constructive comments on what students write, the assignment can show students what readers expect from good writing. Writing without pursuing a definite purpose, as some writing handbooks urge, though, is difficult to read, since few readers want to read words that can go virtually anywhere and say almost anything. The latter kind of free writing reminds me of the sixteen-year-old teenager who simply wants the car. He or she is ready to drive the car anywhere at any time. However, people are more inclined to read when informed why an essay or a piece of work has been written and prepared.

We are calling our different way of teaching rhetoric and composition "relational writing" because we have not found a better way to connect literacy and critical thinking to speech and to making sense. These four skills—literacy, critical thinking, speaking, and making sense—are intimately related, showing up as they do in one way or another when students write. Dramatizing for students how these skills coalesce to improve academic performance can be demonstrated by showing students some of the smooth connections that skilled writers make. By doing so, instructors can also answer that perennial question: What do *you* want in a paper?

A good essay, we say without hesitation, tells readers what the author thinks people should believe. Papers should convince readers that a writer has a way of interpreting a text or an issue that other writers have overlooked. And writers have not noticed such interpretations or angles because they have been seeing, thinking, and writing about other issues. In earlier writing stages, students should be taught to summarize, to describe, and to analyze texts, artwork, and other assignments to prepare them to do more independent thinking during their junior and senior years in high school and at the college and university levels. The point is that students need to learn that writers who have something different to say tend to be independent thinkers, which certainly explains why we usually admire writers.

The eternal challenge faced by writers, whether starting or full-fledged professionals, is to look at the reality that everybody sees and to notice something else, some particular that is now being seen differently, articulating the matter or issue more engagingly than previously. The goal at that point in a student's development would be for the student to assume the full burden of writing and to explain why people need to read one more essay on a particular subject and perhaps care.

Thinking along these lines has led us to relational writing. All good writing, we now believe, is relational in that effective written communication implicitly emphasizes the nature of the connections that writers make or shape their sentences into establishing with each other. To show what we mean by defining relational writing in this fashion, three selections have been chosen that highlight how each clause has been written by three writers to link smoothly with its neighboring clauses. This issue may seem elementary to more sophisticated writers, but this is exactly the sort of lesson that many Latino and Latina students do not receive while in the K–12 schools and even afterward in college. We bring out the issue here by way of showing caring teachers that they can devise all sorts of useful exercises for students by focusing attention on a few good clauses, sentences, and paragraphs that emphasize specific writing points that students need to learn. Teaching rhetoric and composition by focusing attention on the construction of clauses, indeed, is tantamount to teaching students as the famous Chinese proverb that says that if we teach a young person how to fish, that person has a way of daily feeding herself or himself for the rest of that person's life.

All kinds of materials can be used by creative teachers to engage the interest of students. Connecting literacy skills, critical thinking, oral communication, and making sense can be demonstrated by studying carefully how an author has put together an argument or a point of view. That is why people are asked to apply for positions in writing or to prepare a written statement explaining why they want to enter law, medical, and other professional schools. People on admissions committees simply want to see how a person represents herself or himself on paper. Hispanic or Latino students, experience has taught us, tend to be reluctant about revealing too much about themselves through writing or participating orally in class discussions. We believe this reticence has been acquired as learned behavior during the K–12 years, and, as far as we can see, we do not think schools have sufficiently counteracted the tendency not to participate in class activities. Students who gradually withdraw into themselves, in other words, are left to stay there, meaning that teachers then understandably turn their attention to other more outgoing students and to the children of parents who make their expectations clear to school districts. To encourage the kind of verbal confidence that shows up in better-written essays, we believe teachers have to endeavor to draw out Latino, Latina, and other marginalized students in their classes so that the more socially inclined students will also have to consider views that otherwise remain unexpressed. How writing instructors accomplish such challenges, of course, is up to their ingenuity and training, but here is one way.

A retired plant pathologist wrote the following three paragraphs:

> I've spent a lot of time wondering about an apparent association between post oak and native yaupon, too. Yaupon grows under post oak trees because birds drop seed while perched on tree limbs. This explains its presence, but it doesn't explain why post oaks do so well in association with yaupon.
>
> I don't fully understand the association between post oak and yaupon, but post oaks growing in yaupon stands seldom die. One would think the two might compete for moisture, but that's apparently not the case.
>
> Perhaps the yaupon growth prevents soil compaction and root disturbance round the post oak tree.[3]

Except for other plant pathologists, most people are not likely to understand the terms yaupon, soil compaction, and root disturbance. We certainly do not, and we do not mind telling students, so that they will learn that teachers and instructors do not know everything, as students often suppose. Yaupon and what appear to be processes are connected in this passage to birds, seed, death, competition for moisture, and post oak trees. Central to these paragraphs is the confession that, although a connection exists between post oaks that survive droughts and something called yaupon, experts themselves do not yet sufficiently understand the nature of that association.

If we were responsible for teaching students to write better, in high school and at the university level we would consider beginning by finding out what a student thinks about these words or about another passage that exhibits characteristics that might engage the interest of students. If students do not understand some words, we would direct them to a dictionary. Next we might look at what the student makes out of these statements about the post oak trees, moisture, yaupon, birds, seeds, drought, survival, soil compaction, and root disturbance.

The writing is straightforward, and the passage suggests that the right person could work up this particular issue into a Ph.D. in agriculture, botany, or biochemistry. At the level of a high school or college student, we would be interested in seeing what the student recognizes and says. Such a student might talk about birds and seeds or about the post oak trees themselves. We would write down the words that emerge from the student on 3×5 cards and talk about the things and relationships that she or he sees. The goal would be to extract and to hone in on the connections and angles, the phrases and clauses used by a student to talk about this material to the instructor. Using the student's words, together we would then write down a few carefully chosen clauses to see if together we can jump-start the student's essay.

Consider writing the words voiced by a student, read them out loud, and wait to see if the student finishes a thought or whether she or he will begin to amend the thoughts or ideas expressed in some way. This is a very simple way to show students that speaking clearly will help listeners understand well enough to write what they mean. The objective here is to begin to explain some aspect of what clearly is a complex symbiotic association between yaupon and the post oak tree. If the student is familiar with droughts, she might write about such periods; if he prefers to find out about how yaupon seeds are carried by birds, there is also room for that.

Instructors should allow students to write on virtually anything that engages them, so long as what the student undertakes stays focused on the materials being examined and clarifies something about that matter. Such students could be sent to the library to look up yaupon and the birds who carry seeds (Are they sparrows, mockingbirds, or all birds?) or soil compaction or root disturbance or anything else that attracts the interest of the student. The idea is to create excitement in the student for learning more about a relationship that has stumped even experts who know oak trees and yaupon. Who knows, a student from this class may someday discover the nature of a mutually beneficial association that will save all post oak trees.

*B*ut how exactly can relational writing help students write better essays? In relational writing the words, clauses, and individual sentences and paragraphs are carefully studied to see how a writer glued together an essay or a shorter or longer piece of writing. The idea is to see if a work of writing can be improved to make the sentences and paragraphs work better with other parts of a piece of writing, or if the writer already wrote a work in the best possible way. Whether one works on a book, a sentence or any other print effort that requires an organized strategy, writing constantly challenges writers to use the most appropriate words and clauses effectively. That is what good writing is, and writing well can be taught if we study how good examples of the best kind of writing have been put together, clause by clause. Since writing consists of searching for precise words to convey meaning, the best writers invariably spend a great amount of their time carefully connecting, arranging, and refashioning clauses to other parts of sentences in order to emphasize the relationships that writers want to point out with their statements and paragraphs.

All students need to start enhancing their vocabularies and expanding their word recognition capacities as early as possible. We suggest acquiring this skill because by the time students enter the sixth grade, when they are beginning to see themselves as young adults, they should be in positions to start expressing themselves in ways that will help them begin to have confidence in themselves. If students have not been prepared in the elementary grades so that they later develop the type of self-esteem and self-pride during the middle school years that will eventually make them good citizens, then the door is opened to problems that begin to show up in the teenage years.

Good writing exercises can help students get over these rough years. Attention to language issues and to building good speaking skills can help students establish excellent relationships with their teachers and with their peers. That type of "I can" attitude will also transfer and can be reinforced by showing students how good reading, good writing, and good oral communication skills can all work together to shape them into good, productive students.

Such students can be taught to work on the best relationships that they can see between their clauses and phrases to form smooth, seamless sentences. Our theory is that aside from employing thinking and the writing of sentences and paragraphs to help create self-esteem, prospective writers and speech makers can also be taught to think and to write by focusing attention on clauses or small clusters of words. Writers redact by thinking of groups of connected words that little by little are gradually stretched out into essays and books. The process of turning start-up clauses that form sentences and paragraphs that smoothly flow into each other can begin in a student-teacher conference when the student walks away with several ideas that an instructor has written on a 3 × 5 card. If the student's writing proves good, readers will hardly notice the words selected for the effort because the message or the actual content will drive the rhetoric.

How a group of words are cast will tell us when words need other words to express a self-standing idea or whether they can sufficiently stand alone, making good sense, as in the following two examples:

In any case, and I shall not try to discuss the technical sciences here, I would argue that academics make their intellectual culture look more opaque, rarefied, and remote from normal learning capacities that it is or needs to be. In this essay I want to suggest that the reputation for obscurity in academic writing, though not without foundation, rests on a misperception and that such obscurity is less frequent (or more peripheral and local) than we tend to think in work that makes an impact on its field.[4]

And:

The prevailing idea of truth in both formal and informal epistemology—that is, among academic philosophers and other people who talk about such things—is that a statement or belief is true if it matches up with the way things really are, independent of anyone's statements or beliefs. This idea is quite venerable. So are certain objections to it, notably the observation that, since we can't catch a glimpse of the way things really are around the corner of our own perceptions or descriptions, we have no way to assess statements or beliefs in regard to their reality-matching properties. Arguments have been sought and found to disarm this objection, the combined current upshot of which is that, through the dedicated pursuit of certain epistemic activities, such as rigorous reasoning, extensive archival work, close textual analysis, and controlled experimentation, we may be brought, if not all the way to a full frontal vision of truth, then at least increasingly close to it.[5]

Here one can focus the attention of students on how the dependent and independent clauses are stitched together to form good, sense-carrying sentences. To show students the art and effort required for such sentences, instructors might separate the clauses in these sentences and ask students to connect them again. From such an exercise students will learn that useful sentences don't simply appear, that writers have to work on sentences until they say exactly what an author desires, making the entire piece appear as if the writer prepared the sentences effortlessly. As in a piece of good music, the sour note is noticed as soon as the wrong word appears.

From such patches of good prose, students learn that papers with clear strategies function well because they emphasize the right relationships among the clauses, the words, the sentences, and paragraphs. Aiming for seamless prose connections carries the added advantage of requiring writers to sharpen their judgment. Our reason for using such examples is to demonstrate that writing employs clauses we use to think in, even while such exercises require us to tease and to pull out the necessary sense-making words that help us create the actual rhetoric of our essays.

*T*ime is precious, not only because we live in a sound-bite culture but because students need to see themselves improving every few days. Educators need to recognize and to factor this into their curriculum planning just as we are daily acculturated by everything brought out by the media. We have become increasingly used to encapsulating truths and untruths in a phrase or two. Many of us hardly speak in complete sentences any more, for we have fallen into the habit of communicating with the fewest words possible, relying on facial expressions and other gestures to complete the meaning of our words. Usually the catchy phrase or attractive string of words that stays with us is a clause or two. We point to these developments as evidenced, for example, in the tremendous popularity of rap and hip-hop among students. Although often clichés, rap phrases are a means used by the young to transmit information, suggesting that writing instructors have to learn how to work with prefabricated language and other short-hand ways of communicating rather than fighting them.

Writing has always depended on securing and then maintaining the attention of readers. Keeping readers reading once they have started is usually more difficult than simply attracting a reader with a good title. And judging from papers received, most writing instructors know that students do not spend much time working on either their titles or the words they use in their essays. Although some people may disagree, we believe teaching writing is a way of socializing or resocializing students, that is, making writers aware of how readers are likely to respond to words on a page.

In writing, as in other educational ventures, the goal should not be to replace Spanish or Latino culture with Anglo American habits and manners. Instead, the idea is to allow students to use their identities and cultural experiences to add such mores to the English language experience that Hispanic students already possess, whether considerable or little. The desired goal in writing as well as in speaking is to build on what students already know, not simply to reiterate the fact that the English language is valuable and serviceable since it is the dominant language of the Internet and global commerce. For this reason, we like to read the sentences that students write out loud. Students need to hear what they are actually saying with their own sentences, if only to see whether they are making sense to other people. They should also learn the conventions that govern English usage, such as not ending sentences in prepositions and avoiding sentence fragments, to name two common mistakes that many students make today without being aware that these are not good English oral or writing practices. All students should know that these two errors are unacceptable because educated people frown on such breaches of conventional writing rules. What students learn by hearing their writing efforts read out loud is that what they actually express and what they intended to write are often different, and that, of course, should not be the case. To ask how a sentence reads is to ask how a sentence sounds to the reader's ear, which is to say, "Does it make sense?" Students know that people create an impression by the words they use, but we suspect students feel readers are their friends and will, you know, like, get the point, though they often expressly fail to make their meaning clear.

Students assume that their work will be read, regardless of what they write. But readers do not care for careless writing. Readers are a jittery group of people constantly pressured to stop reading. Ever-present is the danger that readers will read a little and, growing tired, distracted, or bored, will run off. Readers are busy and generally skeptical, and they understandably expect words, sentences, and sense served up to them on a silver platter. Having many things waiting for their attention, readers might sample a writing piece and immediately determine whether they want and have the time to continue reading. When readers look up from their reading material, in effect, they are quietly deciding whether they will continue reading. The moment the writing flags, they disappear.

Such revelations are news to some students. Students believe that since they have spent more time than a sane person ordinarily should on preparing an essay, readers are obligated to read their efforts. But students interested in improving their writing should early be disabused of this erroneous idea. Good writing requires work, and readers expect to see signs within the writing that show that writers have taken pains to write well. That is why good or excellent writing often takes longer than most people think, since it is a matter of arranging clauses in just the right way to show the proper relationships between ideas. Reading, to be sure, also taxes our energies, and most people would rather dance, eat, go to a movie, or engage in any number of more enjoyable activities. To help them understand that writing and reading, indeed, compete against the rest of the world, we ask them to consider looking and studying how their biology, math, and chemistry textbooks are written.

Since writing is a constant challenge, writers may start well, and, up to a point, their words may move engagingly. When revising their own work, though, good authors are astutely aware that readers who have left a piece of writing may never return. Something in the material they have been reading has to make them want to return to the material anew. Once students learning to write realize that all writing implicitly asks people to set time aside to read, they have discovered that writers have little choice but to deliver their messages clearly and effectively.

Chapter 16

A THIRD DIMENSION TO WORDS: CHOREOGRAPHING WRITING

A good way to further emphasize how clauses and words can be used at every grade level to discuss appropriate ideas is to create exercises designed to teach students how to look at class materials in different, more imaginative ways. At the elementary level, for example, teachers can emphasize not only reading out loud, which is an unacknowledged art, but activities that provide children with opportunities to talk about and interpret what they read. Take a story like Leo Leoni's *Swimmy* (1963) or another text in a school district's curriculum that challenges and develops children's thinking and communication skills. Before introducing the story or the lesson material, children need to be told, in language that they understand, what the teacher desires from a class exercise. In reading *Swimmy* or any other story, children need to be encouraged to picture or to imagine what happens in the story in their minds, on their own private mental screens. This objective is not as difficult as it may sound, since students are familiar with television. Indeed, one of the main education problems is that visualization today is done for us by the media, and it is difficult for children to see that words require each one of us to visualize things for ourselves.

The idea is to have every student imagine the story while it is being read. After the story is read, either by the teacher or the students themselves, perhaps in round-robin group readings, learning can be turned into a fun but serious business at the same time. Creative teachers will have more than enough oral responses when students are asked what they saw, what they conjured up in their minds, and, of course, what they think of the story. The goal here is not to elicit monosyllabic responses but to encourage students to read carefully and to start thinking and talking about their reading. The purpose can later evolve into having the students consider how they can articulate their views both to the teacher and to the other students. The idea is not to focus attention on right or wrong answers necessarily but initially to encourage students to begin to feel comfortable talking about what they are noticing and to engage them in dialogues appropriate to their grade level.

From such exercises, it would be an easy step to then ask them to write about their views and later perhaps even to ask them to plan an oral presentation about what they have written or to discuss other class materials that teachers want to see what the students are actually learning. By engaging their minds and as many of their five senses as classroom exercises like these allow, students will be involved in their learning, leaving them little time to be "bored," as they say. At the middle school, the objective should also be to keep the interest of all of the students engaged, for participation in class lessons develops their knowledge base. Such participation also extends their curiosity and hunger for more information. Classroom activities and assignments, for that reason, might be focused on having them learn how different things work and function, everything in keeping with the disciplines and the curricula that students are expected to master at their different stages and grade levels. Challenging students to perform according to their full potential and best talents is always a prime consideration for the best teachers, since what educators want from students at any stage is academic excellence, not mediocre performance.

At the high school level, we would recommend further creative teaching exercises that do not allow students to cut themselves off from class activities and that are specifically organized to provide young people with the kind of attention this age level normally desires and enjoys. One simple and rather engaging year- or semester-long activity, for example, might be reading the entire dictionary. This challenge should preferably be accomplished before students have to take their SAT or ACT examinations and certainly before they graduate from high school. The purpose here is to sell them on the idea of becoming familiar with all of the readily used, bona fide words in the English language. Such a project will also teach students to continue to develop what ought to become a lifelong appreciation for learning, and for all languages, including the ones that have contributed to the development of English, among them Latin, Greek, Spanish, French, and others.

How can this particular task be accomplished? There are twenty-six letters in the English alphabet, and most states require something like at least 180 days of schooling per year. Teachers can break up reading the dictionary in any number of ways. The idea is to devote quality class time to the words under A, B, C, and so forth, so that students can use that knowledge the rest of their lives. Students required to undertake such a project are likely to squirm and laugh when the idea is first broached, but later they will be pleased to say that their class read and had fun remembering almost every single word in the dictionary when they were in high school. Vocabulary development is an integral part of an education, and activities that augment word knowledge and usage should begin in the first grade or before. Appropriate word-learning exercises should be continued by all teachers in all of the grades until students graduate from high school, for higher education and much of life, as we know, revolve around how adults use words and ideas. Since language and words are the commonest means by which human beings communicate, everything should be done to provide students with the necessary tools that will allow them to understand and to achieve the quality education that teachers know is essential not only to Latinos and Latinas, but indeed to all students.

For the purposes of continuing to dramatize some of the ideas that we have in mind, let us imagine that words also have depth or height, as it were, besides the more obvious qualities of length and width. When we attempt to focus attention on what we might call the third dimension of words, we can say that words possess weight or heft. This is harder to explain and a more sophisticated component of literacy that students gradually need to learn how to analyze, as they learn to read. Interpreting the weight or the actual meaning of the words used in the sentences and in the texts they read and about which they should write is a necessary part of a quality education. To visualize the weight or the height of words and thus the significance conferred on words by authors allows us as readers to pay less attention to the more discernible length and width of words, which normally are matters of font, print size, and other technical particulars determined by publishing houses. As in the world of real estate, what often counts in language usage and in the world of communication itself are the actual words that writers select and their location in a sentence, or how words are arranged on a page to deliver messages. These are skills that can be taught, but teachers and students have to make an effort to learn these finer points of writing and communication.

The weight or height that words carry in a text, what we are metaphorically calling the third dimension of words, depends almost entirely on the roles that authors devise for their words in unfolding meaning. Nouns and verbs, for example, tend to particularize ideas, while adjectives and adverbs usually qualify, specify, and provide readers with details. Which nouns and verbs are more important in any one sentence or paragraph depends on the nature of the perspective an author wishes to communicate. In all pieces of writing regardless of genre, certain words tend to stand out more prominently than others. That is why we are interested in ending these series of suggestions by encouraging teachers to look upon words as if readers can literally see their weight, height, and depth. By studying words within the sentences and ideas that elicited them, students can better discern the meaning and the intentions of the writers. Ethnic students, in particular, need help embellishing their vocabularies and in word-building, exercises that provide a foundation that empower them.

Let us reiterate what we are attempting to convey. When we look at the words in a text, all the words are normally printed in the same letter size and format. All the letters and words look much like the ones before them and the ones that follow. The monochromatic page, in other words, does not sufficiently allow a writer to emphasize some words and to downplay others in order to highlight or to enhance the delivery of his or her idea. As technologies develop, software programs permit computer users to **feature** certain words and to minimize the importance of others, providing teachers with opportunities to teach reading, thinking, talking, and writing as imaginatively as they can. On the regular typed page, though, all the words that an author uses are usually represented on the same equal plane, unlike the example above. Visually, none of the words on a page appears to be significantly more important than its neighbors. Yet we know that in any piece of writing, some words are considerably more important than others. High-quality literacy is just that: being able to recognize and to talk about what is more important in a text versus what is less significant.

Students approaching a text usually see many words monotonously arranged. They see lines of prose arranged after other lines of prose, from the beginning of a text to the end. The teacher's challenge is to succeed in making students interact meaningfully with these ostensibly unexciting-looking printed texts. Most students do not understand, even after a good many years of schooling, that it is not until we read how to print words that the modulations of the human voice impart significance to the words in print. That is why pronouncing words out loud often helps students to see words in new and more exciting ways. For a story, any story, in its essential printed form is inert. But when a story is read out loud, suddenly how we pronounce the words can begin to create a rhythm that allows skilled readers to bring words to life, as it were.

Before, up until the moment that the words are pronounced, the words simply lie on a page, ostensibly dead for all practical purposes. But as a reader starts to say the words on a page out loud, they abruptly assume life, and the nature of that life, of course, depends on the skills of the author, first, and then the oral skills of a reader who clearly has the task of turning words into life, bringing out their full meaning.

In such a scenario, a reader can show that certain words are more important and arresting than others, and that is one of the points that we want to underscore in this penultimate chapter. Although readers cannot literally see the weight, height, or depth of words in a text, to learn how words work in a text, teachers can ask students to imagine which words have greater heft, greater presence and significance. If we were, for instance, to graph the landscape of a text full of words on one page, we would see that certain words are bigger or that they tower or stick out above the other words. If we were to imagine, in other words, our regular two-dimensional printed words in a three-dimensional format, I think we could begin to see what a teacher with an imagination can do to teach students to appreciate how a writer has choreographed a text by carefully selecting appropriate words to convey meaning.

For all texts in effect are choreographed by writers, though that is not the way we usually think of printed words on a page. Any time that an author undertakes to write a word or to add or subtract sentence or a clause or part of one, that decision is a product of countless other decisions that a writer constantly has to make when writing. That is why writing is a difficult process and often the truest way of assessing and gauging what students know and what they have truly experienced. The arrangement of the words selected to communicate an idea or a point of view invariably provides readers with many particulars about a subject and what the writer seeks to achieve. And learning how to interpret words in order to express ourselves from kindergarten to adulthood for the rest of our lives is a progressively sophisticated process.

Printed book texts, to elaborate briefly, have rectangular formats or frameworks. In western European culture, authors and readers enter texts from the top left-hand side of a page, selecting and reading words for a page toward the right, word by word until we arrive at the end of a line. Our eyes then move to the following line, again moving from left to right, proceeding line by line until we have read an entire page. For our purpose, let us stop once we have read a hypothetical page. At any juncture, we can stop to ask what point or points are brought out by the writer of that page. Good readers generally focus attention on several words, on a clause or two, or on one or more sentences that have particularly engaged interest. These may be the words that the author of the page intended to highlight or they may not, and that is partly why readers sometimes see something more or other than what writers intended to communicate. Our point is that when we read, we essentially derive the meanings we see by choosing and extracting words from the texts before us.

If we were now to look at the words on that same page by placing them on a flat horizontal plane that would allow readers to see their weight or height and proportional mass against the two-dimensional backdrop of a horizon, as it were, words we regularly see on a page would appear to have a third dimension. By mentally envisioning the page on such a flat plane, we can visualize where we enter a page and how we read every single word, pausing where punctuation marks exist between the clauses and stopping at the end of sentences. We could then also focus attention on the individual words, phrases, or ideas that have caught our attention and the words that we simply went through in order to understand what the author wants us to notice. By asking readers to envision this mental exercise, we are inviting teachers and students to study words differently, that is, in the ways that words are made to work in texts. For all authors strategize by using words, and good writing finally requires both an understanding and an appreciation for the strategies that an author has chosen to deliver his or her point of view.

Because all words employed in a text elicit responses from us, words carry the weight and height that good readers endeavor to notice in the texts we read. The meaning of the words on any one page of a publication for that reason rests mainly on the importance and significance that words have for readers. Words on a page are all placed in such a way that they relate to each other, forming a fabric that leaves readers with an impression or a set response or effect. On any one page where a good piece of writing exists, certain words employed by an author will necessarily stand out in relation to other words, because the task of some words is to loom larger, giving meaning and qualifying the message or ideas being advanced.

Good readers know that on every single page of a book certain words carry the gist of the author's intention, and that is why marking words and passages in books is a useful exercise. Marking texts thus can serve to prompt good, imaginative discussions about an author's text. The goal for a teacher is to try to invent successful ways to engage the interests of students in texts that they know, read, and consciously consider.

Once that purpose is accomplished, students should be ready to talk. If these steps prove fruitful, students should then be ready to express their views in writing. That, at any rate, is the academic challenge that a print and oral approach would offer Latinos and Latinas as well as all other students who need to be taught how to extract a quality education from their studies in all of the grades that they traverse from kindergarten to the university.

We attended a wedding reception recently in a large Texas city. While waiting to enter the reception hall in a room next to a lovely china cabinet with trophies and awards, a young couple who knew us as teachers turned the talk to education. The young man, a blue-collar employee with children, confided that he had graduated from high school unable to read. Startled, we inquired further. Well, I can read this sign on this trophy, he said, and did haltingly and with difficulty. But I cannot understand because of the effort I make in reading the words out loud. He then added that he had been asked by management to apply for supervisory positions three times but that he had not because he had been afraid they would learn he cannot read. We knew him as a bright, sociable young parent. He told us he was able to go through the grades because he joked with his teachers and received passing grades. He was embarrassed. Because he realized this could happen, he was often at his children's school, checking on their progress and taking part in school activities for them. He didn't want what happened to him to happen to them.

Conclusion

	QUALITY EDUCATION AND THE
Chapter 17	TEACHERS IN THE CLASSROOM

*W*e have championed a quality education for Latinos and Latinas, one that can be pursued and dispensed to all students because, we contend, too many Spanish-speaking Americans, in particular, drop out of school in numbers that have hobbled too many generations. Stating how many actually leave their schooling is difficult because most school districts count dropout students differently, and such statistics understandably are not what schools like to inquire into, much less announce to the public. During the past decade, a number of "alternative school programs" have been created by school officials, backed by state and federal government legislative financing, to help students who do not respond to the regular education programs. These programs, variously known with acronymic names that suggest extra or special efforts by school districts, are designed to provide the kind of help and attention to students who have been disruptive, who become pregnant, who lag behind, or who require more time and opportunities to sort out home, personal, or grade-level problems. Reliable statistics on these newer programs are also difficult to secure, again, because the idea is to provide physical spaces in the schools for students to address individual or group issues that interfere with grade-level pursuits.

Although experienced teachers would naturally do the most good in such alternative programs, too many of the regular school classes and programs today are unfortunately being staffed with substitute teachers or with people recruited from other lines of work. Schools, indeed, are now in need of so many teachers, given the burgeoning student population, that hiring competent, fully trained teachers has been a problem for years. A principal who had long served a working-class neighborhood in Los Angeles, for example, was forced to hire "waiters, actresses, butchers, writers and even a Navy chaplain," according to a 2001 newspaper article. "U.S. Census data show a rising tide of school enrollment—a record 49 million students this year—that is due to grow over the next four years before leveling off. Meanwhile, the bulk of the nation's teaching force is nearing retirement age, with most teachers in their mid-40s to early 50s." A Boston-based nationwide agency that recruits teachers "found that nearly all major urban school districts urgently need teachers in at least one subject area, with more crucial needs in specialty areas. The report also states that 60 percent of urban districts, such as Los Angeles, allow non-certified teachers in the classroom under emergency licenses and hire long-term substitute teachers." [1]

Can noncertified teachers recruited from the general working population deliver a quality education to students who have experiences in the schools like the ones that we have presented in these pages? Not likely. A recent study by the National Commission on the High-School Senior Year "says that while 70 percent of today's high-school graduates enroll in some form of postsecondary education, only half of those who enroll at four-year institutions leave with a degree." The main reason for this low retention rate? Such students simply were not prepared well enough in high school for the rigors of college academics, the report concludes. [2]

It remains clear that if educators and legislators do not work together to address the many problems that we have discussed for students of color at some length in this book, we believe that the education of Hispanic as well as non-Hispanic students will continue to decline. Given that prospect, we end by strongly recommending that a coherent comprehensive plan like the print and oral approach that we espouse here be adopted as soon as possible. Until our state legislatures and federal government choose to make K–16 our country's number one priority, with the proper attendant financial support, education in the United States does not have a better alternative that we can see.

End-of-year note from a seventh-grade student:

> *T*hank you very much for many things. For worrying about us, for caring about us. I appreciate you and would defend you as if you were my mother. And please forgive me for what happened, for worrying.
>
> Please forgive us for the bad things that happened. I lost your confidence.
>
> Some day I will repay you for the help that you gave us. May you have much happiness and good health, a great summer, and perhaps I will see you next year.

May 2004

Notes

Introduction

1. *Spirit: News from the Texas A&M Foundation*, fall 1999, cover page quotation. Inside this newsletter, Mr. Cantu continues: "'If you say today we've got 28 million Hispanics . . . and 38 percent don't have a high school diploma, that's 10.6 million,' he says. 'Double that number by 2020, as the experts predict, and you're going to have over 21 million people — darned near half of the Hispanic population then — without diplomas. Imagine what impact that's going to have on America's social structure and the way we compete in the world market.'"

2. "Thousands of Schools to Be Declared 'Failing,'" Associated Press, in *Houston Chronicle*, April 24, 2002. Schools will be under increasing pressure during the next few decades, which means that all kinds of new theories and programs will emerge to improve testing scores. The article continues: "Part of the landmark Elementary and Secondary Education Act, which President [George W.] Bush signed in January [2002], included a requirement that students in grades three through eight be tested annually in reading and math. For the first time, students in schools where scores don't improve adequately over three or four years would be given federally funded tutoring or allowed to transfer to another public school with most of their transportation costs paid."

3. See Marco Portales, "Examining the Recruitment and Enrollment of Eligible Hispanic and African American Students at Selective Public Texas Universities," in *Education of Hispanics in the United States: Politics, Policies, and Outcomes*, edited by Charles Teddlie, Abbas Tashakkori, and Salvador Hector Ochoa, volume 16 of the Readings on Equal Education Series (New York: AMS Press, 1999), 201–222. This collection of essays by leading educators, including Eugene E. Garcia, Angela Carrasquillo, Richard A. Figueroa, Raynoldo F. Macias, Amaury Nora, Yolanda N. Padrón, Laura I. Rendon, Nadeen T. Ruiz, and others underscores the deplorable condition of K–16 education for Latinos throughout the United States. At a conference hosted on January 26, 2001, by the Center for Mexican American Studies at the University of Texas at Austin, titled "Latinos and Educational Equity: A Public Forum on High-stakes Testing and Percent Plans," scathing reports were presented on "the quality of the educational pipeline for historically underprivileged youth in Texas," California, and wherever Hispanic and minority students are attending U.S. schools.

1. Thinking About Our Spanish-speaking Students in the Schools

1. In the *Chronicle of Higher Education* of August 17, 2001, Vartan Gregorian, president of the Carnegie Corporation of New York and former president of Brown University and the New York Public Library, cites Carnegie Corporation statistics and a study that estimates that "'of 600 students who enter a four-year teaching program, only 180 complete it.'" Gregorian has brought to bear his considerable academic experience and expertise on this most important of education issues and concluded that "'higher-education institutions, in fact, must accept much of the responsibility for the dismal state of public-school teaching today.'" For an argument that cannot be easily obviated or avoided any longer in the training and curricula of colleges of education as well as higher education institutions in general see "Teacher Education Must Become Colleges' Central Preoccupation," *Chronicle of Higher Education,* Chronicle Review, Section 2, August 17, 2001, B7. This is the type of academic issue that should set the agenda of education colleges and universities at least for the next decade.

2. In "Hispanic School Achievement Pivotal to Texas' Future," *Houston Chronicle,* June 4, 2002, Kim Cobb and James Kimberly write:

And the stakes are high. The economic well-being of Texas soon will rest on the shoulders of Hispanic wage-earners. While fairness was the goal of early public school desegregation, equity may prove to be the state's economy.

When the U.S. Supreme Court banned segregated schools in 1954 in *Brown v. Board of Education of Topeka, Kansas,* the justices were attempting to close the educational divide between black and white children. Hispanic children weren't even part of the equation.

Nearly 50 years later, Hispanics now rival blacks as the nation's largest minority group. They make up a third of the Texas population and a majority in several Houston-area school districts. But Hispanic schoolchildren, like black students, frequently do not perform as well academically as whites. Closing the achievement gap for all minority students, and subsequently improving their earning potential, will have economic implications for Texas as whites lose majority status.

3. Systems theory is multifaceted and widely applicable. Practitioners are still in the process of articulating how different systems, both natural and artificial or created ones, work and can be improved. Biologist Ludwig von Bertalanffy is usually credited as the founder of general systems theory, views that he initially formulated to counter the growing compartmentalization of science. Change is central to systems theory, and most systems can be described as either open or closed. Since studying the field of education consists of understanding a highly dynamic process that consists of many professional relationships, points of view, and behaviors, schools are open systems in which interdependence is constantly being tested by new factors and considerations that alter the teaching environ-

ment. See W. Richard Scott, *Organizations: Rational, Natural, and Open Systems* (Upper Saddle River, New Jersey: Prentice Hall, 1997) for a useful text in the field.

4. In an Associated Press article dated August 12, 2001, in the *Houston Chronicle*, Connie Mabin quotes Texas Governor Rick Perry:

"Fifty percent of the new jobs that are created out there require a deep math background. Math is the language of technology," says Texas Governor Rick Perry. Yet "45 percent of [all] Texas students fail algebra class final exams." Like children nationwide, Texas students struggle with math. Short-staffed schools also find it difficult to keep certified, qualified instructors.

National Assessment of Educational Progress scores released last week show that overall, Texas fourth-graders scored an average of 233, while the national average was 226.

But eighth-grade scores fell just below the national average, and minority students in all grades continued to lag behind whites. Perry hopes his [math initiative] program, which focuses on middle grades, also helps end the state's dropout problem. Most children quit school around the ninth grade, when they begin to take advanced math courses.

Although struggles with math aren't the only reasons children quit, "I think it is a substantial part of the formula for failure," Perry said.

5. Sarah Flannery, for example, was taught by her father, a mathematician, how to appreciate the beauties of mathematics. See her book *In Code: A Mathematical Journey* (New York: Workman, 2001) for a delightfully engaging story that reveals how she was taught and how she learned to be curious about mathematical problems. If Latino and Latina children were seen as worth the investment of time and effort Sarah's father spent on his daughter, their curiosity, too, could be engaged enough to create an interest in mathematics or any other discipline by creative instructors.

6. See Guadalupe San Miguel's *"Let All of Them Take Heed": Mexican Americans and the Campaign for Equality in Texas, 1910 –1981* (Austin: University of Texas Press, 1987) for one of the best histories on the education of Spanish-speaking American citizens over three generations.

7. An editorial titled "Closing the Achievement Gap" in *The New York Times*, May 16, 2000, deserves to be quoted at length:

Over the last five years, the New York State Board of Regents has enacted a series of public school reforms that have placed the state in the lead of the national movement for standards and accountability. At the same time, however, local educators and politicians who claim to want reform have sometimes reacted with skepticism and resistance when confronted with the discomfort that comes with change. Defenders of the status quo whipped up a fuss, for example, when the Regents raised graduation standards across the state, demanded a tougher curriculum and began to issue "report cards" that exposed as mediocre schools that many citizens thought were excellent.

A similar backlash has emerged since the Regents announced that they will soon begin reporting student performance by income and race, to focus attention on the achievement gap that often exists between rich and poor and between white and minority students within the same school. Critics say that holding districts accountable for closing the achievement gap is onerous and unfair, some of them suggesting that nothing can be done. But national studies indicate that the gap can indeed be closed and that disaggregating data by race and income is a crucial first step in the process.

Pessimism about closing the performance gap is widespread, but it is not supported by the facts. The most recent study of national achievement data by the Education Trust, a Washington foundation devoted to school reform, shows that while black and Latino students continue to trail white students on reading scores, schools that serve those students made great strides in recent decades. Between the mid-seventies and mid-nineties, the gap in achievement between African-American and white students, as measured by a federally sponsored test called the National Assessment of Educational Progress, narrowed by about half. The progress stopped in the late eighties, when poverty became more concentrated and educators began to focus on remedial studies instead of much-needed high-level instruction.

Several states now report performance by race, most notably Texas. It began its effort in the eighties with the Perot Commission, whose work culminated a decade later in a novel accountability system that rates the public schools on the academic performance of their minority students in particular. Simply put, a school cannot receive the highest state rating unless 90 percent of its students—including 90 percent of minority students—perform at the highest levels on all state assessments. Texans looked at the data and recognized that the schools were jeopardizing the state's future by writing off minorities—who make up more than half of the public school enrollment. Since the reform effort, more minority students than ever are taking the Scholastic Assessment Tests, setting their sights on college.

8. The situation is not receiving due attention, as Marta Tienda and Susan Simonelli note in a 2001 article:

Hispanic people drop out of high school at almost four times the rate of non-Hispanic white people, which narrows the pool of potential Hispanic college applicants. As a result, despite growing numbers of Hispanic students in higher education, the gap between the proportions of Hispanic students and non-Hispanic white students has widened. In 1980, 27 percent of all 18- to 24-year-old non-Hispanic white students attended college, compared with 16 percent of all college-aged Hispanic students. By 1997, the respective shares were 41 and 22 percent.

Of the total campus population, more than 70 percent of all students enrolled in college are white and 11 percent are black, while only 8 percent are Hispanic.

College graduation rates tell a similar story. In 1970, almost 11 percent of white adults 25 and older held college degrees; that figure had jumped to 28 percent by 1999. But the comparable shares of Hispanic graduates were 5 and 11 percent. If current demographic trends continue, we will see even greater enrollment and graduation disparities in the future.

Meanwhile, the type of postsecondary institutions that Hispanic students usually attend also encourages inequality. In 1996, more than half of the Hispanic students who attended college were enrolled in two-year institutions, in contrast to 37 percent of white students. Two-year colleges provide relatively inexpensive, local access to higher education, but research shows that only about one-fourth to one-half of community-college students eventually transfer to four-year institutions. ("Hispanic Students Are Missing from Diversity Debates," *Chronicle of Higher Education*, May 31, 2001.)

9. "Lower Education: Too Few Texans Prepared for College Studies," *Houston Chronicle*, August 30, 2002.

2. Latino and Latina Students and the Schools We Could Create

1. In *The Bell Curve: Intelligence and Class Structure in American Life* (New York: Free Press, 1996), Richard J. Herrnstein and Charles Murray posited a controversial connection designed to show that intelligence is related to a person's ethnicity. This idea was successfully countered the following year by twenty-nine scholars in *Measured Lies: The Bell Curve Examined* (New York: St. Martin's Press, 1997), edited by Joe L. Kincheloe, Shirley R. Steinberg, and Aaron D. Gresson, among other responses that Herrnstein and Murray elicited. More recently, two studies have provided evidence that affirmative action does improve the lives of its recipients and that the Scholastic Aptitude Test, or SAT, maintains considerable inequities and injustices in place that keep minority students from qualifying for and entering the better higher education institutions. See *The Shape of the River: The Long-Term Consequences of Considering Race in College and University Admissions* (Princeton: Princeton University Press, 1998) by William G. Bowen and Derek Bok, respectively the presidents of Princeton and Harvard. See also *The Big Test: The Secret History of the American Meritocracy* (New York: Farrar Straus and Giroux, 1999) by Nicholas Lemann.

2. Educators have long known that the education of children should begin early in life. Maria Montessori (1870–1952), in particular, extended the parameters of how children learn by advancing her early childhood education theories in *The Montessori Method* (1912; reprint, New York: Schocken Books, 1988). E. D. Hirsch, mentioned previously, was motivated in writing *Cultural Literacy: What Every American Needs to Know* (Boston: Houghton Mifflin, 1987) to

provide separate resource guides to accompany the book, with other authors, for parents and teachers on American Civilization and Life Science in the Core Knowledge Series, which he edits for the Core Knowledge Foundation. When these books were being published, we innocently hoped that multi-ethnic materials would be included, but that is what Hirsch's books apparently and unfortunately set out to sidestep. Recent books more sympathetic to Hispanic issues are Guadalupe Valdés' *Learning and Not Learning English: Latino Students in American Schools* (New York: Teachers College Press, 2001) and *Educating Latino Students: A Guide to Successful Practice,* edited by Maria Luisa González, Ana Huerta-Macias, and Josefina Villamil Tinajero (Lanham, Maryland: Scarecrow Press, 1997).

3. Betty Hart and Todd Risley in *Meaningful Differences in the Everyday Experience of Young American Children* (Baltimore, Maryland: Brookes Publishing, 1996) have further explored the following statement by Jim Trelease of the famed *The Read-Aloud Handbook* (1979; reprint New York: Penguin Books, 2001), 5th edition:

The professional [couple's] child heard 32 compliments an hour, working class [children] averaged 12 affirmations, and the poverty child heard just 5 encouragements in an hour. Imagine the impact on a child's self-esteem and confidence from 32 positive statements an hour—one every other minute!

Conversely, the professional child heard the fewest negatives in the space of an hour—5, compared to 7 for the working-class child and 11 for welfare. For America's children who are at-risk, that comes to a total of 104,000 encouragements and 228,000 discouragements by age four. The professional child arrives at the kindergarten door thinking he's a world-beater, while the at-risk child arrives with a mindset of "can't do" because people at home have been telling him so for years.

The message of *Meaningful Differences* is unambiguous: It is not the toys in the house that make the difference in children's lives; it is the words in their ears. The least expensive thing we can give a child outside of a hug turns out to be the most valuable: *words.* We do not need a job, a checking account, or even a high school diploma to talk with a child. Sadly, we have not heard even one of the nation's political "education candidates" address the kinds of issues found in *Meaningful Differences.*

4. Among the best of the more comprehensive education studies of Latino students is Harriet D. Romo and Toni Falbo, *Latino High School Graduation: Defying the Odds* (Austin: University of Texas Press, 1996). For another assessment of the state of education for Latinos and Latinas see *Education of Hispanics in the United States: Politics, Policies, and Outcomes* (New York: AMA Press, 1999), edited by Charles Teddlie, Abbas Tashakkori, and Salvador Hector Ochoa, volume 16 of Readings on Equal Education Series.

5. See Steve H. Murdock, Nazrul Hoque, Martha Michael, Steve White, and Beverly Pecotte, *The Texas Challenge: Population Change and the Future of Texas* (College Station: Texas A&M University Press, 1997). Chapter 4, "Population Change and Income: Implications for Business Activity and Fiscal Resources," is particularly instructive: "In the absence of changes in the income differentials among race/ethnicity groups, future population patterns would lead to lower household income in Texas" (61).

6. In Texas, for example, Steve Murdock, the state demographer and the lead author of *The Texas Challenge,* told the Texas Coordinating Board that oversees all public education in Texas at its July 19 – 20, 2001, meeting in Austin, "In 1990, Texas was 39th in the ranking of states by percent of high school graduates and has now fallen to 46th." Wanda Mills, the executive director of the Council of Public University Presidents and Chancellors, wrote in her minutes of that meeting that Murdock

stressed that if the educational achievement of the people in Texas did not change, a smaller percentage of the population would be well educated and thus there would be more poor people. Dr. Murdock showed a graph indicating that if the graduation rate of Anglo college and university students remained constant, while the graduation rates of Blacks and Hispanics changed at the same rates as from 1990 – 1998, it would be 2045 before there was parity between the Anglo and Black graduation rates, and 2080 before the college and university graduation rate of Hispanics equaled that of Anglos. Dr. Murdock concluded his statements with slides and remarks about average lifetime income and its relationship to education. He stressed that education paid.

The state demographer's Microsoft PowerPoint presentation is available from the Texas State Data Center Web site, http://txsdc.tamu.edu/presentations.

3. But Our Education Systems Are Distended

1. In *Redesigning Education* (New York: Henry Holt, 1994), physics Nobel Prize winner Kenneth G. Wilson and journalist Bennett Daviss discuss various leading school reform programs that have received national attention and federal or state funding. They promote mentoring in a "school-based design" model that they hope will be embraced: "Through mentoring, designers and teachers can collaborate to create and test their own reforms in pilot programs or other small settings, evaluate the results, and then share the results with colleagues. This is the approach to educational change that is proving most effective in individual reforms already underway" (199). To facilitate such interaction, school systems would have to embrace smaller classes and grant more autonomy to teachers and to the administrators working on redesigning education. That is not what we now have in place in most school districts throughout the country, and the

George W. Bush administration's emphasis on more teacher "accountability" is a move in another direction.

2. The emphasis on discipline both in the schools and within the juvenile justice system appears to be disproportionately levied against students of color, according to a report authored by Nancy Walker, associate director of the Institute for Children, Youth, and Families, and Francisco Villarruel, associate professor of family and child ecology, both at Michigan State University. "Treatment of Latino youths in the U.S. juvenile justice system is harsher than that for non-Hispanic white juveniles — and it's getting worse, according to a report commissioned by several groups that sponsor a campaign to end such inequities." The report said

the percentage of Latino juveniles in the nation's detention centers rose by 84 percent between 1983 and 1991, compared with an 8 percent increase for non-Hispanic white youths over the same period and a 46 percent increase for all youths.

"[Latino youths] are arrested more often, stopped more often, detained more often, incarcerated more often and for longer periods of time," said Walker.

Even when Latino kids are charged with the same offense as their white counterparts, they're punished more severely, the report found. Latino youths who've never been detained are 13 times more likely to be incarcerated for drug offenses than non-Hispanic white youths — and they'll spend more than twice as much time in jail, the report said.

"It's bad, but chances are it's worse," said Villarruel. "This is only what we can see." The data are inadequate because state and county governments don't have a single category for 'Hispanic' or 'Latino,'" he said. (Leslie Miller, "Youth Justice System Harsher for Latinos," Associated Press, in *Houston Chronicle*, July 19, 2002.)

3. According to *The Handbook of Texas Online*, "Until the late 1940s the public education system in Texas for Mexican Americans offered segregated campuses with often minimal facilities and a curriculum frequently limited to vocational training. The 1950 U.S. Census showed that the median educational attainment for persons over twenty-five was 3.5 years for those with Spanish surnames and, by comparison, 10.3 years for other white Americans; about 27 percent of persons over twenty-five with Spanish surnames had received no schooling at all." See *Handbook* entry on *Delgado v. Bastrop ISD*.

4. In *Change Forces: The Sequel* (Philadelphia: Falmer Press, 1999), Michael Fullan, former dean of the College of Education at the University of Toronto, correctly states: "A strong public school system, as I shall argue, is the key to social, political and economic renewal in society. In postmodern society, more than ever before, a strong commitment to the role of moral purpose in educational

reform is crucial. But because of worldwide diversity, and because of chaotic complexity, figuring out moral purpose, getting or staying committed to it and making progress in achieving it are enormously difficult. At the very time we need more of a moral commitment to the public good, the forces of change are creating confusion, frustration and discouragement" (1). To see an example of the social context from which we are working, see Pulitzer Prize–winning journalist Jonathan Freedman's book *From Cradle to Grave: The Human Face of Poverty in America* (New York: Atheneum, 1993).

5. In a *Dallas Morning News* article of August 19, 2002, titled "Disparities Found in School Discipline," Tawnell D. Hobbs writes:

Black and Hispanic students are kicked out of their regular classrooms more frequently and for longer periods than white students, according to a first-of-its-kind report from the state education agency. Texas Education Agency officials said their study, generated because of a new state law, warrants a closer look at how school officials across the state mete out one of the harshest measures available: removal to alternative disciplinary programs.

"One of the issues is to do more studies on why this is happening," said Billy Jacobs, senior director of the TEA safe schools division. The agency sent individual reports to school districts in March but has not publicized the results.

According to the report, the disparities appear across the board, both statewide and in most individual school districts: Black and Hispanic students tend to be over represented in alternative disciplinary placement, and whites tend to be under represented.

The Texas Education Code gives principals no option but alternative placement for some serious offenses, such as sexual assault, arson or gun possession. But most placements are for code of conduct violations, such as disrupting class or fighting, and they come at the discretion of campus officials.

Statewide, 87,990 of about 4 million students (2.2 percent) were placed in disciplinary alternative programs in 2000–2001. White students, who made up 42 percent of all students that year, accounted for 34.4 percent of alternative placements. Black students were 14.4 percent of students but 21.6 percent of placements, and Hispanics were 40.6 percent of students and 42.7 percent of those punished . . .

"That is just a pattern that we see across the country," said Joanne McDaniel, director of the Center for the Prevention of School Violence. "It's a very broad picture we have to draw when looking at it. The reality of this is a bigger issue than any one school."

She said the disparities are not unlike those seen in other areas of society, and the reasons for them are complex.

"There are probably multiple explanations of why . . . community issues, societal issues, a lack of understanding of difference in our cultures," she said.

"This type of disproportional minority representation is also the same type we see in [the] juvenile justice and the adult prison system."

Jacobs said school districts should be using alternative disciplinary placement as a last resort.

6. Partisan squabbling by Republicans and Democrats in the U.S. Congress and throughout the country on what monies should be used for what education initiatives have not helped and have only exacerbated the nationwide turmoil in the education field.

7. James Herndon's *The Way It Spozed to Be* (New York: Simon and Schuster, 1968) was one of the first books that successfully called national attention to "the crisis in our schools," a crisis that has continued to simmer now for more than thirty years, as Jonathan Kozol's *Savage Inequalities* (New York: HarperPerennial Library, 1991) and other books have periodically reminded us.

8. Public Agenda is a nonpartisan, nonprofit public opinion research and citizen education organization based in New York City. This report was made available to the general public by Public Agenda on October 22, 1997.

4. Why Students Drop Out

1. Jeremy Schwartz writes in "Confronting Our Dropout Problem: 'It Has an Effect on the Entire Region,'" *Corpus Christi Caller-Times,* March 25, 2001: "Since leaving West Oso High School without finishing his senior year, Jesse Corpus, 18, has had a hard time figuring out what to do with his future. 'Career-wise, I have no idea,' he said. 'I don't even think about it. Maybe I should, but I'm not.'"

Latino and Latina students express the same aimlessness, the same kind of uncertainness about their futures, in media accounts all over the Southwest, whether in Houston, San Antonio, Austin, Dallas–Fort Worth, El Paso, Las Cruces, Tucson, Phoenix, Denver, Las Vegas, San Diego, Los Angeles, or Oakland, but also in the Midwest, in Chicago and Milwaukee, the metropolitan areas in and around New York and Philadelphia, as well as in rural areas. These are sad cases that a wealthy society like ours, led by politicians who insist that they are serving the best interests of the people, should not tolerate any longer.

2. As suggested earlier, the disparities in how school dropouts are counted is distressing. The National Education Association reported in May 2000 that the national dropout rate was 11.8 percent for 1998. NEA estimated that 29.5 percent of the students who dropped out were Hispanic, 13.8 percent were black, 7.7 percent were white, and 4.1 percent were Asian/Pacific Islanders. Other NEA statistics can be found at http://www.nea.org/publiced/edstats/statsata.html. Most school districts, however, count students who leave school before graduation differently. Students who leave but work toward securing their General Educational Development (GED) high school equivalency diplomas, for example, are

counted by some districts and not by others. Also, some districts count students who drop out from their alternative school programs, and other districts do not. State education agencies also seem reluctant to establish standardized ways of counting that will uniformly inform local citizens just how many young people are not being educated, much less provided with a quality education, as we propose. For two examples of the nature of this debate in education see "Dropout Rate Is Near 20%, Study Suggests," an Associated Press story published in the *Bryan – College Station Eagle* on May 21, 2001, in which Jay Smink, the executive director of the National Dropout Prevention Center at Clemson University in South Carolina states: "Every state puts out numbers that are completely bogus. Numbers that low just aren't accurate."

See also "State's Dropout Tally Called 'Silly'" in the *San Antonio Express-News* of August 18, 2001, written by reporter Lucy Hood: "The new [Texas Education Agency] figures sparked criticism from groups like the Civil Rights Project and the San Antonio–based Intercultural Development Research Association that closely monitor dropout issues. IDRA's figures, based on the difference between the freshman class and the number of graduates four years later, show a dropout rate of 40 percent for all students and 56 percent for Hispanics. 'That's entirely unacceptable, not only for the Latino community but for all communities in the state of Texas,' IDRA Director Martha Robledo Montecel said."

An editorial in the *Bryan – College Station Eagle* of August 22, 2002, titled "Quit Playing Games with Texas Dropouts" states the situation well:

The [National Dropout Prevention] Center at Clemson [University] estimates 5 percent of Texas high school students dropped out [for 1999–2000]. Yet the TEA [Texas Education Agency] says the rate was only 1.3 percent. Why the difference? The Center at Clemson—as does the federal government—calculates rate based on the number of students who drop out in high school—grades nine through 12. The TEA, however, also includes in its calculations the number of students who drop out in grades seven and eight. While that is a concern, of course, the drop out rate is far lower in those grades than it is in high school. By including those grades, the TEA can make the drop out rate appear far lower than it is. If the agency included the elementary grades, it most likely would look even better, but that's not the point of issuing the statistics. Further, the TEA doesn't count any high school dropout who says he or she will work toward a General Educational Development equivalency certificate, even if that work is never completed or even started.

5. A Mexican American Mother Who Will Not Visit School

1. See Marco Portales, "A History of Latino Segregation Lawsuits," in *The Unfinished Agenda of Brown v. Board of Education*, edited by the editors of *Black Issues in Higher Education*, with James Anderson and Dara N. Byrne, Landmarks

in Civil Rights History (Hoboken, New Jersey: John Wiley and Sons, 2004), 123–136.

2. In "Study Cites Inability among Many Latino Parents to Advise Children about College," Richard Morgan writes, "Latino parents are largely unable to provide their children with basic information or assistance about attending college, according to a new report by the Tomás Rivera Policy Institute, an independent agency based in California" (*Chronicle of Higher Education*, Today's News, July 15, 2002, online at <http://chronicle.com/cgi2-bin/printable.cgi>).

3. These data are in *The Handbook of Texas Online* under the court case known as *Delgado v. Bastrop ISD*. See http://www.tsha.utexas.edu/handbook/online/articles/view/DD/jrd1.html. The court ruled in 1948 that separate schools then available for Hispanics, African Americans, and whites were illegal and unconstitutional. It should be noted that it took exactly one hundred years from the signing of the Treaty of Guadalupe Hidalgo, which in 1848 ended the U.S. war with Mexico during the James Polk administration, for the U.S. courts to recognize officially that Spanish-speaking Americans had been receiving inferior educations. This history of discrimination, which also occurred in California, Arizona, New Mexico, and other lands that previously belonged to Mexico, is still part of the legacy that educators cannot forget if we are consciously to address past wrongs successfully. Recognizing that the cause of parents' supposed "lack of involvement" might be due to years of educational disenfranchisement ought to help educators understand why it is particularly difficult for some students to succeed.

4. See Derrick Bell, *Faces at the Bottom of the Well: The Permanence of Racism* (New York: Basic Books, 1992), and Cornell West, *Race Matters* (New York: Vintage Books, 1993). Paul Kivel, in *Uprooting Racism: How White People Can Work for Racial Justice* (New York: New Society Publishers, 1995), actively challenges readers to make a difference.

6. The Tribal Mentality and Favoritism

1. On this issue see David Roediger, *Toward the Abolition of Whiteness: Essays on Race, Politics, and Working-Class History* (New York: Verso, 1994), and George Lipsitz, *The Possessive Investment in Whiteness: How White People Profit from Identity Politics* (Philadelphia: Temple University Press, 1998).

2. See Marco Portales, "Hopwood, Race, Bakke, and the Constitution," *Texas Hispanic Journal of Law and Policy* 4, no. 1 (spring 1998): 29–44.

3. Readers may remember when people strongly believed that college hazing and smoking would never be eliminated or reduced. These were activities that people thought youngsters simply went through at certain stages and on certain occasions in their lives. Today state legislatures have outlawed hazing, and smoking has been considerably curtailed by national antismoking campaigns. Why not launch a national campaign against racism, too, one that discourages people

from discriminating based on race, color, ethnicity, or gender? The idea is not to be politically correct, as people say, but to promote respect for everyone's civil rights.

4. It is not necessary to show instances of anger, violence, or distrust and discontent, but there is a more insidious practice at work in our schools, a behavior that is difficult for people to believe, were it not for the fact that playing favoritism is occasionally identified. One such instance occurred in Houston when "two judges admitted rigging tryout scores" after they had been directed to do so by the "cheerleaders' faculty sponsor." A number of the cheerleading contestants, that is, the students themselves, said that the faculty sponsor "was motivated by favoritism." This pernicious behavior advances certain students at the expense of other ones who are not favored: "She just wanted certain girls to make it that weren't going to make it," one student said. See "All Cheerleading Candidates Get on Squad; Contest Found Rigged," (*Dallas Morning News,* August 22, 2001).

5. Inés Pinto Alicea writes, "Americans live on wages averaging $6,000 per year in clapboard homes in some 1,700 colonias along the Texas border, from El Paso to Brownsville," in "Dr. Jaime Chahín Produces *Las Colonias: 'The Forgotten Americans,'*" *Hispanic Outlook in Higher Education* 11, no. 25 (September 24, 2001): 20 – 23. Similar settlements also exist on other stretches along the 2,000-mile border between the United States and Mexico, a region that U.S. President George W. Bush and Mexican President Vicente Fox ethically targeted, after many years of neglect, for mutual development. Since September 11, 2001, though, what began as a clear working relationship between the two presidents and the two countries has been awaiting a better day.

7. Crime and Properly Funded Schools

1. The August 28, 2002, *Houston Chronicle* article titled "Jails over Schools: A New Study Shows Texas Has Increased Spending Faster on Prisons than Education," reports:

> Percentage increases in spending for Texas prisons has far outstripped state spending hikes for higher education since the mid-1980s, according to a report released Wednesday.
>
> The study, by the Justice Policy Institute, a Washington advocacy group, also showed Texas now has more black men in state prisons than in state colleges and universities.
>
> Texas was not alone in seeing its spending on prisons rise along a steep curve in the past decade and a half, while money set aside for higher education rose much more slowly, according to the study.
>
> Since 1985, the increase in money spent on prisons nationwide topped $20 billion. That is almost twice the increase in dollars spent on colleges and universities, according to the report titled "Cellblocks or Classrooms." In

1986, Texas spent about $3.1 billion from its general fund on state colleges and universities. That year, $590 million was spent on corrections, or less than one dollar for every five spent on higher education," the JPI study found.

2. See "An NCIC Milestone," FBI National Press Office release, March 23, 2002, available at http://www.fbi.gov/pressrel/pressrel02/ncic032302.htm.

3. In high schools in Texas and the Southwest, teachers of higher-level Spanish courses begin the year with the history and culture of Spain, even though the actual class texts begin with the history and culture of Mexican and Caribbean Americans. Other teachers skip over the text sections on Africa, saying in various ways that they "don't relate to those people." Why, we need to ask, are people with such counterproductive views working as teachers of the young?

4. Two Mexican American families we know moved three times in two years within the same state. Each of the boys in these families presented documentation upon registering that classified them as gifted and talented in their schools of origin. Yet at each new school, each boy was required to be tested again with the same instruments, the WISK I.Q. test being one, before being allowed into the advanced placement program in their new schools. No such retesting was required of new Anglo students classified as AP who transferred from other schools. We know about this practice because we have spoken to at least three parents who have moved and whose children were placed in the AP program without questions. Two of the latter families brought no documentation, yet their children were placed into the AP program immediately while the school awaited the proper forms from their former schools. Unequal practices like these have to be examined and corrected throughout the country.

10. Teachers and Students in the Classroom

1. James P. Comer, *Maggie's American Dream: The Life and Times of a Black Family* (New York: Plume, 1989), 216–217. I wish to thank Hilary Standish for calling our attention to this excellent passage that discusses the student-teacher relationship that we also wish to emphasize. Relationship issues and child development concerns, we believe, have partly been marginalized by American society's emphasis on high technology.

2. An Associated Press story points out that the problems that materialize between teachers and students is due in part to the fact that "24 percent of secondary classes have out-of-field instructors" or teachers who have not been trained to teach the discipline for which they are hired. "Nearly one in four public middle school and high school classes are taught by a teacher not trained in the subject, and the problem is much worse in schools that serve poor and minority students." The Education Trust conducted the study of the 1999–2000 school year. "The group looked at whether classes in four core subjects—English, math, science and social studies—were assigned to a teacher who lacked a college major or

minor in that field or a related field." The study found that "nationally, 24.2 percent of classes met those criteria, but 12 states had more than 30 percent taught by teachers who did not. In schools that serve mostly poor students, nearly twice as many courses are taught by out-of-field teachers as in schools with few poor students, the analysis found. The problem also is worse in schools that mostly serve minority students: 29 percent compared with 21 percent for schools that have low minority enrollments" ("Wrong Teacher, Wrong Subject," Associated Press, in *Houston Chronicle,* August 22, 2002).

3. See "Latinos Logging More Tube Time" by Richard Huff, *New York Daily News,* August 18, 2002, online at http://www.nydailynews.com/entertainment/v-pfriendly/story/11873p-11246c.html.

4. This focus by teachers is the result of the attention that school districts have increasingly placed on test scores and on bright students, interests that have diverted attention through the years away from healthy student-teacher relationships. Young teachers arriving in the schools, eager to establish meaningful relationships with their students, quickly discover that a high test score is the desired focus of years of training. Tests are important, but when testing and test scores become so important that they displace everything else that teachers and students should also be working on developing, both teacher and student lose.

5. The toll on administrators, particularly on principals, these days is reaching crisis proportions, according to some experts:

> A national study of 1,300 districts found that about half had a shortage of qualified candidates. At the same time, many principals are eligible for retirement, contributing to what educators call a crisis in leadership. "We will lose half of our school leaders in the next four years. How's that for a crisis?" said Milli Pierce, director of the Principals' Center at Harvard University. "The bulk will be due to retirements, but many are opting out early due to the stress of the job and the push for higher standards." Twenty years ago, 20 or 30 applicants would apply for a principal's job. Today, openings may attract 10 candidates. "I don't think anyone wants the job," said Chariho [Rhode Island] Schools Superintendent John L. Pini. "People get into this business to be educators and yet principals do a lot of things that have little to do with pure education." (Linda Borg, "Stress Driving Out School Principals: High Expectations, Few Rewards Cited," for *The Providence (Rhode Island) Journal,* published in the *Houston Chronicle,* August 29, 2001.)

6. Teachers inform us that time must be built into their schedules to meet the different types of special attention that different students require. The time required to fill out the enormous amount of paperwork that school districts use to make teachers "accountable" wears on excellent and caring teachers who are genuinely interested in giving students their best pedagogical energies. This encroachment into the teaching time that teachers used to have is a serious problem

that should not be disregarded any longer. Administrators and school boards have it in their power to alter schedules so that the wear and tear that currently afflict most educators in the school system is considerably reduced.

7. When a new teacher enters a school system and a classroom with enthusiasm, school districts, in turn, have the responsibility of maintaining and improving this enthusiasm. Honest, good-faith gestures on the part of the administration can do wonders for the overtaxed teacher, and any type of closed-door policy can discourage teachers and cause them to consider turning to other careers.

11. Understanding and Educating All Students

1. See for example *Latino College Students,* edited by Michael A. Olivas (New York: Teachers College Press, 1986), and the periodic reports such as "Statistics on Hispanics in Community Colleges" in *Hispanic Outlook in Higher Education* 8, no. 16 (April 10, 1998).

2. Only the cream of the Latino student crop every year is very selectively admitted into the best public and private universities and colleges in the United States. See for instance the "Ivy League Pursues Gifted Hispanics" issue, *Hispanic Outlook in Higher Education* 10, no. 1 (September 24, 1999), and for statistics on Latino and Latina students, "Top 100 Colleges for Hispanics," *Hispanic Outlook in Higher Education* 10, no. 16 (May 5, 2000). When compared against the more than 35 million Latinos who live in the United States (roughly 3 million more than the entire population of Canada), college demographics are yet another way of showing that most Latinos and Latinas are simply not being prepared adequately to compete successfully for admission, enrollment, and retention at the better higher education institutions of the United States.

3. See Angela Valenzuela, *Subtractive Schooling: U.S. Mexican Youth and the Politics of Caring* (Albany: State University of New York Press, 1999) for a discussion of how Chicanos and Spanish-speaking Americans see and experience education in U.S. schools. Here the expectations of the students are usefully contrasted to the expectations of the school systems, with the minority students losing out.

4. According to "The 33rd Annual Phi Delta Kappa/Gallup Poll of the Public's Attitudes toward the Public Schools," conducted by Lowell C. Rose and Alec M. Gallup, announced by radio and by Internet (http://www.pdkintl.org/kappan/k0109gal.htm#5a) on August 22, 2001:

Equal opportunities and equal achievement for minorities remain points of contention for the American public schools. In a repeat of a question first asked in 1978, 79% say the opportunities are the same. The 1978 figure was 80%. This question divides whites and nonwhites, with 83% of whites saying "the same" as compared to 57% of nonwhites. This large difference obscures the fact that the 57% for nonwhites is up 19 points since 1978. This is a question on which political affiliation comes into play. Although strong majorities in both parties hold the view that opportunities are the same, the figure for Republicans is 87%, and the figure for Democrats is 72%.

Our position, based on the experiences and the stories we narrate in this book, is that there is no way that the education of American minorities can be "the same" as that of the mainstream white population. Anyone who maintains that position in light of the statistics and the experiences we recount in this volume simply does not want to recognize the realities under which we all live. We suspect that is the case because an admission of such a fact would call for immediate change in how our schools operate.

Consider, for example, the following education record at the national level since 1964, when the Civil Rights Act was passed. In 1978, 80 percent of white Americans polled said that the education opportunities extended to whites and minorities were "the same." But we know that no substantial initiatives were undertaken between 1964 and 1978 that changed the nature of education in the United States during the administrations of presidents Johnson, Nixon, Ford, and Carter. And when we think of the twenty-five years that have passed since 1978, or the administrations of Reagan, Bush, Clinton, and now W. Bush, we see, as in previous years, that there has been considerable talk about education but no real action that has effectively changed the nature of the education provided to American students, including minority ones.

12. The Four K–16 Cultures

1. Good teaching requires imagination and creativity, as many people know. Many educators know that first-grade teaching, when done especially well, can successfully place students on the track to a quality education. Executed poorly, on the other hand, first grade does not prepare children adequately for the second, third, and all the other grades. On teaching well at this level see Ellen A. Thompson, *I Teach First Grade* (Crystal Springs Books, 2001), and Carol Avery and Donald Graves, *And with a Light Touch: Learning about Reading, Writing, and Teaching with First Graders* (Westport, Connecticut: Heinemann, 1993).

2. Readers may have noticed, for instance, that few American ethnic literature texts focus on the school experiences of their main characters. These surprising lacunae in the lives of young people occur precisely because such experiences are not worth dwelling on or articulating to any great length. Writers instead usually focus on all of the other untoward experiences that shape such characters, experiences wherein their schooling, mirroring the larger reality, rarely factors in how they try to cope.

13. Emphasizing All Print and Oral Skills

1. Hirsch, who presents himself as a conservative, has unduly drawn criticism from more liberal educators and thinkers for specifying lists of concepts that all

Americans should know. His *Cultural Literacy* became both an adulated and reviled text when it was published in 1987, depending on whether people aligned themselves with Rousseau and Dewey or with Plato. Hirsch was correct in saying in his preface that "history, not superior wisdom, shows us that neither the content-neutral curriculum of Rousseau and Dewey nor the narrowly specified curriculum of Plato is adequate to the needs of a modern nation" like the United States.

Although we do not prescribe a curriculum of specific books, mainly because every state has different education criteria that need to be met for every grade (and for which students are tested), Hirsch himself has already moved in this direction, as his well-known Core Knowledge Series for kindergarten through sixth grade shows. These texts are resource guides for parents and teachers about some of the better-known American civilization and life science ideas and concepts that any person who considers himself or herself well educated ought to know. Others have followed in his footsteps; see for example Diane Zahler and Kathy A. Zahler's national bestseller, *Test Your Cultural Literacy* (New York: Arco, Simon and Schuster, 1993), now into a second edition.

The standard criticism against such lists of books and concepts by mainstream Americans is that such curricula are mainly concerned with maintaining and disseminating a hegemonic sense of the United States that in one way or another continues to marginalize the contributions of blacks, Latinos and Latinas, and Native Americans. Except for *Don Quixote* in the Zahler volume, for example, Latinos and Latinas are effectively left out, as we are in Hirsch's universe. Although Hirsch could be singled out for this oversight, his contribution is that he does offer readers of mainstream America information we should know, since the "quality education" that people generally recognize is measured by ACT, SAT, and graduate and professional school admission test scores.

2. One of the best ways to dramatize the importance of a discipline to students who may not see how a subject can be useful is to invite guest speakers who are chemists, biologists, architects, construction workers, or businesspeople to explain how the subject area being studied is used in a certain career.

3. Perhaps the best way to see and to understand what we have in mind at this point would be to compare John Gray's *Children Are from Heaven: Positive Parenting Skills for Raising Cooperative, Confident, and Compassionate Children* (New York: HarperCollins, 1999) with Beverly Tatum's excellent study *Why Are All the Black Kids Sitting Together in the Cafeteria? And Other Conversations about Race* (New York: Basic Books, 1997). Gray's book is addressed to parents who hope their children will start life full of confidence about the future, and Tatum's book explains why African American children understandably find comfort in each other at school.

14. Blueprint for Reinstating Social Values and Civic Virtues

1. These *desiderata* are in general agreement with what educators are now suggesting. See *Rediscovering the Democratic Purposes of Education,* edited by

Lorraine M. McDonnell, Michael Timpane, and Roger Benjamin (Lawrence: University Press of Kansas, 2000). This collection of essays addresses issues connected to the role of the schools as social places for the necessary transmission of civic and communal values.

15. A Print and Oral Approach That Champions the Importance of Clauses

1. Grammarians break out clauses into noun, adjectival, and adverbial clauses. Adjectival clauses are either restrictive or nonrestrictive, and studying how clauses are used can significantly help students with the writing suggestions we make in this chapter.

2. See for example D. Biber, *Variation across Speech and Writing* (Cambridge, England: Cambridge University Press, 1988); M. A. K. Halliday and R. Hasan, *Cohesion in English,* English Language Series No. 9 (London: Longman, 1976); Holly Jacobs' *Testing ESL Composition: A Practical Approach* (Rowley, Massachusetts: Newbury House, 1981); W. Mann and S. Thompson, *Rhetorical Structure Theory: A Theory of Text Organization* (Marina del Rey, California: Information Sciences Institute, 1987); W. Mann, *The RST Relation Definitions,* online at http://www.sil.org/linguistics/RST/toolnote.htm; T. Odlin, *Language Transfer: Cross-Linguistic Influence in Language Learning,* Cambridge Applied Linguistics Series, edited by M. H. Long and J. C. Richards (Cambridge, England: Cambridge University Press, 1989); T. Sander and C. Van Wijk, "PISA: A Procedure for Analyzing the Structure of Explanatory Texts," *Text* 16, no. 1 (1996): 91–132; M. A. Walker, *Centering Theory in Discourse* (New York: Oxford University Press, 1998).

3. Wendell Horne, "Post Oak Trees Deal Well with Drought," *Bryan – College Station (Texas) Eagle,* September 29, 2000.

4. Gerald Graff, "Scholars and Sound Bites: The Myth of Academic Difficulty," *PMLA* 115, no. 5 (October 2000): 1042.

5. Barbara Herrnstein Smith, "Netting Truth" *PMLA* 115, no. 5 (October 2000): 1089.

17. Quality Education and the Teachers in the Classroom

1. Greg Toppo, "Districts Strive to Find, Retain Teachers," Associated Press, in *Bryan – College Station (Texas) Eagle,* August 15, 2001. These kinds of news reports appear quite frequently throughout the year. We do not think it an exaggeration to say that in the more than thirty years that we have been teaching, we tend to see one or two similar laments per month. The tragedy is that so few do anything about this serious social problem. We firmly believe that, if repaired, our schools can offer all of our students quality educations instead of contributing to the social problems that we have attempted to point out in this book. Legislators, who talk to each other continually, often wring their hands over the deplorable state of this country's education at the national and state levels. Then

they proceed to use (the little) tax money (that they apparently have) to take care of other interest groups first. Education commonly receives the money left over, even though education is the first item on which many of our leaders run for office. This state of affairs tells us that students and educators simply do not matter, but they should. Educators should be among the most respected members of society, and they should be appropriately paid for their professional services, like lawyers, medical doctors, accountants, engineers, and other businesspeople. Lobbying groups for education are disregarded, essentially because they have few resources ($) and other perks to offer, while educational conditions worsen. At this rate, quality education for all students, including K–16 Latino youngsters, who have always been sidelined, remains a shiny illusory goal that appears to be out of reach. Will no one in a position of power or influence, from our presidents down to the members of our local school boards, bravely exercise the leadership that education requires and actualize quality educations for our young people, our future citizens? We cannot think of a broader, more worthy public service.

2. The 2001 report described by Alex P. Kellogg in *Chronicle of Higher Education* continues:

> "Too many of our students are being left behind. Too many leave high school unprepared for further study or work," said Gov. Paul E. Patton of Kentucky, chairman of the commission, which was formed last year by the U.S. Education Department, with support from the Carnegie Corporation of New York, the Charles Steward Mott Foundation, and the Woodrow Wilson National Fellowship Foundation.
>
> Although 90 percent of freshmen say they expect to complete college, the study's authors say that only 44 percent have taken a college-preparatory curriculum in high school that positions them successfully to do so. "The other 30 million are being prepared for a future that has already vanished, in courses of study that lack rigor or coherence," the report says.
>
> Its recommendations echo those made in similar reports released this year on the need for secondary-school educational reform. They include calls for the comprehensive restructuring of high-school curriculums to better prepare students for the rigors of college studies, and a closer alignment of high schools' curriculums and graduation requirements with colleges' own standards. ("Report Finds the Majority of U.S. Students Not Prepared for College," *Chronicle of Higher Education*, October 5, 2001, online at http://chronicle .com/daily/2001/10/2001100501.htm.)

ßIBLIOGRAPHY

"All Cheerleading Candidates Get on Squad; Contest Found Rigged," Associated Press, published in *Dallas Morning News,* Texas and Southwest Section, August 22, 2001. Online at http://www.dallasnews.com/texas_southwest/450583_cheer22e.html.

Avery, Carol, and Donald Graves. *And with a Light Touch: Learning about Reading, Writing, and Teaching with First Graders.* Westport, Connecticut: Heinemann, 1993.

Bell, Derrick. *Faces at the Bottom of the Well: The Permanence of Racism.* New York: Basic Books, 1992.

Biber, D. *Variation across Speech and Writing.* Cambridge, England: Cambridge University Press, 1988.

Borg, Linda. "Stress Driving Out School Principals: High Expectations, Few Rewards Cited." *Houston Chronicle,* August 29, 2001.

Bowen, William G., and Derek Curtis Bok. *The Shape of the River: The Long-Term Consequences of Considering Race in College and University Admissions.* Princeton: Princeton University Press, 1998.

Bryant, Tamera, and Pamela Schiller. *The Values Book: Teaching Sixteen Basic Values to Young Children.* Beltsville, Maryland: Gryphon House, 1998.

"Closing the Achievement Gap." *New York Times,* May 16, 2000.

Cobb, Kim, and James Kimberly. "Hispanic School Achievement Pivotal to Texas' Future." *Houston Chronicle,* June 4, 2002.

Comer, James P. *Maggie's American Dream: The Life and Times of a Black Family.* New York: Plume, 1989.

"Dropout Rate is Near 20%, Study Suggests." Associated Press, published in *Bryan–College Station (Texas) Eagle,* May 21, 2001.

Federal Bureau of Investigation (FBI), National Crime Information Center. "An NCIC Milestone." March 23, 2002. Online at http://www.fbi.gov/pressrel/pressrel02/ncic032302.htm.

Flannery, Sarah, with David Flannery. *In Code: A Mathematical Journey.* New York: Workman, 2001.

Freedman, Jonathan. *From Cradle to Grave: The Human Face of Poverty in America.* New York: Atheneum, 1993.

Fullan, Michael. *Change Forces: The Sequel.* Philadelphia: Falmer Press, 1999.

González, Maria Luisa, Ana Huerta-Macias, and Josefina Villamil Tinajero. *Educating Latino Students: A Guide to Successful Practice.* Lanham, Maryland: Scarecrow Press, 1997.

Graff, Gerald. "Scholars and Sound Bites: The Myth of Academic Difficulty." *PMLA* 115, no. 5 (October 2000): 1042.

Gray, John. *Children Are from Heaven: Positive Parenting Skills for Raising Cooperative, Confident, and Compassionate Children.* New York: HarperCollins, 1999.

Gregorian, Vartan. "Teacher Education Must Become Colleges' Central Preoccupation." *Chronicle of Higher Education,* August 17, 2001.

Halliday, M. A. K., and Rugaiya Hasan. *Cohesion in English.* No. 9, English Language Series. London: Longman, 1976.

Handbook of Texas Online. Online at http://www.tsha.utexas.edu/handbook/online.

Hart, Betty, and Todd Risley. *Meaningful Differences in the Everyday Experiences of Young American Children.* Baltimore, Maryland: Brookes Publishing, 1996.

Hedges, Michael. "Jails over Schools: A New Study Shows Texas Has Increased Spending Faster on Prisons than Education." *Houston Chronicle,* August 28, 2002.

Herndon, James. *The Way It Spozed to Be.* New York: Simon and Schuster, 1968.

Herrnstein, Richard J., and Charles Murray. *The Bell Curve: Intelligence and Class Structure in American Life.* New York: Free Press, 1996.

Hirsch, E. D. Jr. *Cultural Literacy: What Every American Needs to Know.* Boston: Houghton Mifflin Company, 1987.

Holdren, John, and E. D. Hirsch Jr. *Books to Build On: A Grade-by-Grade Resource Guide for Parents and Teachers.* Delta, 1996.

Hobbs, Tawnell D. "Disparities Found in School Discipline." *Bryan–College Station (Texas) Eagle,* August 19, 2002.

Hood, Lucy. "State's Dropout Tally Called 'Silly.'" *San Antonio Express-News,* August 18, 2001.

Huff, Richard. "Latinos Logging More Tube Time." *New York Daily News,* August 18, 2002.

"Ivy League Pursues Gifted Hispanics." *Hispanic Outlook in Higher Education* 10, no. 1 (September 24, 1999). Online at http://www.HispanicOutlook.com.

Jacobs, Holly. *Testing ESL Composition: A Practical Approach.* Rowley, Massachusetts: Newbury House, 1981.

Kellogg, Alex P. "Report Finds the Majority of U.S. Students Not Prepared for College." *Chronicle of Higher Education,* Today's News, October 5, 2001. Online at http://chronicle.com/daily/2001/10/2001100501n.htm.

Kincheloe, Joe L., Shirley R. Steinberg, and Aaron D. Gresson, editors. *Measured Lies: The Bell Curve Examined.* New York: St. Martin's Press, 1997.

Kivel, Paul. *Uprooting Racism: How White People Can Work for Racial Justice.* New York: New Society Publishers, 1995.

Kozol, Jonathan. *Savage Inequalities: Children in America's Schools.* New York: HarperPerennial Library, 1991.

Lemann, Nicholas. *The Big Test: The Secret History of the American Meritocracy.* New York: Farrar Straus and Giroux, 1999.

Lipsitz, George. *The Possessive Investment in Whiteness: How White People Profit from Identity Politics.* Philadelphia: Temple University Press, 1998.

Mabin, Connie. "Perry Wants Improved Numbers in Math Scores." *Houston Chronicle,* August 12, 2001.

Mann, William, and S. Thompson. *Rhetorical Structure Theory: A Theory of Text Organization.* Marina del Rey, California: Information Sciences Institute, 1987.

———. *The RST Relation Definitions.* Online at http://www.sil.org/linguistics/RST/Toolnote.htm.

McDonnell, Lorraine M., Michael Timpane, and Roger Benjamin. *Rediscovering the Democratic Purposes of Education.* Lawrence: University Press of Kansas, 2000.

Miller, Leslie. "Youth Justice System Harsher for Latinos; Study: Inequities in Arrests, Sentences." Associated Press, published in *Houston Chronicle,* July 19, 2002.

Montessori, Maria. *The Montessori Method.* 1912. Reprint, New York: Schocken Books, 1988.

Morgan, Richard. "Study Cites Inability among Many Latino Parents to Advise Children about College." *Chronicle of Higher Education,* July 15, 2002. Online at http://chronicle.com/cgi2-bin/printable.cgi.

Murdock, Steve H., Nazrul Hoque, Martha Michael, Steve White, and Beverly Pecotte. *The Texas Challenge: Population Change and the Future of Texas.* College Station: Texas A&M University Press, 1997.

Odlin, Terence. *Language Transfer: Cross-Linguistic Influence in Language Learning.* Cambridge Applied Linguistics Series, edited by M. H. Long and J. C. Richards. Cambridge, England: Cambridge University Press, 1989.

Olivas, Michael A., editor. *Latino College Students.* New York: Teachers College Press, 1986.

Pinto Alicea, Inés. "Dr. Jaime Chahín Produces *Las Colonias: 'The Forgotten Americans.'*" *Hispanic Outlook in Higher Education* 11, no. 25 (September 24, 2001): 20–23.

Portales, Marco. *Crowding Out Latinos: Mexican Americans in the Public Consciousness.* Philadelphia: Temple University Press, 2000.

———. "Examining the Recruitment and Enrollment of Eligible Hispanic and African American Students at Selective Public Texas Universities." In *Education of Hispanics in the United States: Politics, Policies, and Outcomes,* edited by Charles Teddlie, Abbas Tashakkori, and Salvador Hector Ochoa. Volume 16 of Readings on Equal Education Series. New York: AMS Press, 1999.

———. "A History of Latino Segregation Lawsuits." In *The Unfinished Agenda of Brown v. Board of Education*, edited by the editors of *Black Issues in Higher Education*, with James Anderson and Dara N. Byrne, Landmarks in Civil Rights History Series (Hoboken, New Jersey: John Wiley and Sons, 2004).

———. "Hopwood, Race, Bakke, and the Constitution." *Texas Hispanic Journal of Law and Policy* 4, no. 1 (spring 1998): 29–44.

Public Agenda. Online at http://www.publicagenda.org.

"Quit Playing Games with Texas Dropouts." *Bryan–College Station (Texas) Eagle*, August 22, 2002.

Roediger, David. *Toward the Abolition of Whiteness: Essays on Race, Politics, and Working-Class History*. New York: Verso, 1994.

Romo, Harriet D., and Toni Falbo. *Latino High School Graduation: Defying the Odds*. Austin: University of Texas Press, 1996.

Rose, Lowell C., and Alec M. Gallup. "The 33rd Annual Phi Delta Kappa/Gallup Poll of the Public's Attitudes toward the Public Schools," August 22, 2001. Online at http://www.pdkintl.org/kappan/k0109gal.htm#5a.

San Miguel, Guadalupe. *"Let All of Them Take Heed": Mexican Americans and the Campaign for Educational Equality in Texas, 1910–1981*. Austin: University of Texas Press, 1987.

Sander, T., and C. Van Wijk. "PJSA: A Procedure for Analyzing the Structure of Explanatory Texts." *Text* 16, no. 1 (1996): 91–132.

Schiller, Pamela, and Kay Hastings. *The Complete Resource Book: An Early Childhood Curriculum with Over 2000 Activities and Ideas!* Beltsville, Maryland: Gryphon House, 1998.

Schwartz, Jeremy. "Confronting Our Dropout Problem: 'It Has an Effect on the Entire Region.'" *Corpus Christi Caller-Times*, March 25, 2001.

Scott, W. Richard. *Organizations: Rational, Natural, and Open Systems*. Upper Saddle River, New Jersey: Prentice Hall, 1997.

Smith, Barbara Herrnstein. "Netting Truth." *PMLA* 115, no. 5 (October 2000): 1089.

Spirit: News from the Texas A&M Foundation. Fall 1999.

"Statistics on Hispanics on Community Colleges." *Hispanic Outlook in Higher Education* 8, no. 16 (April 10, 1998). Online at http://www.HispanicOutlook.com.

Tatum, Beverly. *Why Are All the Black Kids Sitting Together in the Cafeteria? And Other Conversations about Race*. New York: Basic Books, 1997.

Teddlie, Charles, Abbas Tashakkori, and Salvador Hector Ochoa, editors. *Education of Hispanics in the United States: Politics, Policies and Outcomes*. Volume 16 of Readings on Equal Education Series. New York: AMA Press, 1999.

Tienda, Marta, and Susan Simonelli. "Hispanic Students Are Missing from Diversity Debates." *Chronicle of Higher Education*, May 31, 2001. Online at http://chronicle.com/weekley/v47/i38b01301.htm.

Thompson, Ellen A. *I Teach First Grade.* Crystal Springs Books, 2001.

"Thousands of Schools to Be Declared 'Failing.'" Associated Press, published in *Houston Chronicle,* April 24, 2002.

"Top 100 Colleges for Hispanics." *Hispanic Outlook in Higher Education* 10, no. 16 (May 5, 2000). Online at http://www.HispanicOutlook.com.

Toppo, Greg. "Districts Strive to Find, Retain Teachers." *Bryan–College Station (Texas) Eagle,* August 15, 2001.

Trelease, Jim. *The Read-Aloud Handbook.* 5th edition. New York: Penguin Books, 2001.

Valdés, Guadalupe. *Learning and Not Learning English: Latino Students in American Schools.* New York: Teachers College Press, 2001.

Valenzuela, Angela. *Subtractive Schooling: U.S. Mexican Youth and the Politics of Caring.* Albany: State University of New York Press, 1999.

Walker, Marily, Aravind K. Joshi, and Ellen F. Prince, editors. *Centering Theory in Discourse.* New York: Oxford University Press, 1998.

West, Cornell. *Race Matters.* New York: Vintage Books, 1993.

Wilson, Kenneth G., and Bennett Daviss. *Redesigning Education.* New York: Henry Holt and Company, 1994.

"Wrong Teacher, Wrong Subject." Associate Press, published in *Houston Chronicle,* August 22, 2002.

Zahler, Diane, and Kathy A. Zahler. *Test Your Cultural Literacy.* New York: Arco, Simon and Schuster, 1993.

INDEX

academic excellence, 14, 19, 112–114
academic expectations: improvements in, 42–43, 71; lowered, 4, 11, 89, 117, 151; raised, 5, 71; and values, 67, 74
academic freedom, 146
adjectives and adverbs, 179–180
administrators. *See* teachers and administrators
Advanced Placement courses, 141, 151, 204n4
Affirmative Action policies, 75, 195n1
African American students, 5, 16, 49, 54, 57, 74–75, 97, 99, 117, 133; dropout rate among, 60; and Hispanics, 5, 192n2. *See also* minority students
alternate education programs, 45–46, 187
Anderson, James, 201–202n1
And with a Light Touch: Learning about Reading, Writing, and Teaching with First Graders (1993), 207n1 (Ch. 12)
anxiety: costs of, 38; frustrations of, 42–43, 45, 52–69, 91; and lawsuits, 45; as seen in struggling students, 91, 96, 151; students as cause of, 46
athletics, 27, 28, 32, 125
Avery, Carol, 207n1 (Ch. 12)

barrio stories, 17, 24, 42, 43–44
behavior. *See* classroom behavior problems
Bell, Derrick, 74, 202n4
Bell Curve, The: Intelligence and Class Structure in American Life (1996), 195n1
Benjamin, Roger, 208–209n1

Biber, D., 209n2
Big Test, The: The Secret History of the American Meritocracy (1999), 195n1
bilingual education, 72–73, 78, 83, 108–111, 123–124, 126, 150
bilingual personnel, 60, 109
Black English, 133
Black Issues in Higher Education, 201–202n1
boards of education. *See* school boards and boards of education
Bok, Derek, 19, 195n1
bonds, school, 18, 128
Bowen, William, 19, 195n1
Brown University, 192n1
Brown v. Board of Education (1954), 15–16, 192n2, 201–202n1
Bryan–College Station Eagle, 200–201n2, 209n3, 209–210n1
bureaucracy of education, 47, 103–111
Bush, George W., 198n1, 203n5
Byrne, Dara, 201–202n1

Carlos H. Cantu Hispanic Education and Opportunity Endowment at Texas A&M University, 1, 191n1
Carnegie Corporation of New York, 192n1, 210n2
Carrasquillo, Angela, 191n3
Center for Mexican American Studies at the University of Texas at Austin, 191n3
Center for the Prevention of School Violence, 199–200n5
Centering Theory in Discourse (1998), 209n2

Chahín, Jaime, 203
Change Forces: The Sequel (1999), 198–199n4
Charles Steward Mott Foundation, 210n2
charter schools, 156
Children Are from Heaven (1999), 208n3
choreographing writing, 177–183
Chronicle of Higher Education, The, 192n1, 194–195n8, 202n2 (Ch. 5), 210n2
Cinco de Mayo, 78
Cisneros, Sandra, 17
civic virtues, 162–165
Civil Rights Act of 1964, 15, 206–207n4
civil rights of students, 164
classroom behavior problems, 107; interrupting a teacher, 155
class size, 118, 119
clauses, importance of, in writing, 166–176
clichés, 175
Clinton, Bill, 78
Cobb, Kim, 192n2
Cohesion in English (1976), 209n2
college and university curricula, 158
college-bound students, 140; and advanced courses, 21; and graduation from college, 151, 194–195n8; minority students as, 54, 61, 117, 150–151, 195n1. *See also* higher education
college entrance examinations, performance of minority vs. white students on, 9, 19, 54, 117, 195n1
college hazing, 202–203n3
colleges of education, 156, 192n1, 198–199n4
colonias, 83, 203n5
color-blindness, 77
Comer, James P., 117, 204n1
communication: professional, 49, 80, 96, 103, 108–110, 121; skills, nourishment of, 154, 160, 179
community colleges, 129, 194–195n8
complaints, 33, 34, 40, 107; of administrators, 9; of teachers, 9, 44, 60, 127
composition and rhetoric, 168–176
Core Knowledge Foundation, 196n2, 207–208n1

Corpus Christi Caller-Times, 200n1
costs of education, new funding for, 2, 89
counselors, school, 37, 41, 107; advising students, 54, 96, 129–130, 139, 141
creativity and imagination: in students, 163, 172; in teachers, 23, 35, 78, 128, 152, 177–183
crime, drugs, and violence, 37, 53, 68, 87, 93; and education, 94, 98
critical thinking skills, 153, 158–159, 161, 162, 163; testing of, 155
Cultural Literacy: What Every American Needs to Know (1987), 146, 207–208n1
culture, school, 136–141
cultural mores: issues regarding, for research, 119, 198n2; sensitivity and respect toward, 50, 83, 133; teacher and administrative responses to, ix, 11
curricular content: care regarding, 38; changing, 23, 160; common components of, 157; and flexing mental muscles, 137; importance of, 66, 117, 148; relevance of, 53, 110, 145; specificity of, 34–35; that engages student attention, 156, 177–183

Dallas Morning News, 46, 199–200n5, 203n4
Daviss, Bennett, 197–198n1
Delgado v. Bastrop Independent School District (1948), 44, 198n3, 202n3 (Ch. 5)
delinquency, 73
demography and the twenty-first century, 1–4, 38–39, 46, 63, 89, 93, 187–188, 194–195n8
desegregation, 80
detention hall, 59
Dewey, John, 146, 207–208n1
Día de los Muertos, El, 78
dictionary activity/challenge, 167, 178–179
discipline: in the classroom, 25, 91, 199–200n5; importance of, 43; need for, 48, 117. *See also* classroom behavior problems
discrimination, 54, 62, 71, 80, 87–88, 198n2

documentation by teachers, excessive, 64, 104, 120, 205–206n6

Don Quixote (1605; 1614), 207–208n1

"Driving while Black" (DWB), 77

dropouts, 91, 96; and alternative education, 45–46; rates of, ix, 1, 16–17, 60, 194–195n8, 200nn1,2; reasons for, 52–69, 97, 117

drugs. *See* crime, drugs, and violence

economic disparities. *See* social and economic disparities

Educating Latino Students: A Guide to Successful Practice (1997), 195–196n2

education: and the uncertain future, 157, 192n2; change in, 43, 156; defined, 153; news coverage of, 98–99; pipeline, 38, 89–90; players/roles, 41; purpose of, 4, 37–38, 40, 136, 147, 149, 159, 198–199n4; reforms, 3, 9, 39, 117, 156, 192n1, 197–198n1; theories of, 31, 40, 80, 148, 153, 198–199n4; uses of, 150, 153. *See also* education, inferior; educational outcomes

education, inferior: and alternative education programs, 45–46; and *Brown v. Board of Education*, 15; and the Civil Rights Act of 1964, 15; and lower expectations, 11, 19, 71, 193; reports of, 10, 52, 191n2; resulting from deplorable conditions, 191n2, 202n3 (Ch. 5); and test results, 1, 19, 194–195n8

education agencies, 103–111

educational outcomes: and crime, 94, 97–98; creating excitement for learning in students, 170–172; differences in, 11, 121, 151; evaluations of, 113; and lower expectations, 11, 19, 71; and low test scores, 13; print and oral skills approach to determining, 17, 145–161; purpose of, 40, 80, 93, 147, 153

education courses: teaching realities, 41; and school needs, 48, 192n1

Education of Hispanics in the United States: Politics, Policies, and Outcomes (1999), 191n3, 196n4

Elementary and Secondary Education Act (2002), 191n2

elementary school level, 138, 177

Ellis, Rodney, 16

Ellison, Ralph, 77

Emerson, Ralph Waldo, 36

Émile, The (1762), 116

empowering students, 87, 93, 133, 145–161, 163, 180

English alphabet, 178

English language usage, 133

enrollment in schools, 187–188

ESL (English as a Second Language), 47, 58, 73, 108, 141

essay writing, 166–178

ethics, 73; unethical practices and behaviors, 82

ethnicity, 87

exclusion from higher education, 96, 151, 194–195n8, 199–200n5

Faces at the Bottom of the Well (1992), 74, 202n4

Falbo, Toni, 196n4

favoritism, 76–88, 203n4

Federal Bureau of Investigation (FBI), 94; FBI National Press Office, 204n2 (Ch. 9)

Figueroa, Richard A., 191n3

First Amendment, 81, 162

Flannery, Sarah, 193n5

Fox, Vicente, 203n5

Freedman, Jonathan, 198–199n4

freedom of speech, 81

From Cradle to Grave: The Human Face of Poverty in America (1993), 198–199n4

Fullan, Michael, 198–199n4

Gallup, Alec M., 206–207n4

gang stories, 43–44, 53, 67

Garcia, Eugene E., 191n3

GED (General Education Development), 200–201n2

George Washington Gomez (1940; 1990), xii

gifted and talented programs, 65, 150

González, Maria Luisa, 195–196n2

grades, improvement in, 51, 126, 129
graduation, 48, 136, 140, 188, 194–195n8
Graff, Gerald, 173, 209n4
Graves, Donald, 207n1 (Ch. 12)
Gray, John, 208n3
Gregorian, Vartan, 192n1
Gresson, Aaron D., 195n1

Halliday, M. A. K., 209n2
Handbook of Texas Online, The, 198n3, 202n3 (Ch. 5)
Hart, Betty, 196n3
hate speech/talk, 81, 162
hazing. *See* college hazing
Herndon, James, 48, 200n7
Herrnstein, Richard J., 195n1
Herrnstein Smith, Barbara, 173–174, 209n5
higher education: degrees sought, 158; exclusion from, 151. *See also* college-bound students
high school level, 139, 178, 200n1; and low retention rates, 188, 194–195n8
hip-hop. *See* rap and hip-hop
Hirsch, E. D., 146, 195–196n2, 207–208n1
Hispanic/Mexican American communities, 54, 57, 62, 73, 85–86, 108, 126, 127, 129, 155, 198n3; and African Americans, 5, 192n2; and Aztec heritage, 42; parents in, 202n2 (Ch. 5); and tracking, 16; values of, 79, 119, 175; and word-of-mouth beliefs, 5, 18, 20. *See also* history, Mexican American; Latino and Latina students
Hispanic Outlook in Higher Education, The, 203n5, 206n2
history, Mexican American, 62, 198n3
history of education: and Latinos, 2, 62–63; and global economy, 42; inclusion in, and politics, 15; since World War II, 12
Hobbs, Tawnell D., 199–200n5
Horne, Wendell, 170–172, 209n3
House on Mango Street, The (1984), 17
Houston Chronicle, 16–17, 89, 198n2, 203–204n1, 204–205n2, 205n5
Huerta-Macias, Ana, 195–196n2
Huff, Richard, 205n3

identity and writing, 175
imagination and creativity. *See* creativity and imagination
immigrants, 22, 58, 141, 202n3 (Ch. 5); opportunities for children of, 55–56
inclusion: in schools, 15, 133; and exclusion perceptions, 61, 93
In Code: A Mathematical Journey (2001), 193n5
information society, 146
Initiative Media, 119
Institute for Children, Youth, and Families at Michigan State University, 198n2
instructional delivery/technology, 123, 126, 157
instructional time, 120
Internet, 99
interpretive skills. *See* critical thinking skills
Invisible Man (1947), 77
I Teach First Grade (2001), 207n1 (Ch. 12)

Jacobs, Holly, 209n2
Jim Crow laws, 77
Justice Policy Institute, 203–204n1
juvenile justice, 198n2, 199–200n5

Kellogg, Alex P., 210n2
Kimberly, James, 192n2
Kincheloe, Joe L., 195n1
Kivel, Paul, 202n4
Koerner, Stacey Lynn, 119
Kozol, Jonathan, 48, 200n7
Ku Klux Klan (KKK), 135

language: adjustments of minority students, 67, 153, 155; and learning, 154
Language Transfer: Cross-Linguistic Influence in Language Learning (1989), 209n2
Latino and Latina students: attendance problems of, 91; dropout rates of, 1, 16–17, 56, 60, 91, 96–97, 117, 194–195n8; and educational equity, 191n1, 194–195n8, 197n6, 199–200n5, 204n4, 206–207n4; graduation as goal

for, 96, 191n1, 192n1; as problem pupils, 3, 45, 53; respect of, for schooling, 10; responses of, to school, 9, 16, 70; and school dialogues, 16, 191n3. *See also* Hispanic/Mexican American communities; Mexican Americans; minority students

Latino College Students (1986), 129, 206n1

Latino High School Graduation: Defying the Odds (1996), 196n4

lawsuits. *See* litigation

leadership, 105

learning: and language, 154; as a lifetime endeavor, 163

Learning and Not Learning English: Latino Students in American Schools (2001), 195–196n2

learning environments: and boredom, 21, 53; and effective learning, 30, 127, 146; frustrations of, ix, 9, 45–46, 52; lack of, 47, 91; main beneficiaries of, 33, 133; process of creating, 13, 120, 133; psychology of, 21, 61; transformation of, 3, 17, 159

legislators, 103–111

Lemann, Nicholas, 195n1

Leoni, Leo, 177

"Let All of Them Take Heed": Mexican Americans and the Campaign for Equality in Texas, 1910–1981 (1987), 193n6

Lipsitz, George, 202

litigation: and Latinos, 44–45, 70, 201–202n1; and teachers, 44, 64–65, 104

Mabin, Connie, 193n4

Macias, Raynoldo F., 191n3

Maggie's American Dream: The Life and Times of a Black Family (1988), 117, 204n1

Mann, W., 209n2

math scores, 193n4

McDaniel, Joanne, 199–200n5

McDonnell, Lorraine M., 208–209n1

Meaningful Differences in the Everyday Experiences of Young American Children (1996), 21, 196n3

Measured Lies: The Bell Curve Examined (1997), 195–196n2

media: and advertising, 91, 93; and books and films, 146; and hype, 162; negative images in, 67, 77, 98, 200n1; positive images in, 42; reports in, 45, 89, 98; and sound-bite culture, 174; and Spanish-language programs, 119; and television, 53, 98, 119; and visual culture, x–xi, 146, 177

Mexican American and U.S. Latino Research Center (MALRC) at Texas A&M University, xiii

Mexican Americans, 5, 16, 54, 57, 62, 73, 85–86, 108, 126, 127, 129, 155, 198n3. *See also* Hispanic/Mexican American communities; history, Mexican American; Latino and Latina students; minority students

middle school level, 138, 155, 178; sample activity at, 164

migrant programs, 108, 111, 150

minority students: qualified, lack of, 5, 9, 19, 45–46, 192n2; and language adjustments, 67, 153, 155; psychological challenges of, 67–69, 91. *See also* African Americans; Hispanic/Mexican American communities; Latino and Latina students; Mexican Americans

miseducated youngsters or adults, 3–5, 37, 52, 91, 191n3

Montessori, Maria (1870–1952), 195–196n2

Montessori Method, The (1912), 195–196n2

Morgan, Richard, 202n2 (Ch. 5)

motivating students, 52, 117, 133, 145–161, 163

Murdock, Steve H., 197n6

Murray, Charles, 195n1

National Assessment of Educational Progress scores, 193n4

National Commission on the High-School Senior Year, 188

National Crime Information Center (NCIC), 94

National Dropout Prevention Center at Clemson University, 200–201n2
National Education Association, 200–201n2
national test standards, 156
No Child Left Behind Act (2001), 3, 16, 63
Nora, Amaury, 191n3
nouns and verbs, 180; sample first-grade lesson on, 152
nurturing, 56, 58, 60, 63, 65–66, 78, 85, 121, 127, 129

Ochoa, Hector, 191n3
Odlin, T., 209n2
Olivas, Michael A., 206n1
oral communication, emphasis on, 18, 39, 133, 160. *See also* print and oral skills; speaking; speech
Organizations: Rational, Natural, and Open Systems (1997), 192–193n3
overtime pay, 104

Padrón, Yolanda N., 191n3
paperwork, 104, 120, 205–206n6
Paredes, Américo, xii
parents: resources of, 11, 49, 54, 96; and students, 129, 141; and teachers, xii, 11, 19, 54, 70, 96, 125
pedagogy: and alternative education, 45–46, 145; effective, 37, 103–107, 122, 145, 163; reform of, 43, 48, 162
Perry, Rick, 193n4
Phi Delta Kappa/Gallup Poll on the Public's Attitudes toward the Public Schools, 206–207n4
Pierce, Milli, 205n5
Plato (427?–347 B.C.), 146, 207–208n1
political correctness, 68, 74, 133
Polk, James, 202n3 (Ch. 5)
Portales, Marco, 191n3, 201–202n1, 202n2 (Ch. 6)
Possessive Investment in Whiteness: How White People Profit from Identity Politics (1998), 202n1 (Ch. 6)
potential, full: of teachers and administrators, x, 25, 29; of students, 5, 24, 121
power: lack of, 47; in relationships, 4, 11, 113–114

principals, 47, 112–115, 205n5
Principals' Center at Harvard University, 205n5
print and oral skills: basic, 23, 37, 159; in the classroom, 17, 26, 158; practicality of this approach, 38, 51, 145, 154–155; recommendations about, 14, 145–161; renewed emphasis on, 3, 42, 151, 159; and students, 36, 42; and story about Africa, 155–156; ubiquity of, 151, 159. *See also* oral communication, emphasis on; reading; speaking; thinking; writing
prisons, 68, 73, 91, 198n2, 203–204n1
progressive mastery, 136
Public Agenda, 48, 200n8
public policy, 75

quality education: and students of color, 3, 25, 27, 71–72; as a goal, 80–81, 112, 146, 187–188; and better schools, 11, 136; long-term nurturing of, 19, 159
quinceañeras, 78

Race and Ethnic Studies Institute (RESI) at Texas A&M University, xiii
Race Matters (1993), 74, 202n4
race relations, 78
racism, 74–79
rap and hip-hop, 133, 175
Read-Aloud Handbook, The (1979), 196n3
reading, 130–133, 181–182; combined with thinking, writing, and speaking, xi, 131, 153, 157, 159, 176; inability, 131, 183; and interpreting texts, 155; out loud, 180–181. *See also* print and oral skills
Redesigning Education (1994), 197–198n1
Rediscovering the Democratic Purposes of Education (2000), 208–209n1
reforming education, 9, 117, 156
relational writing, 168–176
Rendon, Laura I., 191n3
respect: for the law, 89; for others, 85, 93–95, 117, 163
Rhetorical Structure Theory (1987), 209n2
rhetoric and composition, 168–176
Roediger, David, 202n1 (Ch. 6)
Romo, Harriet, 196n4
Rose, Lowell C., 206–207n4

Rousseau, Jean-Jacques (1712–1778), 116, 146, 207–208n1

RST Relation Definitions, The, 209n2

Ruiz, Nadeen T., 191n3

safety, school, 43, 48, 67, 98, 128

Sander, T., 209n2

San Miguel, Guadalupe, xii, 193n6

SAT (Scholastic Aptitude Test), scores on, 16, 195n1

Savage Inequalities (1991), 48, 200n7

scholarships, 16–17, 22

school boards and boards of education: accountability of, 27, 30, 33, 39, 105, 141; and alternative education programs, 45–46; assessing teachers, 106, 113; beliefs of, 15; easing education burdens, 40, 107, 145–161; roles of, 41, 103–111

school building bonds. *See* bonds, school

school cultures. *See* culture, school

school enrollment. *See* enrollment, school

schools: as boring places, 2, 91, 128, 130; division of labor in, 30–33, 107; as local entities, 15, 105; reason for, 4, 25, 40, 136; record-keeping in, 10; yearly calendar of, 123

school safety. *See* safety, school

school spirit. *See* spirit, school

school systems: accountability of, 27, 34, 112, 141; basically sound, 3, 31, 105; destabilized, 27, 41; and the pipeline, 37, 38, 47–48, 89–90; repairing of, 3, 26, 31, 34, 43, 47, 50, 90, 115, 122–123; roles in, 32, 107, 126

Schwartz, Jeremy, 200n1

Scott, W. Richard, 192–193n3

self-esteem, 57, 87, 91, 145, 173

self-reliance, 57, 96

Shape of the River, The (1998), 19, 195n1

Simonelli, Susan, 194–195n8

slang, 133

smoking, 202–203n3

social and economic disparities, 73, 141; long-standing, 1, 47, 84, 141; and new needs, 3–4, 16; at school, 24, 58, 133, 140

social values, 162–165

sound-bite culture, 174

Spanish in the classroom, 123–124, 133

Spanish-language [media] program, 119

Spanish-speaking personnel, 20, 22, 58; lack of, 67, 108–110; and parents, 70, 109; and youngsters, 14, 78–79, 91

speaking, 157, 183; combined with reading, thinking, and writing, 153, 172. *See also* oral communication, emphasis on; print and oral skills; speech

special education, 150

speech: freedom of, 81; and need for oral skills, 38, 182–183; student, 18. *See also* hate speech/talk; oral communication, emphasis on; print and oral skills; speaking

spirit, school, 34

sports. *See* athletics

stakeholders in education: as defenders of status quo, 31; duties of, 40, 103–104, 112–115; and other school district interests, 30

state education agencies, 103–111

Steinberg, Shirley R., 195n1

student learning: and articulating views, 52, 177–178; and boredom, 40–41; and disaffected youngsters, 42, 46, 70–72, 91, 149; first priority in, xi, 27; and indifference toward teachers, 46, 60, 116, 121; and motivation, 60, 62, 117; and nurturing and planning, 67, 91, 118–119, 136; and sensitivity, 36, 52, 163; and solving problems, 37; and talking about class materials, 62, 182–183. *See also* motivating students

student records: interpretation of, 41, 118; for lawsuit purposes, 45

substitute teachers, 52, 58, 187–188

Subtractive Schooling: U.S. Mexican Youth and the Politics of Caring (1999), 206n3

Swimmy (1963), 177

systems theory, 12–15, 26–28, 29–34, 192–193n3

Tashakkori, Abbas, 191n3

Tatum, Beverly, 208n3

TEA (Texas Education Agency), 46, 199–200n5, 200–201n2

teacher assessment, 113

teachers and administrators: and accountability, 34, 39, 112; agreements between, 49; leadership among, 30, 103–111, 116, 121, 145–161, 206n7; and noncertified teachers, 188; and powerlessness, 47, 117; relationships among, xiii, 30–32, 41, 63–64, 106, 112–114, 122, 125; responsibilities of, 33, 41, 103–111, 141; stress and burnout in, 122; and substitutes, 187–188

teachers and students: approaching relationship constructively, 116–117, 149, 152; and articulation of student views, 177, 182–183; centrality of relationship, 30, 35–36, 64, 96, 105, 107–108, 124; and clear explanation of disciplines, 150; creating excitement for learning, 170–172; and creative exercises to stimulate thinking, 177–183; and critical thinking skills, 153, 155; and demonstrating understanding of taught materials, 153, 155; and disrespect, 155; and dissipation of good energies, 44, 52, 154; and enhancing student vocabularies, 172; and goodwill gestures, 119; and the inability to read, 183; interactive relationship between, 33, 60, 112, 120; and interference, 24; and learning and language use, 154; and listening, 44, 145; and monosyllabic student responses, 177; and motivation, 117, 133, 145–161; relationship, smoothness of, 30, 41, 112–114; sensitivity between, 85, 116

teacher education, 192n1

teaching: dissatisfactions of, 9, 47, 117; effective, 120–125, 166–176, 177–183; force, nearing retirement, 188; fundamental skills, 2, 25, 64; and low test scores, 16; and overtime pay, 104; realities of, 41, 64, 94, 116; suggestions and recommendations for, 12, 13, 30, 105, 121, 126, 141, 145, 164; workload in, 118

teaching environment, 29, 64, 103–104, 121, 145, 192–193n3

teaching evaluations, 113

team approach diagram, 115

technology, 157

Teddlie, Charles, 191n3

teen pregnancies, 49, 53

Testing ESL Composition, 209n2

tests: defined, 137; national standards for, 156; and pressures on teachers, 119, 121, 205n5; stories about, 36, 118; standardized, 50, 118, 205n5

Test Your Cultural Literacy (1993), 207–208n1

Texas Challenge, The: Population Change and the Future of Texas (1997), 197n6

Texas Coordinating Board, 197n6

Texas Education Code, 199–200n5

Texas Hispanic Journal of Law and Policy, 202n2 (Ch. 6)

thinking: combined with writing, speaking, and reading skills, 153, 157, 159; and writing clearly, 155, 166–176. *See also* print and oral skills

Thompson, Ellen A., 207n1 (Ch. 12)

Tienda, Marta, 194–195n8

Timpane, Michael, 208–209n1

Tomás Rivera Policy Institute at the University of California/Riverside, 202n2 (Ch. 5)

Toppo, Greg, 208–209n1

Toward Excellence, Access and Success grant program, 16

Toward the Abolition of Whiteness: Essays on Race, Politics, and Working Class History (1994), 202n1 (Ch. 6)

traditional education, 71–72

translators in schools, 60, 109

Treaty of Guadalupe Hidalgo (1848), 202n3 (Ch. 5)

Trelease, Jim, 196n3

tribalism and favoritism, 76–88, 203n4

Unfinished Agenda of Brown v. Board of Education, The (2004), 201–202n1

university curricula. *See* college and university curricula

Uprooting Racism: How White People Can Work for Racial Justice (1995), 202n4

U.S. Census, 187; of 1950, 71, 198
U.S. Constitution, 4, 75, 81, 83

Valdés, Guadalupe, 195–196n2
Valenzuela, Angela, 206n3
values. *See* social values
Variations across Speech and Writing (1988), 209n2
verbs and nouns. *See* nouns and verbs
Vietnamese students, 134–135
Villamil Tinajero, Josefina, 195–196n2
violence. *See* crime, drugs, and violence
visual culture, 146
visual symbols, 146
vocabulary: enhancement of, 172, 178–183; usage, in high- vs. low-income families, 21, 133
von Bertalanffy, Ludwig, 192–193n3

Wadsworth, Deborah, 48
Walker, M. A., 209n2
Walker, Nancy, 198n2

Way It Spozed To Be, The (1968), 48, 200n7
West, Cornell, 74, 202n4
Why Are All the Black Kids Sitting Together in the Cafeteria? (1997), 208n3
Wilson, Kenneth G., 197–198n1
WISK I.Q. Test, 204
Woodrow Wilson National Fellowship Foundation, 210n2
words: importance of, 154, 155, 179; monotonous arrangement of, 180; on a page, requiring responses from readers, 182; third dimension of, 179
writing: better essays, 168–169, 178, 181; combined with thinking, speaking, and reading, 153, 157, 164, 166–176; importance of clauses in, 166–176; and student identity, 175; relational, 168–176. *See also* print and oral skills

Zahler, Diane, 207–208n1